ECL시험 대비
New ALC
必 필수어휘 완성

이준용 / 황기동

연경문화사

ECL시험 대비
New ALC 必 필수어휘 완성

저 자 소 개

이 준 용 교수

1981년 해군사관학교를 졸업하고 1998년 인디애나 볼 주립대학교에서 영어교수법 박사학위를 취득하였으며,
현재 해군사관학교 영어과에 재직 중이다. 〈아메리칸 애드미럴십〉〈미 해군 영문서 작성법〉〈해군 리더십〉
〈Daily Expressions for Leadership〉〈American English: 미국사회와 언어의 이해〉 등 다수를 번역하고 저술하였다.

황 기 동 교수

1992년 부산대학교에서 박사학위를 취득하였으며, 미 국방 언어학교(DLI)에서 고급 영어교육 과정 우등상을 수상하고,
영국 버밍엄 대학교 TESL/TEFL 과정을 연수하였으며, 현재 해군사관학교 영어과에 재직 중이다.
〈Teach English Using English〉 외 다수를 저술하고 번역하였다.

서문

　미 국방성 언어연구소가 발행한 New ALC[New American Language Course] 시리즈는 연합군의 일원이 습득해야 할 가장 기본적인 영어 관련 내용을 담고 있습니다. New ALC는 미국에서의 연수 혹은 훈련이 예정되어 있는 외국군 장병들이 반드시 익혀야 할 자료들을 정리한 것으로 현재 미군에 실시하는 ECL 시험의 모든 문제는 이 시리즈를 기준으로 출제되고 있습니다. 그러나 이 시리즈는 34권의 방대한 책자로 구성되어 단기에 효과적으로 학습하기가 쉽지 않습니다. 같은 내용이 계속해서 반복되기도 하며, 구성 또한 매우 단조로워서 학습자들의 조기 학습포기가 우려되기도 합니다. 효과적인 개별 학습을 위한, 보다 짜임새 있는 교재의 등장을 오랫동안 기다려 온 이유도 여기에 있을 것입니다.

　이 책에서는 New ALC 시리즈에 등장하는 모든 어휘와 관용어를 보다 쉽게 그리고 체계적으로 학습할 수 있도록 구성하였습니다. 제1권부터 34권까지의 시리즈에 사용된 필수어휘를 새로운 문장으로 재구성하고, 편집 체계 또한 재정비하였습니다. 단기적으로는 ECL 시험 등에 대비하고, 장기적으로는 자신의 영어능력 향상에 도움이 되도록 구성과 편집을 새롭게 정리하였습니다. 내용의 구성은 학습효과를 높이는데 중점을 두었습니다. 수십 권의 책에서 산발적으로 출현하는 어휘를 종합한 후 이를 8개 분야로 나누어 정리하였습니다. 각 분야는 세부적으로 명사, 동사, 형용사, 관용어 및 어법 등의 순서로 나열하였으며, 각 세부 분야를 기본어휘와 연습 문제로 나누어 학습토록 함으로써 배운 내용의 장기 기억이용이하게 하였습니다.

　이 책으로 필요한 어휘를 단기간에 효과적으로 습득할 수 있기를 바랍니다. ECL시험뿐 아니라, TEPS, TOEFL, TOEIC 등 여러 종류의 영어 관련시험에 효과적으로 대비하면서, 또한 개인의 영어능력 발전에도 적지 않은 도움이 되기를 기원합니다.

이 준 용 / 황 기 동

New American Language Course

ECL시험 대비 NEW ALC 필수어휘 완성

차례

New American Language Course

New American
Language Course

일상생활 1

A. 명사   B. 동사   C. 형용사   D. 어휘, 관용구, 문형 종합

ECL시험 대비 NEW ALC 必 필수어휘 완성

명사

기본어휘 / 연습 문제

A

New American Language Course

1. 기본어휘　명사

allure / 유혹 (attraction, fascination)

The allure of wealth caused the man to abandon his friends and lead a life of crime.
(부에 대한 유혹으로 그 사람은 친구를 버리고, 죄를 범하였다.)

angle / 각도 (the direction that something is leaning or pointing)

Thanks to the angle I stood, I could just see the sunset.
(내가 서있는 각도 때문에 일몰을 볼 수 있었다.)

appliance / 기구, 설비 (machine or piece of equipment that you have in your home)

We stock a wide range of kitchen appliances.
(우리는 여러 가지 다양한 부엌 기구들을 확보하고 있다.)

assistance / 도움, 조력 (aid, help)

South Korea has decided to resume economic assistance to North Korea.
(남한은 북한에게 경제적 지원을 재개하기로 결정했다.)

beard / 턱수염 (hair that grows on a man's chin and checks)

His beard grows on the face of an animal such as a goat.
(그의 턱수염은 염소수염이다.)

birth / 출생 (the occasion of a baby being born)

We are happy to announce the birth of our son, Nick.
(우리 아들 닉이 태어났음을 알리게 되어 기쁩니다.)

booth / 칸막이 (an enclosed space)

Three persons were in the small booth. (세 사람이 그 작은 부스에 있었다.)

broom / 빗자루 (a brush with a long handle, used for sweeping dirt)

We need a lot of brooms to sweep all the rooms.
(우리는 모든 방을 청소할 다수의 빗자루가 필요하다.)

cleaner / 세제 (a chemical substance used for cleaning things), 청소기

Using cleaner is not good for your body. (세제를 사용하면 몸에 좋지 않다.)

community / 지역사회 (a social, religious, or occupational group)

He is well known in the local community.
(그는 그 지역사회에서 잘 알려져 있다.)

correspondence / 편지, 서신 (a letter or letters)

My correspondence with her lasted many years.
(그녀와의 서신은 수년간 지속되었다.)

deal / 합의, 거래 (a formal agreement, especially in business or politics)

I've got a really good deal living at Sophie's house.
(나는 타협이 잘 되어 소피의 집에서 살게 되었다.)

discrepancy / 불일치, 차이 (disagreement, inconsistency)

There is always some discrepancy between press and television reports.
(보도자료와 TV보도와는 항상 약간의 차이가 있다.)

drink / 음료, 주류 (an alcoholic drink)

Hector ordered drinks at the bar. (핵터는 술집에서 술을 주문하였다.)

ease / 편이, 편함 (lack of difficulty)

The computer is popular for its practical design and ease of use.
(그 컴퓨터는 실용적인 디자인과 사용의 편이성으로 인기가 있다.)

effort / 노력, 시도 (an attempt to do something)

We must spend our life in an effort to do good.
(우리는 선을 행하고자 노력하는 인생을 살아야 한다.)

favor / 호의, 친절 (an act of gracious kindness)

We sailed under favor of cloudless skies.
(우리는 구름 한 점 없는 하늘 아래에서 항해하였다.)

figure / 모습 (person's shape)

A small figure appeared in the doorway.
(한 조그만 물체가 문간에 모습을 드러냈다.)

flaw / 결점, 실수 (a mistake or fault in something)

There are serious flaws in the way we train our teachers.
(우리가 우리 교사를 훈련시키는 방법에는 심각한 문제가 있다.)

flashlight / 손전등 (a portable electric light)

The soldiers were searching the immediate area by flashlight.
(군인들은 인접지역을 손전등으로 수색하고 있었다.)

foray / 침입, 급습 (venture, sudden attack, attempt to do something)

His foray into the dense forest ended up with his getting lost and breaking a leg.
(우거진 숲으로 모험하다가 그는 길을 잃고 다리를 부러뜨리게 되었다.)

fume / 증기, 가스 (gas, smoke, or vapor)
Some debtors killed themselves by breathing car exhaust fumes in a locked garage.
(몇몇 채무자들이 잠긴 차고에서 차의 배기가스를 흡입하여 자살했다.)

feature / 특징, 특색 (a prominent or conspicuous part)
Tall buildings were a new feature on the skyline. (큰 건물은 도심평면의 새로운 특징이다.)

guidance / 조언, 지도 (advice or assistance)
My academic advisor gave me a lot of guidance when I was writing up my Ph.D.
(내가 박사학위 논문을 쓸 때 나의 학업지도 교수는 많은 조언을 했다.)

hook / 고리, 걸쇠 (a curved piece of metal or plastic for hanging things on)
He hung his coat on a hook on the back of the door. (그는 방 뒤의 옷걸이에 코트를 걸었다.)

infant / 유아 (baby, a very young child)
Children under one year of age are considered infants. (한살 아래의 아이는 유아라고 한다.)

inquiry / 문의, 조회 (a request for information, a question about something)
The police made some inquires about the accident.
(경찰은 그 사고에 대해 몇 가지 물어 보았다.)

invitation / 초대, 초청 (a request asking someone to come to a social event)
The wedding invitations went out yesterday. (그 결혼 청첩장은 어제 발송되었다.)

intention / 의향, 의도 (aim, end, purpose)
A man's good intentions rarely seem to last long.
(인간의 선의는 오래 지속되는 경우가 드물다.)

lounge / 휴게실, 담화실 (a room for waiting)

The hotel guests are having a drink in the lounge before dinner.
(호텔 손님들이 저녁식사 전에 라운지에서 음료수를 마시고 있다.)

mass / 다수, 많음 (a large quantity or number of)

The article is covered with a mass of figures.
(그 기사는 많은 수치로 범벅되어 있다.)

maverick / 독자적인 인간, 이단자 (one who act independently of a group)

When I first witnessed young Benjamin refusing to be pressured by his friends, I knew he'd always be a maverick. (내가 처음 어린 벤자민이 그의 친구들로부터의 압력을 거부하는 것을 보았을 때, 나는 그가 항상 독자적인 인간이라는 것을 알았다.)

obligation / 의무, 은혜 (indebtedness, a debt of gratitude)

I always feel an obligation to my teacher.
(나는 항상 나의 선생님에게 빚을 지고 있다.)

privacy / 사생활, 사적 자유 (the freedom to do things without other people watching)

They don't want their privacy invaded by reporters.
(그들은 기자들로부터 사생활이 침해당하는 것을 싫어한다.)

reflection / 반사, 반영 (an image that you see when you look in a mirror)

We could see the reflection of clouds on the water.
(우리는 물에 구름이 반사된 모습을 볼 수 있었다.)

relationship / 관계, 혈연 (connection, kinship)

We should keep close family relationship.
(우리는 가족 간의 유대를 공고히 유지해야 한다.)

resident / 주거, 주택 (a house or other place where someone lives)
The building is partly a museum and partly a private residence.
(그 빌딩의 일부분은 박물관이고 일부분은 개인 거주지역이다.)

reservoir / 저수지, 저장소 (a place in an engine where a liquid is kept)
The truck has a huge oil reservoir. (그 트럭은 큰 기름통을 가지고 있다.)

routine / 일과, 일정 (regular procedure), 지루한 (ordinary and boring)
There's no fixed routine at work. (직장에는 정해진 일과가 없다.)
Yesterday was a routine and uninteresting day. (어제는 따분하고 재미없는 날이었다.)

rust / 녹 (the red or orange coating on iron when exposed to air and moisture)
The steady dripping of water rusted the metal stopper in the sink.
(물이 계속 떨어져서 싱크대의 금속 마개에 녹이 쓸게 하였다.)

security / 안전, 보안 (freedom from fear, anxiety, or care. free from danger)
The visit took place amidst tight security.
(그 방문은 철저한 보안 하에서 이루어졌다.)

suggestion / 제안, 제의 (an idea or plan that you offer for someone to consider)
If you're looking for last-minute Christmas present, here are somesuggestions.
(크리스마스 마지막 시즌의 선물을 찾으신다면 몇 가지 제안을 드리겠습니다.)

sympathy / 연민, 공감 (natural feeling of kindness and understanding)
The movie describes, with considerable sympathy, the problems faced byeconomic migrants.
(그 영화는 상당한 연민의 정으로 경제적 이유로 이주한 사람들이 겪는 문제를 그려내고 있다.)

tidbits / 토막뉴스, 소문 (small pieces of information , gossip, etc)

In reading the letter from home, Andrew was delighted to discover all kinds of tidbits – who was getting married, who had been promoted, who was sick, and who was well.
(집에서 온 편지를 읽으면서, 앤드류는 온갖 종류의 토막뉴스-누가 결혼할 것인지, 누가 승진했는지, 누가 아픈지, 누가 잘 있는지-를 듣고 기뻐하였다.)

windshield / 바람막이 (windscreen, the window in front of a car)

The driver usually looks through a windshield.
(운전사는 대부분 전면 유리를 통해 본다.)

yearning / 갈망 (longing, desire)

After being away for ten years, Linda has a strong yearning to return home and see her family.
(10년 동안 가족들과 멀리 떨어져 있던 린다는 고향에 돌아와 가족을 보고 싶은 강한 욕구가 있다.)

2. 연습문제

1. Our _____ is to build our own home for ourselves someday.

   ⓐ tip   ⓑ addition   ⓒ drill   ⓓ aim

2. Do you want some tea? It'll just take _____ to make.

   ⓐ an instance   ⓑ a capacity   ⓒ an instant   ⓓ an intention

3. She wore her hat at a(n) _____ to shade her eyes.

   ⓐ angel   ⓑ dimension   ⓒ angle   ⓓ sight

4. We offered to help Liza, but she didn't need any _____ .

   ⓐ consistency   ⓑ assistance   ⓒ prevention   ⓓ arrangement

5. John didn't forget to shave. He's growing a _____ .

   ⓐ curly   ⓑ beard   ⓒ bone   ⓓ bald

6. After my 17th _____ , I moved away from home so I could go to the university.

   ⓐ couple   ⓑ turn   ⓒ coming   ⓓ birthday

7. The telephone is located in that very small enclosed area at the end of the hall. It's in a telephone _____ .

   ⓐ segment   ⓑ tunnel   ⓒ air   ⓓ booth

8. Pvt Roland, go get the _____ . I want you to sweep this room.

    ⓐ mop   ⓑ shape   ⓒ broom   ⓓ polish

9. Even the _____ couldn't get this spot out of my suit.

    ⓐ furnace   ⓑ research   ⓒ cleaners   ⓓ fire

10. Karl is kind, honest, and hardworking. He has a good _____ .

    ⓐ character   ⓑ dependable   ⓒ charming   ⓓ appearance

11. She grew up in a little _____ in the countryside.

    ⓐ community   ⓑ commitment   ⓒ compartment   ⓓ companion

12. I didn't receive any _____ this month because no one wrote to me.

    ⓐ distribution   ⓑ correspondence   ⓒ destination   ⓓ contribution

13. Mr. Nick: Let's make a _____ . You wash the dishes tonight, and I'll cook dinner tomorrow.

    Mrs. Nick: Okay.

    ⓐ deal   ⓑ sale   ⓒ free   ⓓ chance

14. I dropped my car key. Can you shine the _____ over here?

    ⓐ lightening   ⓑ lighthouse   ⓒ flashlight   ⓓ sunlight

15. When he gets into trouble, Tom goes to his older brother for _____ .

    ⓐ confidence   ⓑ mission   ⓒ guidance   ⓑ capability

16. James has such a peaceful _____ . He never fights or argues with anyone.

    ⓐ potential   ⓑ outfit   ⓒ nature   ⓓ cruelty

17. They are looking for an apartment building that provides plenty of _____ for the residents.

ⓐ service   ⓑ furniture   ⓒ protection   ⓓ secret

18. You have a mark on your face. Here, look at your _____ in the mirror.

ⓐ reflection   ⓑ harvest   ⓒ location   ⓓ hand

19. What is his _____ to the woman in the red dress?

ⓐ tolerance   ⓑ relationship   ⓒ knowledge   ⓓ correction

20. Gregory lives in Maine. He's a _____ of Maine.

ⓐ relation   ⓑ reside   ⓒ resident   ⓓ residue

21. If you occasionally change your _____ to work, you can make your trip more exciting.

ⓐ tray   ⓑ destination   ⓒ route   ⓓ duty

22. You don't have to follow a _____ this weekend. You can do what you feel like doing.

ⓐ mission   ⓑ attendance   ⓒ skill   ⓓ routine

23. I found a _____ in his statement. He said he stayed at home all day, but his roommate said he went shopping in the afternoon.

ⓐ disarmament   ⓑ a discrepancy   ⓒ discontent   ⓓ discrimination

24. One _____ of working for myself is that I can set my own hours.

ⓐ advantage   ⓑ habit   ⓒ obligation   ⓓ responsibility

25. Mike and Nina want to furnish the kitchen with modern _____ .

ⓐ utilities   ⓑ appliances   ⓒ ingredients   ⓓ cars

A 명사 / 일상생활

26. I'm almost ready to start. I'll be there in a small amount of time.
 ⓐ a capacity ⓑ an instant ⓒ a range ⓓ at short intervals

27. George hasn't shaved the hair on his face for two months.
 Now he has a ______ .
 ⓐ trust ⓑ check ⓒ beard ⓓ demand

28. Please help yourself to a ______ .
 ⓐ company ⓑ party ⓒ pickles ⓓ drink

29. Alice is really good She doesn't seem to have any ______ in her character.
 ⓐ flaws ⓑ influence ⓒ inventories ⓓ minors

30. She tried to improve her ______ by dieting.
 ⓐ figure ⓑ words ⓒ speech ⓓ hook

31. Don't close the garage door while the car's motor is running. The poisonous gases could damage you.
 ⓐ fumes ⓑ waste ⓒ surroundings ⓓ guest

32. Sandra' bright black eyes are her most noticeable ______ .
 ⓐ lens ⓑ beauty ⓒ feature ⓓ patience

33. Several times, Jim made an ______ about his sweetheart's address.
 ⓐ inquire ⓑ inquiry ⓒ inquisitive ⓓ inquiring

34. Though their ______ were the best their plans fell through.
 ⓐ enthusiasm ⓑ intentions ⓒ intension ⓓ extension

35. The Bakers will throw a party to pay back all the people who helped them in their homes. They have a lot of social ______ .

ⓐ advantages   ⓑ obligations   ⓒ disadvantages   ⓓ orientations

36. Not many people come to this are There's a lot of _____ here.

ⓐ public   ⓑ privacy   ⓒ relevance   ⓓ work

37. After he gets up in the morning, June exercises for half an hour. Then he takes a shower, gets dressed, eats breakfast, and go to work. He follows the same ______ every day.

ⓐ routine   ⓑ route   ⓑ skill   ⓒ success

38. What was her ______ for wanting to postpone her trip? She never told me why.

ⓐ reason   ⓑ excuse   ⓒ cause   ⓓ order

39. Water is dripping on the edge of metal. There's a lot of ______ on it.

ⓐ burst   ⓑ rust   ⓒ dust   ⓓ lust

40. Every car should keep a little ______ of water under the hood to wash the windshield with.

ⓐ conserve   ⓑ reservoir   ⓒ reserve   ⓓ conservation

41. After someone dies, people show their ______ to the family by sending flowers and letters.

ⓐ service   ⓑ decoration   ⓒ sympathy   ⓓ office

42. Thank you for your advice. I'm going to follow your ______ .

ⓐ suggestion   ⓑ suffocation   ⓒ relaxation   ⓓ activities

A 명사 / 일상생활

43. I can't drive in a rainy day because the _______ gets so blurre.
   ⓐ windward　　ⓑ windshield　　ⓒ windmill　　ⓓ windproof

44. I have a mass of laundry to do.
   ⓐ large amount　ⓑ little amount　ⓒ small amount　ⓓ some amount

45. The party area was in a state of chaos. No one knew what to do with the leftover food or where to put all the trash left on the tables and floor.
   ⓐ utter confusion　ⓑ organization　　ⓒ communication　　ⓓ ordered condition

46. Mr. Simmons gave his five-year old grandson twenty dollars for his birthday. From the perspective of a five-year old, the money seemed like a fortune.
   ⓐ the calculation　ⓑ the point of view　ⓒ the prospection　ⓓ the expectation

47. Juliet had one problem after another after moving to Seoul. She never realized there could be so many pitfalls living in a big city.
   ⓐ a big hole in the street.　　　　　ⓑ unexpected difficulties.
   ⓒ damage while having the oil changed.　ⓓ much argument

정답 / 해석

1. ⓓ 우리의 목적은 언젠가 우리 혼자 힘으로 집을 짓는 것이다.

2. ⓒ 차 마실래? 잠깐이면 끓일 수 있어.

3. ⓒ 그녀는 눈을 가릴 수 있는 각도로 모자를 쓴다.

4. ⓑ 우리는 리자를 도우려고 했으나, 그녀는 아무 도움이 필요하지 않았다.

5. ⓑ 존은 면도하는 것을 잊지 않았다. 그는 턱수염을 기르고 있다.

6. ⓓ 열일곱 번째 생일 이후에 나는 집을 떠나 대학에 진학할 수 있었다.

7. ⓓ 그 전화는 그 건물의 모퉁이에 있는 벽으로 둘러싸여 있는 작은 공간에 있다. 그것은 전화박스에 있다.

8. ⓒ 로랜드 일병은, 비를 갖고 와라. 이 방을 청소해라.

9. ⓒ 세탁소 주인(세제)도 내 옷의 점을 없애지 못했다.

10. ⓐ 칼은 친절하고, 정직하고, 또한 열심히 일한다. 그는 훌륭한 성격의 소유자다.

11. ⓐ 그녀는 그 시골의 작은 지역에서 자랐다.

12. ⓑ 아무도 나에게 편지를 쓰지 않았기 때문에 나는 이 달에 편지를 받지 않았다.

13. ⓐ 닉: 이렇게 합시다. 당신이 오늘 밤 설거지를 하고, 나는 내일 요리를 하면 되겠죠?

14. ⓒ 내 차 열쇠를 떨어뜨렸다. 여기에 손전등을 비추어 줄 수 있니?

15. ⓒ 곤란한 상황에 처하면 톰은 그의 형님에게 가서 조언을 구한다.

16. ⓒ 제임스는 온순한 성격의 소유자다. 그는 누구와도 싸우거나 다투지 않는다.

17. ⓒ 그들은 거주자의 신변을 잘 보호해 주는 아파트를 찾고 있다.)

18. ⓐ 얼굴에 흔적이 있구나. 여기 봐, 거울에 나타난 모습을.

19. ⓑ 붉은 옷을 입은 여자와 그는 어떤 관계냐?)

20. ⓒ 그레고리는 메인 주에 살고 있다. 그는 메인 주의 거주자이다.

21. ⓒ 때때로 출근길을 바꾸면, 통근이 더 재미있다.

22. ⓓ 이번 주말은 일과에 따르지 않아도 된다. 하고 싶은 대로 해라.

23. ⓑ 나는 그의 말에서 모순을 발견했다. 그는 온 종일 집에 있었다고 말했지만, 그와 같은 방을 사용하는 친구는 오후에 그가 쇼핑을 했다고 말했다.

24. ⓐ 혼자 일하는 것의 장점은 내가 내 시간을 정할 수 있다는 것이다.

25. ⓑ 마이크와 니나는 부엌을 현대식 가구로 꾸미려고 한다.

ECL시험 대비 New ALC 필수어휘 완성

26. ⓑ 곧 출발할 준비가 되어 있다. 나는 거기에 곧 갈 것이다.

27. ⓒ 조지는 두 달 동안 면도를 하지 않았다. 지금은 털보다.

28. ⓓ 많이 마시세요.

29. ⓐ 앨리스는 정말 멋있다. 그녀의 성격은 아무런 문제가 없다.

30. ⓐ 그녀는 다이어트로 몸매를 가꾸려고 노력하였다.

31. ⓐ 차의 모터가 움직이는 동안은 차고 문을 닫지 마라. 유독가스가 해롭다.

32. ⓒ 산드라의 밝고 검은 눈은 그녀의 가장 두드러진 특징이다.

33. ⓑ 몇 번씩이나, 짐은 자신의 애인의 주소에 대해 문의하였다.

34. ⓑ 그들의 의도는 매우 좋았지만 그 계획은 실패하였다.

35. ⓑ 베이커 가족은 그들을 도와 준 모든 사람들에게 보답하기 위해서 집에서 파티를 열 것이다. 그들은 갚아야 할 많은 사회적인 빚이 있다.

36. ⓑ 이 지역에는 많은 사람들이 오지 않는다. 여기는 사생활이 충분히 보호된다.

37. ⓐ 준은 아침에 일어나서 30분 동안 운동을 한다. 그런 뒤 샤워를 하고 옷을 차려입고 아침을 먹고 직장으로 간다. 그는 매일 같은 일정을 따른다.

38. ⓐ 그녀가 여행을 연기하려고 하는 이유는 무엇인가? 나에게는 아무런 이유도 말하지 않았다.

39. ⓑ 물이 쇠끝에 떨어지고 있다. 그 위에는 많은 녹이 있다.

40. ⓑ 모든 차는 앞 유리를 씻기 위해 덮개 아래에 약간의 물을 비축할 저장통이 있어야 한다.

41. ⓒ 사람이 죽으면, 사람들은 가족들에게 꽃을 보내거나 편지를 써서 연민의 정을 표시한다.

42. ⓐ 충고에 감사드립니다. 당신의 제안을 따르도록 하겠습니다.

43. ⓑ 나는 비오는 날이면 전면 유리가 흐려지기 때문에 운전을 할 수 없다.

44. ⓐ 나는 세탁물이 많다.

45. ⓐ 그 연회장은 혼란스러운 상태였다. 아무도 남은 음식을 어떻게 해야 할 지, 탁자와 마루에 있는 쓰레기를 어디에 두어야 할 지 몰랐다.

46. ⓑ 시몬씨는 자신의 다섯 살 난 손자의 생일에 이십 달러를 주었다. 다섯 살 아이에게 그 돈은 큰 재산이었다.

47. ⓑ 줄리엣은 서울로 이사한 후 계속해서 문제가 생겼다. 그녀는 대도시에 살면 많은 어려움이 있다는 것을 깨닫지 못했다.

동사

기본어휘 / 연습 문제

B

New American
Language Course

accumulate / 모으다, 축적하다 (to pile up, collect)

Have you accumulated enough wood for the fireworks tonight?

(오늘밤 불꽃놀이를 위한 충분한 나무를 비축했나요?)

activate / 작동시키다, 활성화하다 (to make a device or chemical process start working)

A burglar alarm is activated if a stranger come into the house.

(낯선 사람이 집에 들어오면 침입경보가 작동된다.)

advantage / 이익, 이득 (benefit, profit, gain)

The system advantages the rich. (그 제도는 부자들에게 이익이 된다.)

alienate / 멀어지게 하다 (to cause to be unfriendly)

Because of his relentless gossiping, Frank alienated his friends.

(쉴 새 없는 험담 때문에 프랭크는 친구들과 멀어졌다.)

assume / 당연히 여기다, 가정하다 (to take for granted, postulate)

If a present is wrapped well, we assume that the contents are valuable.

(선물의 포장이 잘 되어 있으면, 우리는 그 내용물이 가치가 있다고 생각한다.)

bear / 참다, 견디다 (withstand, endure)

We should bear all these sufferings gently.

(우리는 이 모든 고통을 점잖게 참아야 한다.)

bend / 굽다, 구부러지다 (to become curved or crooked)

The road bent toward the south.

(길은 남쪽으로 굽었다.)

connote / 내포하다 (suggest, imply)

Living a big, crowded city often connotes a lack of personal friendships.

(번잡한 대도시에 산다는 것은 개인적인 우정의 결핍을 의미한다.)

convince / 납득시키다, 설득시키다 (to make someone believe that something is true)

You don't have to convince me you're the right person for the job.

(당신이 그 직업에 꼭 맞는 사람이라는 것을 설득해야 하는 것은 아니다.)

exacerbate / 악화시키다 (to aggravate or make worse)

Although Emma tried to help, she only exacerbated the problem. It seemed she couldn't do anything right.

(엠마는 도우려고 노력했지만 문제를 악화시킬 뿐이었다. 그녀는 아무것도 잘할 수 없는 것 같았다.)

enclose / 둘러싸다, 에워싸다 (to surround someone or something)

Her arms enclosed him. (그녀의 팔이 그를 에워쌌다.)

frighten / 겁주다, 놀라게 하다 (to make someone feel afraid, especially suddenly)

Stop it! You're frightening the children.

(그만 해! 너는 아이들에게 겁을 주고 있어.)

furnish / 구비하다, 갖추다 (to provide furniture for a room or house)

Her study was furnished with an antique desk and chair.

(그녀의 연구실에는 골동품 책상과 의자로 구비되어 있다.)

1. 일상생활

grip / 쥐다, 붙잡다 (to grasp or seize firmly)

They gripped the sides of the boat as the waves tossed them about.
(파도로 몸이 흔들리자 그들은 배의 양 옆을 꽉 쥐었다.

hesitate / 머뭇거리다, 주저하다 (to pause before doing something)

He hesitated a moment, and then knocked on the door.
(그는 잠시 머뭇거린 후 방문을 노크했다.)

imitate / 따라하다, 흉내내다 (to seek to follow, to act the same as)

Parrots can imitate human speech.
(앵무새는 인간의 목소리를 흉내 낼 수 있다.)

install / 설치하다, 설비하다 (to make a piece of equipment ready for use)

Have you installed a smoke alarm in your office?
(당신 사무실에 연기 경보기를 설치하였나요?)

iron / 다림질하다 (to push a heated iron to make clothes smooth)

She's finished ironing.
(그녀는 다림질을 끝냈다.)

involve / 포함하다, 연루시키다 (to include or entail)

The new system involves little, if any, new technology.
(그 새로운 제도에는 새로운 기술이 거의 포함되어 있지 않다.)

irritate / 자극하다, 화나게 하다 (to annoy, provoke)

Soap can irritates our eyes.
(비누는 눈을 자극한다.)

judge / 판단하다, 재판하다 (to form a judgment or opinion of, decide upon critically)

You can't judge a book by its cover.

(책을 표지로 판단해서는 안 된다.)

limit / 제한하다, 한정하다 (to restrict, to confine or keep within limits)

Please limit answers to less then 30 words.

(30 단어 이내로 답을 쓰세요.)

lock / 잠그다, 닫다 (to put something in a (safe) place and lock it)

The front door slammed behind her and she was locked in the house.

(앞문이 그녀 뒤에서 닫혀서 그녀는 집 안에 갇히게 되었다.)

locate / 위치를 정하다, 두다 (to exist in a particular place)

The hotel is located in downtown Harford.

(그 호텔은 하포드의 도심지역에 있다.)

misplace / 잘못두다 (to put in a wrong place, to mislay)

I often misplace my reading glasses.

(나는 종종 독서용 안경을 잘못 놓아둔다.)

mop / 자루걸레(로 닦다) (to wash a floor using a mop)

Don't go in the kitchen, I've just finished mopping the floor.

(부엌에 가지 마세요. 방금 마루의 걸레질을 끝냈습니다.)

notice / 알아채다, 주의하다 (to become conscious of something by seeing, hearing, or

feeling them)

I noticed that the door was open.

(나는 문이 열려 있다는 것을 알았다.)

overcome / 극복하다, 이겨내다 (to conquer or control, to get the better of)

All of us must overcome the obstacles of poverty.

(우리 모두는 가난이라는 장애물을 극복해야 한다.)

owe / 빚을 지다, 은혜를 입다 (to have am obligation to pay, be indebted)

Tell me how much I owe, and I'll give it to you.

(얼마만큼 빚졌는지 말해 주면 갚아 드리겠습니다.)

pour / 붓다, 따르다 (to serve a drink, fall heavily)

Today the rain continues to pour.

(오늘은 비가 계속 퍼붓는다.)

precede / 선행하다, 앞서다 (to happen or exist before another person or thing)

The paragraph that precedes this one is unclear.

(그 문단 앞에 다른 문단이 앞서 오는 것인지 분명하지 않다.)

prohibit / 금지하다, 막다 (to forbid, hinder, prevent)

Smoking is prohibited here.

(여기서는 흡연이 금지되어 있다.)

radiate / 발산하다, 퍼지다 (to show a particular feeling or attitude in your expression or behavior)

Nervous tension was radiating from her.

(그녀에게서는 신경질적 긴장감이 감돈다.)

raise / 부양하다, 돌보다 (take care of children while they are growing up)

For most parents, raising a family is positive challenge.

(대부분의 부모들에게 있어 가족을 부양하는 일은 실질적으로 부딪치는 문제이다.)

regulate / 조절하다, 통제하다 (to control, direct, govern)

Hormones regulate our bodily functions and control growth.

(호르몬은 우리의 신체기능을 통제하고, 성장을 조절한다.)

revolve / 회전하다, 자전하다 (to be oriented, to spin or turn around a center)

The discussion revolved around the question of changing our attitude of mind.

(그 토의는 우리의 마음가짐을 어떻게 변화시킬 것인가 하는 문제에 맴돌았다.)

recognize / 인식하다, 알아보다 (to identify or know, to be aware of)

Though all of them were wearing the same jacket, I could recognize my uncleby the red sleeve.

(그들 모두는 꼭 같은 윗도리를 입었지만, 나는 붉은 소매를 보고 내 삼촌을 알 수 있다.)

seal / 밀봉(하다), 봉인(하다) (to fasten or close tightly, a piece of wax or soft metal used to close)

The seal on the jar is tight. (그 단지가 단단히 밀봉되어 있다.)

sew / 달다, 꿰매다 (to make repair clothes using a needle and thread)

He was sewing a new button on his jacket.

(그는 자신의 자켓에 단추를 달고 있었다.)

spoil / 망치다, 못쓰게 하다 (to makes something worse or less attractive)

The whole show was spoiled by the lack of decent actors.

(그 전체 공연은 행실 좋지 않은 배우들로 인해 망쳐 버렸다.)

store / 저장하다 (to put something in order to use later)

We should store fresh eggs in a refrigerator in summer.

(우리는 여름에는 신선한 달걀을 냉장고에 저장해야 한다.)

1. 일상생활

stream / 흘러들다, 흘러나오다 (flow or come out in large amounts)

Sunlight streamed through high windows at Kennedy Airport's new immigration arrival hall.
(케네디공항의 새 이민자 도착광장의 높은 창문을 통해 햇볕이 쏟아져 들어왔다.)

tackle / 부딪치다, 처리하다 (to try to do, undertake)

Grace decided to take a nap before she tackled the big stack of dirty dishes in the kitchen.
(그레이스는 부엌에 있는 한 무더기의 더러운 접시들을 설거지하기 전에 낮잠을 자기로 했다.)

trim / 다듬다, 손질하다 (to cut down, to make smaller or neater)

My hair needs trimming.
(내 머리를 다듬을 필요가 있다.)

2. 연습문제

1. Garbage usually _______ in the kitchen very fast everyday.

   ⓐ accomplishes   ⓑ accommodates   ⓒ accounts   ⓓ accumulates

2. Mother, could I please be _______ to play soccer this afternoon?

   ⓐ allowed   allowable   ⓒ asked   ⓓ accepted

3. My parents don't _______ of my smoking.

   ⓐ approve   ⓑ apprehend   ⓒ distinguish   ⓓ improve

4. Since you didn't say no, I _______ you did want to attend the meeting tonight.

   ⓐ assumed   ⓑ consumed   ⓒ resumed   ⓓ preceded

5. Please turn the volume down. I can't _______ it anymore!

   ⓐ bring   ⓑ bear   ⓒ replace   ⓓ reduce

6. When you lift a heavy object, you have to _______ your knees to avoid injuries.

   ⓐ vend   ⓑ bend   ⓒ touch   ⓓ stretch

7. You just don't try hard enough. It takes _______ to succeed.

   ⓐ effort   ⓑ effect   ⓒ expert   ⓓ affect

8. The wild dog was put in a yard with a high fence, so it could not _______ .

   ⓐ squeeze   ⓑ bounce   ⓒ embark   ⓓ escape

9. We should _____ the steering wheel tightly with both hands in the rainy street.
    ⓐ glue   ⓑ grip   ⓒ drill   ⓓ grapple

10. This argument is between you and me. I don't want to _____ anyone else.
    ⓐ consider   ⓑ endanger   ⓓ revolve   ⓓ involve

11. He has a terrible voice, so it is _____ to listen to him make a speech.
    ⓐ irritating   ⓑ disturbed   ⓒ irritated   ⓓ upset

12. We shouldn't _____ other people just by their appearance.
    ⓐ interpret   ⓑ represent   ⓒ rescue   ⓓ judge

13. When we found the miners who were buried under the ground, they were _____ only bread and water.
    ⓐ living on   ⓑ living for   ⓒ living down   ⓓ eating away

14. Judy's _____ her wallet and can't find it.
    ⓐ replaced   ⓑ misplaced   ⓒ prevented   ⓓ displaced

15. There will be a gas shortage in a few days, so we'll have to _____ the amount of gas we use.
    ⓐ limit   ⓑ increase   ⓒ supply   ⓓ calculate

16. Pvt Theresa: Where did they build the new mess hall?
    Pvt Johnson: They _____ it on McGuire Street.
    ⓐ destroyed   ⓑ reflected   ⓒ located   ⓓ spent

17. I _______ that the door was open.

   ⓐ prepared   ⓑ ordered   ⓒ pretended   ⓓ noticed

18. Many rules _______ our behavior. They tell us how to act.

   ⓐ illustrate   ⓑ eliminate   ⓒ regulate   ⓓ rub

19. Hard work doesn't always _______ success.

   ⓐ results with   ⓑ results in   ⓒ results   ⓓ results from

20. Did you _______ the envelope before you put it in the mailbox?

   ⓐ lock   ⓑ seal   ⓒ shape   ⓓ ceil

21. When the power goes off in the building, they start the emergency generator.

   ⓐ overcome   ⓑ activate   ⓒ leave   ⓓ displace

22. The police are going to find out about the robbery.

   ⓐ investigate   ⓑ detect   ⓑ explain   ⓒ expose

23. The box is big enough to _______ all the tools necessary for the job.

   ⓐ contain   ⓑ form   ⓒ seal   ⓓ content

24. Because there was a gas leak in the hall, they had to _______ the electricity to prevent a fire.

   ⓐ cut off   ⓑ check up on   ⓒ put off   ⓓ surge

25. Jack _______ me to write this letter.

   ⓐ convinced   ⓑ discuss   ⓒ disagreed   ⓓ definitely

26. I have to _____ my front yard so my dogs won't run away.

    ⓐ amplify   ⓑ enclose   ⓒ encircle   ⓓ radiate

27. What a great day! Everything's _____ !

    ⓐ gone right   ⓑ gone away   ⓒ gone wrong   ⓓ gone left

28. He _____ before he went in because he wasn't sure it was the right room.

    ⓐ inverted   ⓑ originated   ⓒ delighted   ⓓ hesitated

29. Anthony injured himself while he was repairing his car. He _____ himself.

    ⓐ hurt   ⓑ consulted   ⓒ bled   ⓓ taught

30. Your shirt looks like you slept in it. You need to _____ it.

    ⓐ dry   ⓓ dirt   ⓒ polish   ⓓ iron

31. The child tries to talk like his father. He _____ his voice.

    ⓐ challenges   ⓑ impels   ⓒ imitates   ⓓ immigrate

32. After we bought the refrigerator, we had to _____ it in the kitchen before we could use it.

    ⓐ print   ⓑ install   ⓒ assemble   ⓓ copy

33. There's water on the floor. Please _____ it up.

    ⓐ sweep   ⓑ polish   ⓒ mop   ⓓ scrub

34. A pair of blue pants will _____ a white shirt.

    ⓐ match   ⓑ tie   ⓒ button   ⓓ pin

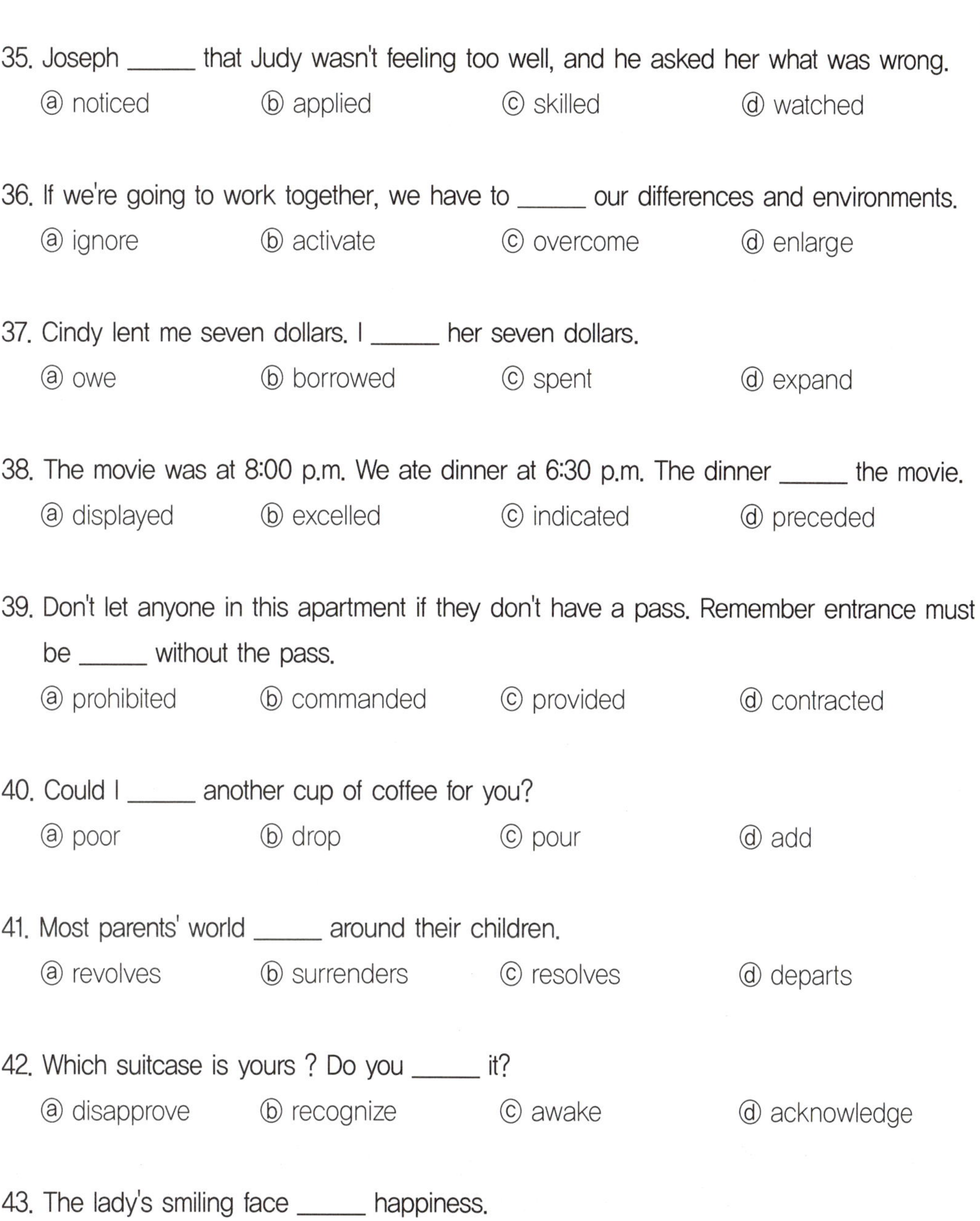

35. Joseph _____ that Judy wasn't feeling too well, and he asked her what was wrong.

ⓐ noticed   ⓑ applied   ⓒ skilled   ⓓ watched

36. If we're going to work together, we have to _____ our differences and environments.

ⓐ ignore   ⓑ activate   ⓒ overcome   ⓓ enlarge

37. Cindy lent me seven dollars. I _____ her seven dollars.

ⓐ owe   ⓑ borrowed   ⓒ spent   ⓓ expand

38. The movie was at 8:00 p.m. We ate dinner at 6:30 p.m. The dinner _____ the movie.

ⓐ displayed   ⓑ excelled   ⓒ indicated   ⓓ preceded

39. Don't let anyone in this apartment if they don't have a pass. Remember entrance must be _____ without the pass.

ⓐ prohibited   ⓑ commanded   ⓒ provided   ⓓ contracted

40. Could I _____ another cup of coffee for you?

ⓐ poor   ⓑ drop   ⓒ pour   ⓓ add

41. Most parents' world _____ around their children.

ⓐ revolves   ⓑ surrenders   ⓒ resolves   ⓓ departs

42. Which suitcase is yours ? Do you _____ it?

ⓐ disapprove   ⓑ recognize   ⓒ awake   ⓓ acknowledge

43. The lady's smiling face _____ happiness.

ⓐ radiated   ⓑ stringed   ⓒ enclosed   ⓓ focused

44. The lawn looked nice after he ______ it.

   ⓐ trimmed   ⓑ pulled   ⓒ reprimanded   ⓓ repaired

45. We often ______ the blanket to expose the other side to sunlight.

   ⓐ turned over   ⓑ turned down   ⓒ turned out   ⓓ turned off

46. Just ______ that glass on the table in the kitchen.

   ⓐ set   ⓑ fly   ⓒ support   ⓓ raise

47. ______ the light before you fall asleep.

   ⓐ Generate   ⓑ Produce   ⓒ Switch off   ⓓ Switch on

48. Do you have a needle and thread I can borrow? I need to ______ this button on.

   ⓐ sale   ⓑ see   ⓒ sew   ⓓ discard

49. Sophia really ______ her little boy. She gives him everything he wants.

   ⓐ accuses   ⓑ spoils   ⓒ warms   ⓓ blames

50. The persimmon tree is growing over the fence into the neighbor's yard. I have to ______ it.

   ⓐ trim   ⓑ slim   ⓒ treat   ⓓ grip

51. They embraced the concept of eating dinner together.

   ⓐ hugged   ⓑ hindered   ⓒ welcomed   ⓓ mistake

52. Tyler was punished for lopping the blossoms off his mother's prize roses. She was very upset when she saw her bushes without any blooms.

   ⓐ removing   ⓑ sprinkling   ⓒ running in circles around   ⓓ sprouing

정답 / 해석

1. ⓓ 쓰레기는 매일 매우 빨리 부엌에 쌓인다.

2. ⓐ 엄마, 오후에 축구해도 되나요?

3. ⓐ 나의 부모는 나의 흡연을 용인하지 않는다.

4. ⓐ 너가 반대하지 않았기 때문에, 나는 너가 오늘밤 회합에 참석하고 싶어한다고 생각하였다.

5. ⓑ 볼륨을 낮추세요. 더 이상 참을 수 없습니다.

6. ⓑ 무거운 물체를 들 때에는 부상을 피하기 위해 무릎을 구부려야 한다.

7. ⓐ 너는 열심히 노력하지 않는다. 성공하려면 노력이 필요하다.

8. ⓓ 그 거친 개는 높은 울타리가 쳐진 마당에 가두어져서, 도망갈 수 없다.

9. ⓑ 비에 젖은 거리에서는 양손으로 운전대를 단단히 잡아야 한다.

10. ⓓ 이 논쟁은 너와 내가 연관된 문제이다. 그 밖에 다른 사람이 개입되지 않았으면 한다.

11. ⓐ 그는 매우 나쁜 목소리를 가지고 있다. 그가 연설하는 것을 들으면 짜증난다.

12. ⓓ 우리는 다른 사람들을 단지 외모로 판단하지 않아야 한다.

13. ⓐ 우리가 땅 속에 묻힌 광부들을 찾았을 때, 그들은 빵과 물만 먹으며 살고 있었다.

14. ⓑ 쥬디는 자기의 지갑을 잘못 놓아두어서 찾을 수가 없다.

15. ⓐ 며칠 후 가스가 부족할 것이다. 그래서 우리는 우리가 사용하는 가스의 양을 제한해야 할 것이다.

16. ⓒ 테레사 일병: 새 사병 식당은 어디에 지었지?

    존슨 일병: 맥과이어 거리에 있지.

17. ⓓ 나는 문이 열려 있다는 것을 알았다.

18. ⓑ 많은 규칙이 우리의 행동을 규제하고 있다. 그것들은 우리의 행동방식을 지시하고 있다.

19. ⓑ 노력이 항상 성공을 낳는 것은 아니다.

20. ⓑ 우편함에 넣기 전에 봉투를 봉했습니까?

21. ⓑ 건물에 전기가 나가면, 그들은 비상발전기를 가동한다.

22. ⓐ 경찰은 그 도난에 대해 조사할 예정이다.

23. ⓐ 그 상자는 그 일에 필요한 모든 도구를 담을 수 있을 정도로 크다.

24. ⓐ 복도에 가스누출이 있었기 때문에, 그들은 화재를 예방하기 위해서 전기를 차단해야 했다.

25. ⓐ 잭은 나에게 이 편지를 써야 하는 당위성을 깨닫게 했다.

26. ⓑ 나는 개들이 뛰어다니지 못하도록 이 정원을 폐쇄해야겠다.

27. ⓐ 멋진 날이군! 모든 것이 잘 되었다.

28. ⓓ 그는 방에 들어가기 전에 맞는 방인지 확신되지 않아 머뭇거렸다.

29. ⓐ 앤소니는 자기 차를 수리하는 도중에 다쳤다. 스스로에게 상처를 입힌 것이다.

30. ⓓ 당신 셔츠가 엉망이다. 다림질을 할 필요가 있다.

31. ⓒ 그 아이는 자기 아버지처럼 말하려고 한다. 그는 아버지의 목소리를 모방한다.

32. ⓑ 냉장고를 구입한 후, 사용하기 전에 부엌에 설치해야 했다.

33. ⓒ 마루에 물이 있다. 걸레로 닦아라.

34. ⓐ 푸른색 바지가 흰 셔츠에 어울린다.

35. ⓐ 조셉은 쥬디의 상태가 별로 좋지 않다는 것을 알아차리고, 무슨 일인지 물어보았다.

36. ⓒ 우리가 함께 일하려면 서로의 차이점과 환경을 극복해야 한다.

37. ⓐ 신디는 나에게 7달러를 빌려주었다.

38. ⓓ 그 영화는 8시에 시작되었다. 우리는 6시 30분에 저녁을 먹었다. 저녁시간이 영화시간보다 빨랐다.

39. ⓐ 허가증이 없으면 이 아파트에 누구도 들여 놓지 마라. 허가증 없이는 출입할 수 없다는 것을 명심해라.

40. ⓒ 커피 좀 더 드릴까요?

41. ⓐ 대부분의 부모의 세계는 아이들 주위에서 맴돈다.

42. ⓑ 어느 가방이 너의 것이냐? 너는 알아 볼 수 있느냐?

43. ⓐ 그 여자의 웃는 얼굴은 행복을 번지게 한다.

44. ⓐ 그가 다듬은 뒤에 잔디가 멋져 보인다.

45. ⓐ 우리는 반대편에도 햇볕을 쬘 수 있도록 종종 담요를 뒤집는다.

46. ⓐ 부엌 안의 테이블은 그 잔으로 놓아라.

47. ⓒ 잠자기 전에 스위치를 끄세요.

48. ⓒ 바늘과 실을 빌릴 수 있을까요? 이 단추를 꿰매야 하거든요.

49. ⓑ 소피아는 그의 어린 시절을 망쳐버렸다. 그녀는 그가 원하는 모든 것을 주었다.

50. ⓐ 감나무가 울타리 넘어 이웃마당으로까지 자라고 있다. 가지치기를 해 주어야 한다.

51. ⓒ 그들은 함께 식사하는 생각을 환영하였다.

52. ⓐ 타일러는 그의 어머니의 멋진 장미꽃을 잘라 벌을 받았다. 그녀는 꽃이 없는 장미 관목을 보고 매우 낙담하였다.

형용사

기본어휘 / 연습 문제

C

New American
Language Course

1. 기본어휘 — 형용사

abrupt / 갑작스러운, 느닷없는 (coming or happening suddenly)
I caught cold because of an abrupt change in the weather.
(날씨가 갑자기 변하여 감기가 걸렸다.)

appropriate / 적당한, 적절한 (proper, suitable)
Appropriate gestures can be very effective in public speaking.
(적당한 손짓은 대중연설에서 매우 효과적이다.)

bucolic / 전원의, 목가적인 (rustic, rural, peaceful)
Powell spent all his hard earned money on a farm in order to live a more bucolic life.
(포웰은 보다 목가적인 삶을 살기 위해 힘들게 번 모든 돈을 농장에 투자했다.)

bumpy / 울퉁불퉁한, 요철이 많은 (not even, uncomfortable and rough)
We had a bumpy and hot ride across the desert.
(우리는 사막을 가로질러 요철이 많고 무더운 차량여행을 했다.)

convincing / 설득력 있는 (causing one to believe or agree)
She offered a totally convincing argument.
(그녀는 아주 설득력 있는 주장을 제시했다.)

crusty / 성격이 거친 (rude or harsh in speech and manner)
Although the crusty old sailor was foulmouthed and quick to anger, those who knew him well saw through his tough exterior.

(성질 나쁜 늙은 선원은 입이 상스럽고 성을 잘 내었지만, 그를 잘 아는 사람들은 그의 투박한 외모의 이면을 꿰뚫어 보았다.)

dependent / 의지하는, 의존하는 (controlled, determined, subordinate)

The harvest is dependent largely upon the weather. (수확은 대개 날씨에 좌우된다.)

generous / 관대한, 온화한 (giving people more of your time or money than is usual or expected)

Merton is clearly a warm and generous human being.
(멀톤은 따뜻하고 온화한 사람임이 분명하다.)

former / 앞의, 이전의 (past. preceding in order)

The former suggestion was preferred to the latter. (앞의 제안이 뒤에 나온 제안보다 더 낫다.)

independent / 독립한, 자립의 (free from others, not connected with others)

An independent school is a school which does not receive money from thegovernment.
(자립 학교는 정부로부터 금전을 받지 않는 학교이다.)

ingrained / 뿌리박힌, 생성된, 각인된 (firmly fixed or established)

Adam's parents have always taught him to be considerate and thoughtful toothers.
Consequently, good manners have been ingrained in him sincechildhood.
(아담의 부모는 그에게 다른 사람들을 사려 깊게 생각해라고 가르쳤다. 그 결과, 어린 시절부터 좋은 태도가 그에게 생성되었다.)

innocuous / 악의가 없는, 해가 없는 (harmless, not offensive)

You have no reason to be upset; what I said was perfectly innocuous.
(너는 기분 나빠 할 필요가 없다. 내가 말한 것은 전혀 악의가 없었다.)

mean / 비열한, 잔인한 (cruel, angry, violent)

Don't be so mean to your sister. (여동생에게 너무 치사하게 행동하지 않도록 하라.)

messy / 더러운, 지저분한 (not neat or dirty)

Politics has always been a messy business. (정치학은 항상 지저분한 분야다.)

nonverbal / 말을 사용하지 않는, 비언어적인 (not involving words or speech)

Unable to speak, the elderly woman communicated her ideas in a nonverbal manner.
(말을 할 수가 없어서 그 중년의 여자는 몸짓으로 자신의 생각을 전달하였다.)

parochial / 편협한 (limited or narrow in scope), 지방적인

Although Logan has studied and traveled in other countries, his views are still rather
parochial. You'd think his outlook would have been broadened by the traveling he's done.
(로간은 외국에서 공부하고 여행도 했지만, 그의 사고는 여전히 편협하다. 너는 그가 여행을 해서 사고
방식이 관대할 것으로 생각했을 것이다.)

previous / 이전의, 앞의 (coming before something else, before, prior to)

The previous owner of the house built an extension on the front.
(그 집의 이전 소유자가 앞 쪽으로 건물을 확장하였다.)

prior / 이전의, 앞의 (before, previous)

I can't attend the wedding ceremony because a prior engagement.
(나는 선약 때문에 결혼식에 참가할 수 없다.)

reliable / 믿을 만한, 신뢰할 만한 (a reliable person is someone you can trust to behave well, work hard, or do what you expect them to do

This is a better and more reliable car than my last one.
(이 차는 이전의 차보다 더 좋고 믿음직하다.)

remote / 먼, 먼 장래의 (far away from the cities, towns, or people)

The idea of a vacation seems so remote I can hardly even imagine it.

(휴가 가려면 한참 기다려야 하기에 휴가는 생각하기 힘들다.)

restricted / 제한된, 한정된 (limited to or admitting only members of a group orclass)

Building in this area of the city is restricted.

(이 지역에서의 건물 신축은 금지되어 있다.)

self-confidence / 자신감 (confidence in one's ability)

It takes a lot of self-confidence to travel abroad by yourself for the first time.

(처음 혼자서 외국으로 여행하기 위해서는 많은 자신감이 필요하다.)

2. 연습문제

1. Susan doesn't make many mistakes. She's usually _______ .
   ⓐ accurate　　　ⓑ attributive　　　ⓒ auditory　　　ⓓ strict

2. I'm so happy here, so I don't want to move _______ else.
   ⓐ no place　　　ⓑ anyplace　　　ⓒ someplace　　　ⓓ every place

3. He _______ passed his course. He got a 70.
   ⓐ rarely　　　ⓑ idly　　　ⓒ barely　　　ⓓ mostly

4. Dorothy bounced up and down on her way home because the road was so _______ .
   ⓐ twisted　　　ⓑ smooth　　　ⓒ bumpy　　　ⓓ even

5. The electricity went off last night; _______ , my alarm clock didn't ring, so I got up late this morning.
   ⓐ however　　　ⓑ otherwise　　　ⓒ consequently　　　ⓓ at once

6. Bill slept well last night. His bed was _______ .
   ⓐ uneasy　　　ⓑ comfortable　　　ⓒ dirt　　　ⓓ pretty

7. When I talk about something with my wife, I usually end up agreeing with her. She's very _______ .
   ⓐ convincing　　　ⓑ entire　　　ⓒ preventable　　　ⓓ argumentative

8. Do you know how many ______ Koran Presidents are still living?

ⓐ before　　　ⓑ former　　　ⓒ formal　　　ⓓ front

9. Although the box was quite heavy, Jack lifted it with ______ .

ⓐ peace　　　ⓑ sight　　　ⓒ ease　　　ⓓ comfort

10. The house is ______ with many beautiful items.

ⓐ open　　　ⓑ made　　　ⓒ included　　　ⓓ furnished

11. "He'd give you the shirt off his back" is an expression that is used to describe a ______ person.

ⓐ rich　　　ⓑ mean　　　ⓒ handsome　　　ⓓ generous

12. The woman has lives alone for a long time and is very ______ .

ⓐ independent　　ⓑ dependent　　ⓒ distinguished　　ⓓ unreliable

13. After the children played, their clothes were torn and dirty. They were ______ .

ⓐ neat　　　ⓑ nice　　　ⓒ messy　　　ⓓ attractive

14. People can not remember what Barbara looks like because she's very ______ .

ⓐ plain　　　ⓑ homely　　　ⓒ patient　　　ⓓ friendly

15. I didn't talk to Smith last week; I talked to him the ______ week.

ⓐ secondary　　ⓑ opposite　　ⓒ previous　　ⓓ second

16. We should pt on our socks ______ putting on our shoes.

ⓐ while　　　ⓑ prior to　　　ⓒ preferred to　　　ⓓ beforehand

C 형용사 / 일상생활

17. I only see my friend once every five years. Our visits are ______ .
ⓐ many   ⓑ brave   ⓒ rare   ⓓ direct

18. If John says he's coming at 8:00, he will be here at 8:00. He's a very ______ person.
ⓐ reliable   ⓑ duty   ⓒ neat   ⓓ messy

19. The action took place far away from populated areas. The location was ______ .
ⓐ constant   ⓑ nearby   ⓒ remote   ⓓ vague

20. Nobody can go in there. That area is ______ .
ⓐ stern   ⓑ restricted   ⓒ firm   ⓓ strict

21. Jacky is always sure that she is right. She's very ______ .
ⓐ educational   ⓑ self-confident   ⓒ successful   ⓓ sufficient

22. His reaction to the unendurable situation was absolutely right. I would have acted ______ .
ⓐ strenuously   ⓑ similarly   ⓒ permanently   ⓓ differently

23. Don't play the radio so loudly. Play it ______ .
ⓐ turned up   ⓑ poorly   ⓒ softly   ⓓ quickly

24. The sudden and unexpected noise frightened the sleeping child.
ⓐ abrupt   ⓑ additive   ⓒ ample   ⓓ annoying

25. His sullen expression showed that he wasn't happy with the decision that was made.
ⓐ showing ill humor by gloomy silence
ⓑ meeting between the heads of the state
ⓒ dish of ice cream with fruits, nuts, juice, etc

ⓓ expensive and grand expression

26. Leah's father is very wise and practical. She can always trust him to give her sound advice.

    ⓐ meaningless   ⓑ sensible and reliable

    ⓒ frank   ⓓ sarcastic and negative

27. Jake didn't take enough time to consider all his options so he made a hasty decision.

    ⓐ without much thought   ⓑ withough agreement

    ⓒ over a long period of time.   ⓓ with much thought

정답 / 해석

1. ⓐ 수잔은 많은 실수를 하지 않는다. 그녀는 대개 정확하다.

2. ⓑ 나는 여기에 있는 것이 행복해서 다른 곳으로 옮기고 싶지 않다.

3. ⓒ 그는 과정을 간신히 통과하였다. 그는 70점을 받았다.

4. ⓒ 길이 울퉁불퉁하였기 때문에 도로시는 집으로 오는 도중 아래위로 뛰었다.

5. ⓒ 어젯밤 전기가 나가고, 그 결과 자명종이 울리지 않아서, 오늘 아침 늦게 일어났다.

6. ⓑ 빌은 어제 밤 잘 잤다. 그의 침대는 안락하다.

7. ⓐ 나는 아내와 토의할 때 대개 그녀에게 결국에는 동의하게 된다. 아내는 매우 설득력이 있다.

8. ⓑ 너는 과거 한국 대통령이 몇 명이나 아직 살아 있는지 아느냐?

9. ⓒ 상자는 꽤 무거웠지만 잭은 그것을 쉽게 들었다.

10. ⓓ 그 집은 아름다운 것들이 많이 있다.

11. ⓓ "그는 그의 셔츠를 벗어 줄 것이다" 라는 표현은 그가 관대한 사람이라는 의미다.

12. ⓐ 그 여자는 오랫동안 혼자 살아서, 매우 독립적이다.

ECL시험 대비 New ALC 필수어휘 완성

13. ⓒ 놀고 난 뒤 아이들의 옷은 찢어지고 더러워졌다. 옷들은 엉망이었다.

14. ⓐ 사람들은 바바라가 너무 평범하기 때문에 얼굴이 어떠했는지 기억하지 못한다.

15. ⓒ 나는 지난 주에 스미스와 대화하지 않았다. 나는 그와 그 전 주에 대화하였다.

16. ⓑ 신발을 신기 전에 양말을 신어야 한다.

17. ⓒ 나는 매 5년마다 내 친구를 만난다. 우리 만남은 아주 드물다.

18. ⓐ 만약 존이 8시에 온다고 말했다면, 그는 8시에 올 것이다. 그는 아주 믿음직한 사람이다.

19. ⓒ 그 작전은 인구밀집 지역으로부터 멀리 떨어진 곳에서 행해졌다. 그 장소는 멀리 떨어진 곳이다.

20. ⓑ 아무도 그 안에 들어갈 수 없다. 그 지역은 금지 구역이다.

21. ⓑ 재키는 항상 자신이 옳다고 확신한다. 그녀는 매우 자신감이 있다.

22. ⓑ 참을 수 없는 상황에 대한 그의 반응은 옳다. 나도 유사하게 행동했을 것이다.

23. ⓒ 라디오 소리를 너무 크게 하지 마라. 소리를 줄여라.

24. ⓐ 갑작스런 예기치 않은 소리가 잠자는 아이를 놀라게 했다.

25. ⓐ 그의 못마땅한 표정은 그 결정에 만족하지 않음을 보여 준다.

26. ⓑ 리아의 아버지는 매우 현명하고 실용적이다. 그녀는 항상 아버지가 그녀에게 건전한 충고를 해 줄 것이라고 믿는다.

27. ⓑ 제이크는 모든 대안을 고려할 충분한 시간이 없었다. 그래서 그는 성급한 결정을 내렸다.

어휘, 관용구, 문형 종합

기본어휘 / 연습 문제

D

New American
Language Course

barely / 간신히, 가까스로 (only just, hardly)

We could barely see the street in the thick fog.

(짙은 안개로 인해 거리를 거의 볼 수가 없었다.)

bite the bullet / 정면으로 대응하다 (to confront a difficult situation with courage)

Colin finally had to bite the bullet and tell his father that he had wrecked the car. He had no other alternative.

(콜린은 나쁜 상황에 정면으로 부딪치지 않을 수 없었다. 그의 아버지에게 자신이 차를부수었다고 말했다. 다른 대안이 없었다.)

consequently / 그 결과 (as a result, therefore)

It rained heavily last night; consequently, the street was flooded.

(어제 밤 많은 비로 도로가 범람하였다.)

be fed up / 지겨운 (be disgusted with, be bored or tired with)

I'm fed up with his complaints. (나는 그의 불평이 지겹다.)

bring back / 되돌리다, 상기시키다 (to cause ideas, feelings, or memories to be in your mind again)

Do these stories bring back any memories? (이 이야기들은 어떤 기억을 떠 올리게 합니까?)

calm down / 진정하다 (to begin to feel more relaxed and less emotional)

Calm down and tell us what's going on. (진정하시고 어찌된 일인지 말해보세요.)

cheer up / 격려하다 (to give hope, comfort, encouragement to others)

She often cheer us up with her happy smile.
(그녀는 종종 행복한 미소로 우리를 격려한다.)

drop in (on) / 비공식 방문하다 (to visit informally or unexpectedly)

Why not drop in for a chat? (담소하러 놀러오지 않겠니?)

in all / 전체 (as a total)

There were ten of us in all for the meeting.
(그 모임에 참가한 사람은 모두 우리 열 명이었다.)

in the event / 그럴 경우, 그러면 (if something happens)

There's a possibility of my travel being delayed. In that event I'll phone to letyou know.
(내 여행이 연기될 가능성이 있다. 그 경우에는 내가 전화로 알려 줄께.)

look down on / 깔보다 (to think of as less good or important, to despise)

Nobody looks down on the people who hasn't been to college.
(대학가지 않은 사람들을 경멸하는 사람은 아무도 없다.)

look out for / 주의하다 (to be wary about, to try to avoid something bad)

What are the symptoms to look out for? (주의해야 할 징조는 무엇입니까?)

no matter how / 어떤 방식이든 (however)

Arrange your schedule however you want to. (너의 일과를 원하는 데로 조정하여라.)

nowhere / 아무데도 (없다) (not in any place, not anywhere)

I glanced anxiously at the hall, but she was nowhere to be seen.
(나는 걱정스럽게 실내를 보았지만, 그녀는 어디에도 보이지 않았다.)

put away / 치우다, 잊다 (to put in the right place or out of sight, to stop thinking)

You should put away your worries during the party.

(파티가 진행되는 동안에는 걱정을 잊어라.)

ready to [for] / 준비 된, 기꺼이 하는 (prepared for, willing to)

Can you help me get every food ready for this party?

(이번 파티의 음식을 준비하는 데 도와 줄 수 있니?)

run short of / 부족하다, 바닥나다 (having less than enough)

We are running short of fuel.

(연료가 다 떨어져 간다.)

similarly / 유사한, 비슷한 (in almost the same way)

Most of Japanese people who travel abroad are similarly dressed.

(외국을 여행하는 일본인들은 대부분 비슷하게 옷을 입는다.)

turn down / 줄이다, 작게 하다 (to reduce the amount of sound, heat, or light produced by a piece of equipment by pressing a button or moving a switch

Could you turn down the music down a little?

(그 음악 소리를 좀 줄여 줄 수 있겠어요?)

turn up / 올리다, 높이다 (to increase the amount of sound, heat, or light produced by a piece of equipment by pressing a button or moving a switch)

Can you turn the volume up a little? (볼륨을 좀 더 높여주시면 안될까요?)

underneath / 아래에 (under, below)

The letter was pushed underneath the door. (그 편지는 문 아래쪽으로 밀려들어갔다.)

stay over / 외박하다, 하루 밤 (밖에서) 자다 (to sleep in someone's house as a guest for one night)

It's getting late; do you want to stay over?

(지체되고 있네요. 계속 남아 있겠습니까?)

switch off / 끄다, 중지하다 (to turn off, stop thinking)

He just switched off and ignored me. (그는 스위치를 내리고 나를 무시했다.)

cut off / 차단하다, 막다 (to block or separate)

We are told to pay the bill or the water supply will be cut off.

(요금을 지불하지 않으면 수도공급이 중단될 것이라고 한다.)

live on / 먹고 살다 (to eat only or a particular type of food)

Koreans are living mainly on rice. (한국인은 주식으로 쌀을 먹는다.)

result from / 초래되다 (to come out from)

Many stomach problems result from what you eat.

(많은 위장병은 섭취하는 음식에서 초래된다.)

result in / 초래한다, 원인이 된다 (to spring or arise as a consequence of actions)

Thirty percent of road accidents result in serious head injuries.

(교통사고의 30%는 심각한 두뇌 손상을 초래한다.)

1. Okay, guys, I _______ your fighting!
  ⓐ am satisfied with ⓑ disturbed   ⓒ am fed up with   ⓓ am indulged in

2. No, I didn't tell _______ , _______ .
  ⓐ anything, anybody   ⓑ someone, some thing
  ⓒ anybody, anything   ⓓ everybody, everything

3. You didn't say _______ to _______ , did you?
  ⓐ anything, anybody   ⓑ nothing, nobody
  ⓒ nothing, somebody   ⓓ everything, nobody

4. The children sat _______ their grandmother and asked her to tell them stories.
  ⓐ probably   ⓑ a lot   ⓒ definitely   ⓓ around

5. When Brian heard that song on the radio, it _______ memories of his high school days.
  ⓐ bought back   ⓑ suddenly   ⓒ blamed   ⓓ imagine

6. The kid feels upset today because his friend has moved away to Seoul. Let's ____ the poor child.
  ⓐ hurry up   ⓑ cheer up   ⓒ get up   ⓓ take up

7. We haven't seen Gerry for quite a while. Let's _______ this afternoon.
  ⓐ drop in on him   ⓑ drop out of him   ⓒ drop in with him   ⓓ drop behind him

8. **Calm down.**

    ⓐ Depress down

    ⓑ Don't get so excited

    ⓒ It's around 6.

    ⓓ Please say something

9. He **looks down on** people who do such a pretentious behavior like that.

    ⓐ talks back to   ⓑ does not respect   ⓒ wants to be like   ⓓ keep away from

10. I _____ an old photo of mine taken at the Naval academy while I was looking for some papers yesterday.

    ⓐ came up with   ⓑ came on   ⓒ came down on   ⓓ came across

11. **Jack did me a favor.**

    ⓐ He asked me to help him.

    ⓑ He didn't need help.

    ⓒ He helped me.

    ⓓ He couldn't figure out what I said.

12. My wife worked on knitting a handbag for several days. _____ , I guess it took her about 30 hours to complete it.

    ⓐ For all   ⓑ At all   ⓒ After all   ⓓ In all

13. What do you want me to tell Donna **in the event** she calls?

    ⓐ as long as   ⓑ in case   ⓒ unless   ⓓ before

14. Oh, no! I locked my keys _____ the car.

    ⓐ beside   ⓑ inside   ⓒ on   ⓓ at

15. John's sister is going to _____ the kids while we go shopping.

    ⓐ check out   ⓑ look after   ⓒ turn on   ⓓ take up

16. They say that there are abandoned and dangerous dogs loose around here. You'd better
_____ .
    ⓐ look forward to it
    ⓑ look down on it
    ⓒ look back on it
    ⓓ look out for it

17. My brother always found her purse _____ how it was concealed.
    ⓐ no matter
    ⓑ in spite
    ⓒ even though

18. John: Where are you going this coming Saturday?
    William: _____ . I have no money.
    ⓐ Nowhere
    ⓑ Somewhere
    ⓒ Everywhere
    ⓓ Anywhere

19. Does the jacket that's on the wall belong to you? Does the jacket _____ belong to you?
    ⓐ is the wall
    ⓑ the wall is on
    ⓒ on the wall
    ⓓ that's the wall

20. Now that winter is coming, you'd better store your summer clothes in a wardrobe.
    ⓐ bear in mind
    ⓑ bring out
    ⓒ put away
    ⓓ take off

21. Please _____ the jewel case on the top shelf in the closet.
    ⓐ put away
    ⓑ put across
    ⓒ put up with
    ⓓ put out

22. You need to hurry. You're _____ time.
    ⓐ running short of
    ⓑ going over
    ⓒ distributing
    ⓓ taking

23. Maria: Have you seen Susan anywhere?
    Edward: No, but I suppose she's _____ in this building.
    ⓐ anyplace
    ⓑ anything
    ⓒ something
    ⓓ someplace

24. If the paper isn't on top of the refrigerator, look ______ .

   ⓐ uncomfortable   ⓑ against   ⓒ besides   ⓓ underneath

25. Please ______ the radio. I can't hear it.

   ⓐ put on   ⓑ turn on   ⓒ turn up   ⓓ turn down

26. Dave: Did you hear that loud noise last night?

   Mark: Yes, I was sleeping and it ______ .

   ⓐ threw me out   ⓑ woke me up   ⓒ put me out   ⓓ picked me up

27. He was scared of a big dog.

   ⓐ love very much   ⓑ frightened   ⓒ doesn't care   ⓓ proud

28 Please turn down the TV.

   ⓐ continue the program   ⓑ increase the volume

   ⓒ reduce the volume   ⓓ put off

29. Steven was ready to go out for lunch when he got a long distance phone call from his sister..

   ⓐ was likely to   ⓑ was about to

   ⓒ was reluctant to   ⓓ was possible to

30. She always wants to get anything she needs.

   ⓐ whoever   ⓑ wherever   ⓒ whatever   ⓓ whenever

31. The child begged relentlessly for the new toy. His mother finally gave in and bought it for him.

   ⓐ persistently   ⓑ perpetually   ⓒ softly   ⓒ devotedly

32. Let's give it a shot.

ⓐ Let's give it an injection.   ⓑ Let's try it.

ⓒ Let's fire the gun.   ⓓ Let's take it away.

33. It's out of this world.

ⓐ It's extraterrestrials.   ⓑ It's awful.

ⓒ It's indescribably delicious.   ⓓ It's terribly bitter

34. I'll go for that.

ⓐ I'll look at that.   ⓑ I'll try that.

ⓒ I'll pass on that   ⓓ I'd like to buy it.

35. Everything was super.

ⓐ It was excellent.   ⓑ It was too much.

ⓒ The dishes were very big.   ⓓ It is insignificant

36. I have a sweet tooth.

ⓐ Candy is stuck to my tooth.   ⓑ My tooth is sweet.

ⓒ I like desserts.   ⓓ I like sweet food.

37. Coming right up.

ⓐ It'll be served soon.   ⓑ It's being raised.

ⓒ It's coming up on the right.   ⓓ It will arrive on time.

38. This one's on us.

ⓐ This is our night out.   ⓑ We'll pay this time.

ⓒ The wine spilled on us.   ⓓ I like this one.

39. I'll cover the tip.

    ⓐ I'll pay the whole bill.

    ⓑ I'll cover this sharp point.

    ⓒ I'll leave the waiter money for good service.

    ⓓ I'll not pay the tip

40. Mr. Hunter: That box looks awfully heavy. Can I give you a hand?

    Mrs. Lees: Yes, thank you. It weighs more than I thought.

    ⓐ Let me applaud you.   ⓑ Let me help you.

    ⓒ Let me open the box.   ⓓ Let me work alone.

41. Amy: LT Boga says they eat roaches in his country.

    Pam: Yeah, he was just pullin' your leg.

    ⓐ trying to get her to eat roaches   ⓑ joking with her

    ⓒ trying to make her mad   ⓓ travel with you

42. Sam: Hey Joe, where's Kelly? Doesn't she usually sit behind you?

    Joe: She used to, but I told her to get off my back.

    ⓐ to stop bothering me.   ⓑ not to sit behind me.

    ⓒ to stop lying to me.   ⓓ to stand by me

43. Martin: How'd the meeting go?

    Robert: Okay. We talked about what to do with Keller. Nobody likes him.

    Martin: I wonder if his ears were burning.

    ⓐ he overheard you talking about him

    ⓑ someone told him you were talking about him.

    ⓒ he sensed you were talking about him.

    ⓓ he got into trouble.

44. Sally: Would you like to go to lunch with us today?

Katie: Yes, but I can't. I need to save my money.

Sally: That's okay. Larry's going to foot the bill.

ⓐ pay for everyone ⓑ leave the restaurant without paying

ⓒ make everyone pay him later ⓓ get a part time job

45. Mr. Smith: Oh, no! I can't find the notes for my speech. What am I going to do?

Mr. Riden: I guess you'll just have to talk off the top of your head.

ⓐ memorize the speech. ⓑ shorten your speech.

ⓒ talk to the audience sincerely. ⓓ speak without preparing.

46. Boss: What do you want to talk to me about?

Stan: I want to get something off my chest.

ⓐ see a doctor about my problem today.

ⓑ talk with you in private.

ⓒ talk about something that's bothering me.

ⓓ stop moving heavy boxes around.

47. Oliver is a very optimistic person. He can smile even when the chips are down.

ⓐ the stock market plunges ⓑ having hard luck; ill fortune

ⓒ broken pieces of glass on the floor ⓓ the potato chips are not crunchy

48. Because we're so fond of Michael, we tried to bear with the rude behavior of his children.

ⓐ put up patiently with ⓑ try to like

ⓒ ignore ⓓ get along with

49. Edward is usually so polite and well-mannered. For him to be so rude and thoughtless is totally out of character.

ⓐ the part of an evil person in a play.　　ⓑ inconsistent with his usual conduct.

ⓒ rude at least half of the time.　　ⓓ consistent with his real character

50. A: You were really lucky to meet the President.

B: Yeah, it was the opportunity of a lifetime.

ⓐ stages of one's life　　ⓑ greatest chance of one's life

ⓒ informative meeting

51. No one could pull off that kind of schedule today.

ⓐ cancel　　ⓑ accomplish　　ⓒ approve　　ⓓ admit

52. Julio: What's so funny?

Mario: Velez asked Cruz if his wife was his mother!

Julio: You're kidding? Velez really put his foot in his mouth, didn't he?

ⓐ left very carefully.　　ⓑ made an embarrassing mistake.

ⓒ interrupted his friend.　　ⓓ did the best he could

정답 / 해석

1. ⓒ 그만, 나는 너희들의 싸움이 지겹다.

2. ⓒ 아니, 나는 누구에게도 아무 말도 하지 않았다.

3. ⓐ 너는 누구에게도 아무 말 안했지?

4. ⓓ 아이들은 할머니 주위에 앉아서 이야기 해달라고 졸랐다.

5. ⓐ 브라이언은 라디오에서 흘러나오는 그 노래를 듣고 고등학교 시절을 회상했다.

6. ⓑ 그의 친구가 서울로 이사 가서 그 애는 오늘 기분이 울적하다. 그 가엾은 아이를 격려하자.

7. ⓐ 제리를 본지 오래되었다. 오늘 오후에 들러보자.

8. ⓑ 진정하세요.

9. ⓑ 그는 그와 같이 위선적인 행동을 하는 사람들을 경멸한다.

10. ⓓ 나는 어제 서류를 찾는 동안에 해군사관학교에서 찍은 옛 사진을 우연히 발견했다.

11. ⓒ 잭은 나에게 호의를 베풀었다.

12. ⓓ 나의 아내는 며칠 동안 핸드백 뜨개질 작업을 했다. 그것을 완성시키는 데 모두 합쳐서 약 서른 시간이 걸렸다.

13. ⓑ 그녀가 전화를 걸어오면 너는 내가 도나에게 무엇을 말하기를 원하느냐?

14. ⓑ 아이쿠! 열쇠를 차 안에 놓고 잠구었다.

15. ⓑ 존의 여동생은 우리가 쇼핑하는 동안 아이들을 보살필 것이다.

16. ⓓ 이 주위에 버려진 위험한 개가 있다. 주의하는 게 좋을 거다.

17. ⓐ 지갑이 어디에 감추어져 있어도 나의 동생은 그녀의 지갑을 찾는다.

18. ⓐ 존: 이번 토요일 어디로 갈 예정이니?

   윌리엄: 아무데도 안가. 돈이 없어.

19. ⓒ 벽에 걸린 윗도리는 너의 것이냐?

20. ⓒ 겨울이 다가오니, 여름철 옷은 옷장에 치워두는 것이 좋다.

21. ⓐ 벽장안의 맨 위쪽 선반에 보석함을 치워두어라.

22. ⓐ 서둘 필요가 있다. 시간이 없다.

23. ⓓ 마리아: 수잔 어디서 보았니?

   에드워드: 아니, 그러나 이 건물 어딘가 있을 것으로 생각한다.

24. ⓓ 만약 서류가 냉장고 위에 없으면, 그 아래를 살펴보세요.

25. ⓒ 라디오 소리를 좀 높여주세요. 들리지가 않아요.

26. ⓑ 데이브: 어제 밤 시끄러운 소리 들었지?

마크: 예, 자고 있었는데, 그 소리 때문에 잠을 깼답니다.

27. ⓑ 그는 큰 개를 무서워한다.

28. ⓒ TV 소리를 줄이세요.

29. ⓑ 스티븐이 점심 먹으러 나가려는 순간, 그는 여동생으로부터 장거리 전화를 받았다.

30. ⓒ 그녀는 자신이 필요로 하는 것은 모두 항상 갖고 싶어한다.

31. ⓐ 그 아이는 집요하게 새 장난감을 요구했다. 그의 어머니는 마침내 굴복하고, 그에게 그것을 사 주었다.

32. ⓑ 한번 시식[시험]해 봅시다.

33. ⓒ 그것은 매우 맛있다.

34. ⓑ 내가 한번 시험해볼게.

35. ⓐ 모든 것이 훌륭했다.

36. ⓒ 나는 디저트를 좋아한다.

37. ⓐ 곧 (배달해) 드리겠습니다.

38. ⓑ 이번에는 우리가 지불하겠다.

39. ⓒ 팁은 내가 낼께

40. ⓑ 헌터씨: 그 상자 매우 무거워 보입니다. 도와 줄까요?

리부인: 예, 고마워요. 생각보다 무겁네요.

41. ⓑ 애미: 보가 대위는 자기 조국에서는 바퀴벌레를 먹는다고 했다.

팸: 그래, 그는 너를 놀린거야.

42. ⓐ 샘: 헤이, 조. 캘리 어디있니? 그녀는 항상 너 뒤에 앉지 않니?

죠: 그랬어, 그렇지만 나는 그녀에게 성가시게 굴지마라고 했어.

43. ⓐ 마틴: 회합은 어떻게 되었니?

로버트: 좋아. 우리는 캘러를 어떻게 할지에 대해 이야기했어. 아무도 그를 좋아하지 않아.

마틴: 그의 귀가 간질간질하지 않는지 의심스럽다.

44. ⓐ 셀리: 오늘 우리와 점심먹으러 갈래?

캐티: 그러고 싶지만, 안돼. 돈을 아껴야 해.

셀리: 괜찮아. 래리가 지불할거야.

45. ⓓ 스미스: 내 연설 메모지를 분실했어. 어떻게 하지?

　　라이든: 즉석에서 말해야겠지.

46. ⓒ 상관: 무슨 말을 하려고 하지?

　　스텐: 마음 속의 부담을 털어놓고 싶습니다.

47. ⓑ 올리버는 매우 낙천적인 사람이다. 그는 운이 나쁠 때에도 미소를 짓는다.

48. ⓐ 우리는 마이클을 매우 좋아하기 때문에 그 아이들의 무례한 행동을 참으려고 노력했다.

49. ⓑ 에드워드는 대개 매우 공손하고 예의가 있다. 그가 그렇게 무례하고 사려깊지 못했다는 것은 맞지 않다.

50. ⓑ A: 너는 운 좋게 대통령을 만났구나.

　　B: 그래, 그것은 일생의 기회였어.

51. ⓑ 요즘은 아무도 그런 종류의 계획을 해낼 수 없다.

52. ⓑ 줄리오: 뭐가 재미있니?

　　마리오: 베레즈가 크루즈에게 자기 아내가 그의 어머니냐고 물었어.

　　줄리오: 정말? 벨레즈는 크게 실언을 했군.

New American Language Course

New American
Language Course

사회와 경제 2

A. 명사   B. 동사   C. 형용사   D. 어휘, 관용구, 문형 종합

ECL시험 대비 NEW ALC 必 필수어휘 완성

명사

기본어휘 / 연습 문제

A

New American
Language Course

access / 접근, 출입 (a way or means of approaching)
The main access to the building is at the right side.
(건물에 진입하는 입구는 오른쪽에 있습니다.)

accessory / 액세서리 (a small thing such as a piece of jewelry)
The book offers advice on choosing fabrics, furniture, and accessories.
(이 책은 건조물, 가구, 부속물의 선택에 관해 조언하고 있다.)

accord / 협정, 일치 (formal agreement between countries or groups)
A peace accord was signed by both leaders. (평화협정은 두 지휘관들 간에 조인되었다.)

advantage / 유리, 이익 (benefit, gain, profit)
It will be to his advantage to learn Chinese before going to China.
(중국에 가기 전에 중국어를 배우면 그에게 유리할 것이다.)

agreement / 일치, 합의 (an arrangement or decision about what to do)
Check the terms of your lease agreement right away.
(당신의 계약기간을 지금 즉시 확인하세요.)

allocation / 배분, 배정 (distribution, setting a thing apart for a specific purpose)
Some of the federal agencies weren't satisfied with the government's allocation of funds;
they felt they had been cheated out of badly needed monies.
(몇몇 연방기관들은 정부의 예산할당에 만족하지 않았다. 그들은 필요한 돈을 사기 당했나고 느꼈다.)

allowance / 급여 (an amount of money that is given regularly)

She gets an allowance for looking after the kids.

(그녀는 아이들을 돌보는 데 대한 급여를 받는다.)

approval / 동의, 허가 (agreement, permission)

We must get the commander's approval to use buses.

(버스를 사용하기 위해서는 지휘관의 동의를 얻어야 한다.)

bar / 장애, 막대기 (a long piece of wood or metal, hinder)

A lack of formal education is no bar to becoming rich.

(공식적인 교육을 적게 받았다고 부자가 되는데 장애가 되지는 않는다.)

bargain / 싼 물건, 매매 (something you buy that costs much less than normal)

You should be able to pick up a few good bargains.

(당신은 몇몇 좋은 값싼 물건들을 살 수 있습니다.)

bearer / 지참자, 짐꾼 (one that carries or supports)

A green card is a work permit and proof of legal entry and it entitles the bearer to permanent residence and to apply for citizenship after five years.

(영주권은 노동허가서이며 합법적인 입국에 대한 증거로써, 소지자에게 영주권을 주고 5년 뒤에 시민권을 신청할 자격을 준다.)

bundle / 짐, 묶음 (a group of things that have been tied together)

The women carried heavy bundles on their backs.

(그 여자들은 등에 무거운 짐들을 지고 나른다.)

charisma / 권능, 지도적 재능 (a special charm that inspires loyalty and devotion)

President Roosevelt used his great charisma and other qualities of influence to lead

A 명사 / 사회와 경제

America out of economic depression.
(루즈벨트 대통령은 미국을 경제침체로부터 이끌어가기 위해서 그의 강한 카리스마와 아울러 여러 가지 다른 영향력 있는 자질을 이용했다.)

constitution / 헌법 (a set of basic laws or principles for a country)
The US Constitution guarantees freedom of the press. (미국 헌법은 언론의 자유를 보장한다.)

contents / 내용(물) (the things that are inside something such as box and bottle)
He emptied out the contents of his pockets onto the table.
(그는 자신의 호주머니에 있는 것들을 테이블 위에 놓았다.)

condolence / 애도, 조의 (the things that you say to show sympathy when someone has just died)
We offer our condolences to David and his family on their tragic loss.
(우리는 데이비드와 그의 가족이 당한 비극적 사건에 대하여 애도한다.)

conference / 회의 (a formal meeting)
They sat down at the table for a conference.
(그들은 회의하기 위해 테이블에 앉았다.)

consensus / 합의, 의견의 일치 (an opinion held by all or most)
Because most of the committee members could not agree on the issue, a consensus couldn't be reached.
(대부분의 위원들이 그 문제에 의견이 일치하지 않았기 때문에 합의에 도달할 수가 없었다.)

currency / 돈, 화폐 (money, being commonly known or accepted)
Many internet words are gaining currency in daily newspapers.
(많은 인터넷 용어들이 일간신문에 점점 더 자주 사용되고 있다.)

deference / 경의, 존중 (a yielding in opinion or judgment, courteous respect)

The Vice–President, in deference to his superior, refused to make a decision without first consulting the President.

(부통령은 상관을 존중하여, 대통령에게 먼저 상의하지 않고 결정내리는 일을 거부했다.)

dressing room / 분장실, 옷 갈아 입는 방 (a small room in a clothing store for trying on clothes)

Dressing room is used by a performer or sports player for preparing for a performance or game.

(한복실은 연극 또는 게임을 위해 준비하는 연극인 혹은 스포츠인들이 사용한다.)

discount / 할인 (a reduction in the price of something)

Bus and train discounts are available for people over 60.

(버스와 기차의 할인은 60세 이상의 사람들에게 적용된다.)

document / 문서, 서류 (a piece of paper containing official information)

A secret policy document was leaked to the newspapers.

(비밀 정책 문서가 신문에 유출되었다.)

exchange / 교환, 댓가 (giving something for doing something)

It is illegal for public officials to solicit money or gift certificates in exchanges of favors.

(공무원이 도움의 댓가로 돈이나 상품권을 요구하는 것은 불법이다.)

finality / 종국, 결말 (the fact or feeling that something has ended and has no possible future)

We ought to accept the finality of this outcome.

(우리는 이 결과에 대한 최종적인 내용을 받아들여야 한다.)

first-class / 일등석 (the best and most expensive seats on an airplane or train)

He's sitting in first class.
(그는 일등석에 앉아 있다.)

frequency / 빈도, 주파수 (a number of times that something happens during a period)

Changes in sea temperature will increase the frequency of hurricanes.
(해수 온도의 변화는 허리케인의 발생 빈도수를 증가시키게 될 것이다.)

indictment / 기소, 비난 (charge or accusation)

Ava listened to her employer's harsh indictment and insisted upon her innocence.
(애바는 고용주로부터 심한 비난을 들은 뒤에, 자신의 무고함을 주장했다.)

mechanism / 체제, 과정 (a method or a (working) system)

The mechanism of our city seems very insufficient. They never get anything done.
(우리 도시의 체제가 아주 미흡한 것 같다. 그 체제로는 아무 것도 하지 못한다.)

oppression / 압박, 억압 (cruel or unjust use of authority)

The new immigrants come to escape oppression and to provide a better life forthemselves and their children.
(새로운 이민자들은 억압을 피하고, 자신과 자손들에게 더 좋은 삶을 보장하기 위하여 온다.)

performance / 공연, 수행 (the act of performing a play, dance, or other form of entertainment)

The school drama society will give a performance of Hamlet.
(학교 연극 모임은 햄릿 공연을 할 것이다.)

rate / 율, 요금 (a fixed amount of money that charged or paid for something)

They offer special reduced rates for students. (학생들에게는 특별히 할인된 요금을 받는다.)

reduction / 할인, 축소 (the amount by which the price of something is reduced)

We are offering special price reductions on computers this month.

(이번 달에는 컴퓨터에 대해 특별 할인을 실시합니다.)

refreshment / 다과 (something to eat or drink during an event)

Refreshments are being sold in the lobby.

(다과물은 로비에서 판매한다.)

setting / 배경, 환경 (a particular time or place that a play, movie, etc. happens in)

Today's setting was perfect.

(오늘의 무대장치는 완벽했다.)

senator / 상원 (someone who is a member of a senate)

Do you know how many senators in the US?

(미국에는 몇 명의 상원의원이 있는지 아십니까?)

speedmeter / 속도계 (a device to indicate speed)

A speedmeter is a dashboard instrument that indicates how fast a car is going.

(속도계는 차가 얼마나 빨리 가는지를 나타내는 계기판이다.)

string / 줄, 끈 (thin rope)

The ballon was attached to a long string.

(그 풍선은 긴 줄에 묶여 있다.)

strip / 긴 조각, 긴것 (a piece of something such as cloth, paper, or grass that ismuch longer than it is wide

Cut the turkey into strips. (이 터키 고기를 몇 조각으로 나누어라.)

tenet / 원리, 주의 (principle or doctrine)

A basic tenet of democracy is that government should be controlled directly by the people or through elected representatives.
(민주주의의 기본 원칙은 정부가 직접 국민에 의해 또는 선출된 대표에 의해 통제되어야한다는 것이다.)

variable / 변수 (something that can change and affect the result of a situation)

All these variables can affect a student's performance.
(모든 변수들은 학생의 수행능력에 영향을 미칠 수 있다.)

zone / 구간, 지역 (area, region)

When the needle enters the red zone you will find the engine too hot.
(침이 붉은 구간에 들어가면, 엔진이 가열되고 있다는 것을 알아야 한다.)

2. 연습문제

1. William had already heard about the party, so it wasn't ______ .

   ⓐ comprise   ⓑ an entry   ⓒ a difference   ⓓ a surprise

2. Excuse me. Is this an ______ to the hospital?

   ⓐ access   ⓑ orientation   ⓒ alloy   ⓓ lead

3. The camera by itself is $220, but with ______ it is $320.

   ⓐ characteristics   ⓑ traits   ⓒ terminals   ⓓ accessories

4 The ______ of having a credit card is to be able to order things from a shop by telephone.

   ⓐ responsibility   ⓑ influences

   ⓒ advantages   ⓓ obligations

5. The boss and I are in complete ______ . We're going to buy the two new computers and hire the three new employees.

   ⓐ agreement   ⓑ disagreement   ⓒ exciting   ⓓ point out

6. What kind of ______ do you get for food, clothes, and living expenses?

   ⓐ consumption   ⓑ capacity   ⓒ allowance   ⓓ consideration

7. We need your written ______ to transfer the money to another person.

   ⓐ approve   ⓑ approving   ⓒ approval   ⓓ appropriate

8. We can park across that street, but near the building. We must keep that _____ clear.
   ⓐ area ⓑ guard ⓒ break ⓓ exercise

9. Banks often store gold in the form of _____ .
   ⓐ beams ⓑ bars ⓒ poles ⓓ board

10. The ___ of the country guarantees freedom of speech to its citizens.
    ⓐ record ⓑ condolence ⓒ accord ⓓ constitution

11. The package came open while being transported, and half of its _____ were lost.
    ⓐ break ⓑ blanks ⓒ curvatures ⓓ contents

12. How are you going to pay, in _____ or with a check?
    ⓐ commerce ⓑ currency ⓒ current ⓓ courtesy

13. I like to pay my phone bill early because I get a 3% _____ when I do. That way I save about $1,000 per month.
    ⓐ less ⓑ more ⓒ sales ⓓ discount

14. Customer: Excuse me, where's your _____ ? I'd like to try on this dress.
    ⓐ store ⓑ dressing room ⓒ dining room ⓓ bedroom

15. Take lots of money because the art in that shop is _____ .
    ⓐ usual ⓑ occupied ⓒ first–class ⓓ criticism

16. Dylan makes money by buying old furniture, _____ , and then selling it.
    ⓐ leaving it out ⓑ fixing it up ⓒ pulling it apart ⓓ pushing it out

17. The increasing _____ of crime frightens a lot of people.

    ⓐ frequency   ⓑ measuring   ⓒ bearing   ⓓ grid

18. My saving account didn't balance. Some _____ were missing.

    ⓐ funds   ⓑ letters   ⓒ zones   ⓓ article

19. The Spanish invaders found gold in that _____ !

    ⓐ basis   ⓑ mine   ⓒ origin   ⓓ root

20. Pat: Which show do you want to go to?

    Joe: Let's go to the eight o'clock _____ .

    ⓐ stage   ⓑ theater   ⓒ performance   ⓓ preference

21. We want to show our thanks by giving you this small _____ .

    ⓐ blowout   ⓑ birthday   ⓒ present   ⓓ tiresome

22. There has been a _____ in that store's prices.

    ⓐ reduces   ⓑ reduction   ⓒ to reduce   ⓓ reduced

23. The _____ of the conference was changed to San Fransisco.

    ⓐ timing   ⓑ mobility   ⓒ setting   ⓑ residue

24. We have room for six passengers in our car. We have enough _____ for six people.

    ⓐ office   ⓑ space   ⓒ state   ⓓ formation

25. Sandy looked at the _____ to see how fast her car was going.

    ⓐ steering wheel   ⓑ thermostat   ⓒ speedometer   ⓓ piston

26. They don't have enough _____ space to keep all of these packages.

    ⓐ trenches   ⓑ storage   ⓒ gasoline   ⓓ petroleum

27. Robert: Why were you tying some _____ around the package?

    Joseph: To make the package stronger.

    ⓐ player   ⓑ string   ⓒ space   ⓓ basket

28. They used several _____ of tape when they wrapped the box.

    ⓐ discourse   ⓑ strips   ⓒ networks   ⓓ blanks

29. Flight 209 will arrive at _____ number 2 in about 15 minutes.

    ⓐ graph   ⓑ lounge   ⓒ monitor   ⓓ terminal

30. Is 32" the measurement around the _____ or the length of the pants?

    ⓐ waist   ⓑ leg   ⓒ neck   ⓓ chest

31. The Arabian king possesses a lot of _____ .

    ⓐ leisure   ⓑ wealth   ⓒ success   ⓓ consideration

32. The company has reached a(n) _____ with its working members.

    ⓐ accord   ⓑ top   ⓒ amendment   ⓓ deposit

33. Newspapers are delivered to newspaper stands in _____ of twenty.

    ⓐ goods   ⓑ bundles   ⓒ stocks   ⓓ status

34. On the _____ of their scientific investigation, the prosecutor determined that George had

    not done anything illegal.

    ⓐ basin   ⓑ basic   ⓒ basis   ⓓ bass

35. Ann told Jim how sorry she was in her letter of ______ .

ⓐ appreciation   ⓑ office   ⓒ condolence   ⓓ accord

36. The Declaration of Independence is a valuable ______ in the U.S. A lot of famous men signed it.

ⓐ application   ⓑ certificate   ⓒ document   ⓓ dictionary

37. When Alexander signed the agreement, he didn't realize the ______ of his actions.

ⓐ finality   ⓑ finalize   ⓒ finale   ⓓ finalist

38. I suppose that he has no ______ of paying back all the money he owes to you.

ⓐ intention   ⓑ extension   ⓒ detention   ⓓ intension

39. In America the ______ speed limit on a highway is 45 m.p.h. Driving at a lower speed can often be dangerous.

ⓐ maximum   ⓑ minimum   ⓒ average   ⓓ normal

40. That financial ______ seemed to fail completely and they had to develop another system.

ⓐ extension   ⓑ intention   ⓒ mechanism   ⓓ machinery

41. He's invited to a(n) ______ this Friday afternoon.

ⓐ anniversary   ⓑ reception   ⓒ celebrate   ⓓ ceremony

42. Paul's Garage charges higher ______ for auto repairs than Joe's Garage does.

ⓐ fares   ⓑ money   ⓒ rates   ⓓ fees

43. The flag should be shown respect because it is the ______ of a country.

ⓐ symbol   ⓑ center   ⓒ heart   ⓓ display

ECL시험 대비 New ALC 필수어휘 완성

44. There are many hotels in the ______ of the trade center.
ⓐ virgin   ⓑ vicinity   ⓒ facility   ⓓ vintage

45. The directions he gave me to his house were so ______ I didn't think I could find it.
ⓐ remote   ⓑ systematic   ⓒ vague   ⓓ general

46. They served coffee and cookies at the meeting.
ⓐ drinking   ⓑ refreshments   ⓒ side dishes   ⓓ chances

47. The immigrants were herded like animals through gates and pens while being processed through Ellis Island.
ⓐ recreation rooms   ⓑ barges
ⓒ weapons consisting of long pole   ⓓ fenced enclosures

48. The immigrants possessing particular skills had good prospects for finding employment.
ⓐ prescription   ⓑ expectations   ⓒ evaluations   ⓓ contributions

49. Since our nation was founded on the principles of freedom, individual dignity, and equality of opportunity, we do not cause decay in the body politic by welcoming persons from all nations.
ⓐ House of Representatives   ⓑ one political party
ⓒ a nation's politically organized society
ⓓ the people who make and pass the laws.

50. When asked if he had good prospects for finding employment in the U.S., the immigrant's answer had to be yes because the law excluded those likely to become public charges.
ⓐ people who serves as public officials

ⓑ people who depend on government support

ⓒ people who support large families

ⓓ people who hate to spend money

51. We expect people to move about at parties and be self-starters, introducing themselves and stopping to talk to other guests.
   ⓐ people who are not talkative
   ⓑ people who tackle all the difficulties
   ⓒ people who take the initiative
   ⓒ people who are very shy

52. There are holes in those strategies because you're trying to trick people into buying a product that isn't any good.
   ⓐ flaws
   ⓑ torn spots
   ⓒ ditch
   ⓓ merits

53. She submitted her updated resume of her previous employment along with her applicant for the job.
   ⓐ summary of work experience
   ⓑ a new experience
   ⓒ assume responsibility
   ⓓ a fixed payment

54. The committee member was reliable as well as dependable and showed a great deal of integrity. All the other committee members could depend on him to make an ethical decision.
   ⓐ honesty and sincerity
   ⓑ patience and tolerance
   ⓒ courage and self-confidence
   ⓓ great intelligence

55. Poorer members like Greece and Portugal will need substantial EC subsidies to complete their trains.
   ⓐ reduction in personnel
   ⓑ increased publicity
   ⓒ money for learning in a college
   ⓓ financial assistance

정답 / 해석

1. ⓓ 윌리엄은 그 파티에 대해 들었다. 그래서 그것은 놀라운 일이 아니다.

2. ⓐ 실례합니다. 이것이 병원으로 가는 통로입니까?

3. ⓓ 그 카메라 자체는 220달러다. 그러나 그 부착물이 320달러다.

4. ⓒ 신용카드의 장점은 전화로 가게에서 물건을 주문할 수 있다는 것이다.

5. ⓐ 그 사장과 나는 완전하게 합의하였다. 우리는 컴퓨터 2개를 구매하고 직원 3명을 새로 채용할 것이다.

6. ⓒ 식품, 의복, 생계비를 위해 어떤 종류의 급여를 받고 있습니까?

7. ⓒ 돈을 다른 사람에게 송금하기 위해서는 너의 서명 동의가 필요하다.

8. ⓐ 우리는 길 건너 편, 건물 가까이에 주차할 수 있다. 우리는 그 지역을 정리해 두어야 한다.

9. ⓑ 은행은 종종 막대 형태로 금을 보관한다.

10. ⓓ 그 나라의 헌법은 시민들의 표현의 자유를 보장한다.

11. ⓓ 그 꾸러미는 이송되는 동안 포장이 열렸다. 그리고 그 절반은 분실되었다.

12. ⓑ 현금으로 지불할 것입니까? 아니면 수표로 지불할 것입니까?

13. ⓓ 나는 전화요금을 일찍 지불한다. 3%의 할인을 받을 수 있기 때문이다. 그렇게 함으로써 나는 한 달에 약 1,000달러를 절약한다.

14. ⓑ 고객: 실례지만 옷 갈아입는 방이 어딥니까? 이 옷을 한번 입어보고 싶은데요.

15. ⓒ 돈을 많이 갖고 가세요. 그 가게의 작품들은 일등급들이니까요.

16. ⓑ 딜란은 고가구를 사서, 수리하고, 팔아서 돈을 번다.

17. ⓐ 범죄율의 증가가 많은 사람들에게 위협이 되고 있다.

18. ⓐ 내 저축계좌가 맞지 않는다. 자금이 일부 모자란다.

19. ⓑ 스페인 침략자들은 그 광산에서 금을 발견하였다.

20. ⓒ 펫: 어떤 공연을 보러 갈래?

    조: 8시에 하는 공연에 가자.

21. ⓒ 조그마한 선물로써 감사드리고 싶어요.

22. ⓑ 그 가게에서는 할인가에 판매하고 있다.

23. ⓒ 그 모임 장소는 샌 프란시스코로 바뀌었다.

24. ⓑ 우리는 차에 여섯 명의 승객을 위한 공간이 있다. 여섯 명을 위한 공간이 충분하다.

25. ⓒ 샌디는 차가 얼마나 빨리 가는지 보기 위해서 속도계를 보았다.

26. ⓑ 이 모든 물건을 보관할 충분한 창고가 없다.

27. ⓑ 로버트: 왜 포장물 주위를 줄로 묶고 있지?

　　　조셉: 포장물을 좀 더 단단하게 만들려고요.

28. ⓑ 그들은 박스를 묶을 때 몇몇 테이프 줄을 사용하였다.

29. ⓓ 209 항공기는 약 15분 후 2번 터미널에 도착할 것이다.

30. ⓐ 허리 둘레가 32인치인가 아니면 바지 길이가 32인치인가?

31. ⓑ 그 아리비아왕은 재산이 많다.

32. ⓐ 그 회사는 직원들과 합의하였다.

33. ⓑ 신문은 20부씩 다발로 신문가판대에 배달된다.

34. ⓒ 과학적인 조사 결과를 기초로 검사는 조지가 불법적인 행위를 하지 않았다고 결정하였다.

35. ⓒ 앤은 조문 편지를 써서 짐에게 애도를 표했다.

36. ⓒ 독립선언서는 미국의 귀중한 문서다. 많은 유명 인사가 선언서에 서명하였다.

37. ⓐ 알렉산더가 그 협정에 조인할 때 그는 그 행위의 결말이 어떻게 될 것인지를 알지 못했다.

38. ⓐ 그는 너에게 빌린 돈을 갚을 의도가 없는 것 같다.

39. ⓑ 미국에서 고속도로에서의 최저 속도는 시간당 45마일이다. 더 느리면 종종 위험하다.

40. ⓒ 재정체계가 완벽히 작동되지 않는 것 같아서, 그들은 다른 체계를 개발해야 했다.

41. ⓑ 그는 금요일 오후 어떤 리셉션에 초대받았다.

42. ⓒ 폴의 정비소는 조지의 정비소보다 자동차 수리비용을 더 많이 부과한다.)

43. ⓐ 국기는 한 국가의 상징이기 때문에 존경심을 표해야 한다.

44. ⓑ 무역센터 근처에는 많은 호텔이 있다.

45. ⓒ 그가 알려준 그의 집으로 가는 길은 너무 애매하여 제대로 찾아갈 수 있을지 모르겠다.

46. ⓑ 그들은 모임에서 커피와 과자를 제공했다.

47. ⓓ 이민자들은 엘리스 섬을 통하여 조사 분류되는 과정에서 출입문 유리를 통해 동물처럼 내몰렸다.

48. ⓑ 특별한 기술을 가진 이민자들은 고용될 수 있는 기회가 높았다.)

49. ⓒ 우리 조국은 자유와 개인의 존엄성과 기회의 균등의 원칙하에 설립되었기 때문에, 모든 국가의 사람들을
　　　환영함으로써 정치단체의 부패가 발생되지 않는다.

50. ⓑ 미국에서 직업을 구할 전망이 좋은지 물으면, 이민자들은 예라고 답해야 한다. 왜냐하면 생활보호대상자가

되기 쉬운 사람은 법으로 제한하기 때문이다.

51. ⓒ 파티에서는 돌아다니며 자신을 소개하고 다른 손님과 대화하기 위해 멈추고 솔선하는 사람이 되기를 기대한다.

52. ⓐ 그 전략은 좋지 않은 제품을 사도록 사람들을 속이려고 하기 때문에 문제가 있다.

53. ⓐ 그녀는 그 직장에 갱신한 이력서와 함께 지원서를 제출했다.

54. ⓐ 그 위원회의 위원은 믿을 만하고 의지할 만하였으며 매우 성실하였다. 모든 다른 위원들은 그가 윤리적인 결정을 내릴 것으로 믿을 수 있다.

55. ⓓ 그리스, 포르투갈과 같은 가난한 회원들은 자국의 철도를 완전하게 하기 위해 상당량의 EC 보조금이 필요할 것이다.

동사

기본어휘 / 연습 문제

B

New American Language Course

afford / 여유가 있다, 자금이 있다 (to have enough money to be able to pay for something)

We need a bigger house, but we just can't afford such expensive vacations.
(우리는 좀 더 큰 집이 필요하다. 하지만 그렇게 호화스런 휴가를 지낼 여유는 없다.)

appreciate / 감사하다 (to be grateful for something)

I appreciate this opportunity to put my point of view to the committee.
(저의 소견을 말하게 해 주신 위원회 여러분들께 감사드립니다.)

arrange / 조치하다, 정하다 (to make ready or prepare)

I've arranged to see him on Friday evening. (나는 그를 금요일 저녁에 만나기로 하였다.)

commercialize / 상업화하다 (to develop something so that you can sell it)

Several companies are trying to commercialize the technology.
(여러 회사들이 그 기술을 상업화하려고 한다.)

condense / 응축하다, 압축하다 (to make more dense or compact)

Steam can condense into water when it cools. (증기는 식으면 물로 졸아진다.)

confirm / 확인하다, 확증하다 (give formal approval to)

In minutes an INS inspector confirms that papers are in order and directs the new immigrant to a glass-walled room.
(몇 분 만에 이민 귀화국 조사관들은 서류가 완전한지 확인하고, 새 이민자를 유리벽 사무실로 보낸다.)
(INS : Immigration and Naturalization Service)

contrast / 대조, 대비 (to show a clear difference)

The living standard in South Korea contrasts with that in North Korea.

(한국인의 생계수준은 북한과 대조된다.)

deliver / 배달하다 (to take goods to the person, to carry to a place)

The pizza will be delivered in 20 minutes.

(피자는 20분 후에 배달될 것이다.)

defy / 반항하다, 거부하다 (to refuse to obey someone or something)

The commander defied a direct order to surrender.

(그 지휘관은 항복하라는 직접적인 지시를 거절하였다.)

deny / 부정하다, 부인하다 (to say that you did not do something)

A spokesman denied that the company had acted irresponsibly.

(그 대변인은 회사가 무책임하게 행동하였다는 것을 부정하였다.)

depress / 우울하게 하다, 약화시키다 (to push down something, to make sad)

Loss of self-control always makes me sad.

(자기 통제를 상실하면 항상 기분이 울적하다.)

disregard / 무시하다, 경시하다 (to pay little attention to, to slight, neglect)

I neglected to tell him that I couldn't join them.

(나는 그들과 함께 할 수 없다는 사실을 그에게 말하는 것을 잊었다.)

direct / 가르쳐주다, 지시하다 (to regulate, guide, command, or order)

I directed her to the post office.

(나는 그녀에게 우체국 가는 길을 가르쳐 주었다.)

ECL시험 대비 New ALC 필수어휘 완성

disturb / 괴롭히다 (to upset mentally or emotionally)

I don't want to disturb you but talk softly.

(나는 너를 방해하고 싶지 않지만, 조용히 말해라.)

endorse / 보증하다, 찬성하다 (to write of the back of (a document), to support)

I fully endorse everything the man has said. (나는 그 사람이 말한 모든 것을 보증한다.)

exceed / 초과하다 (to do more than the order)

His performance exceeded our expectations.

(그의 성과는 우리의 기대치를 초과했다.)

exclude / 제외하다, 배제하다 (to deliberately prevent someone or something from being involved in an activity or from entering a place

The committee now has to decide whether to exclude him from the competition.

(그 위원회는 지금 그 경쟁에서 그를 포함시킬 것인지, 제외시킬 것인지를 결정해야 한다.)

export / 수출하다 (to sell and send goods to another country)

Half of the engines are exported to China.

(그 엔진의 절반은 중국으로 수출된다.)

exhaust / 소진하다, 소모하다 (expend or empty completely)

His impolite behaviour nearly exhausted my patience.

(그의 무례한 태도에 나는 더 이상 인내 할 수 없다.)

forge / 단조하다, 형성하다 (make, develop)

The former enemies managed to forge a friendly relationship after one of the countries came to the other's aid.

(그 국가들 중 한 쪽이 다른 쪽을 원조하게 되자, 이전의 적이 친밀한 관계를 형성하게 되었다.)

glance / 힐끗 보다, 얼핏 보다 (to look suddenly and briefly, (take) a quick look)

He took a glance at his watch. (그는 시계를 힐끗 쳐다 보았다.)

guard / 지키다, 억제하다 (to keep under control or restraint)

I can't often guard my temper.

(나는 종종 내 성질을 참지 못한다.)

implement / 수행하다, 이행하다 (to make something such as an idea, plan, or law start to
work and be used)

Attempts to implement change have met with strong opposition.

(변화의 시도는 강력한 반대에 부딪혔다.)

part / 깨지다, 갈라지다 (to be separated from something, to leave, to disagree)

The committee always parted over the urgent issues.

(위원회는 항상 긴급한 문제에 대해 의견이 갈라졌다.)

participate / 참여하다 (to take part in something)

The rebels have agreed to participate in the peace talks.

(그 반대파들은 평화협정에 참여하기로 의견을 모았다.)

persuade / 설득하다 (to make someone agree to do something)

Nobody could persuade her to change her mimd.

(아무도 그녀의 마음을 돌리도록 설득할 수 없었다.)

pose / 제기하다, 주장하다 (offer for consideration, suggest)

The committee posed an interesting solution to the problem of time management.

(그 위원회는 시간관리 문제에 대해 재미있는 해결책을 제안했다.)

prescreen / 미리 선별하다, 미리 조사하다 (examine carefully before a final decisionis made)

For today's immigrant – prescreened and approved by a U.S. embassy or consulate in his or her homeland – entry is streamlined.

(오늘날의 이민자는 자기 나라 미대사관이나 영사관의 사전조사와 승인을 받기 때문에 입국절차가 간결하다.)

publicize / 공표(선전)하다 (to publish or broadcast information about a thing)

They publicized the second plan for the country.

(그들은 그 나라의 두 번째 계획을 대중들에게 알렸다.)

quell / 진압하다, 평정하다 (put an end, quiet)

The police had to use force in order to quell the riot.

(경찰은 폭동을 진압하기 위해 무력을 사용해야 했다.)

realign / 재조정하다, 재편성하다 (to bring into agreement or adjustment)

When the congressmen from California disagreed with everyone else, the Speaker of the House encouraged them to realign their way of thinking.

(캘리포니아 출신 의원들이 다른 사람들과 의견이 틀리자, 하원의장이 그들에게 사고 방식을 재조정할 것을 촉구하였다.)

refer / 언급하다, 조회시키다 (to send for help or advice, to mention or speak about)

This article refers to economic recession. (이 기사는 경제 침체에 대하여 언급하고 있다.)

remark / 말하다, 언급하다 (to say or write)

He remarked that he would go shopping tomorrow. (그는 다음날 쇼핑갈 것이다고 말했다.)

shed / 버리다, 벗어버리다 (to free oneself from something unwanted)

Top level leaders need to shed some particular organizational structures that are no longer effective.

(최고지도자는 효율적이지 못한 세부 조직기관을 정리할 필요가 있다.)

store / 저장하다, 보관하다 (to keep something in a particular place)

Store the cake in an airtight container. (공기가 새지 않는 용기에 케이크를 넣어 두세요.)

trade / 교환하다, 거래되다 (exchange, to be offered for sale)

Korean stocks are trading at lower prices these days.
(한국의 주식은 요즈음 낮은 가격에 거래되고 있다.)

transfer / 이전하다, 환승하다 (change)

All passengers were transferred to another bus. (모든 승객은 다른 버스로 환승하였다.)

transport / 수송하다, 운반하다 (to carry, move, or convey)

Heavy items are expensive to transport by plane. (무거운 물품은 비행기로 우송하면 비싸다.)

utilize / 사용하다 (to use for special purpose)

The teachers were unable to utilize the new computer.
(그 선생님들은 새 컴퓨터를 사용할 수 없었다.)

vary / 바뀌다, 변하다 (to change or be different)

The menu of the restaurant varies with the season. (그 식당의 메뉴는 계절따라 바뀐다.)

welcome / 환영하다 (to greet someone in a polite and friendly way when they have come to see you or help you)

Visitors will be warmly welcomed. (방문객들은 따뜻하게 환영받을 것이다.)

wrap / 싸다, 포장하다 (to enclose in something)

She wrapped her head in a green scarf.(그녀는 머리를 녹색 스카프로 둘러쌌다.)

2. 연습문제

1. Calvin's very interested in becoming an airline pilot. He's already _____ his private pilot's license.

   ⓐ acquired　　　ⓑ appointed　　　ⓒ deprived　　　ⓓ established

2. Tom's boss asked him to _____ a dinner party for the employees.

   ⓐ assist　　　ⓑ insist　　　ⓒ resist　　　ⓓ arrange

3. Sorry to _____ your meal, but there's a long-distance call for you.

   ⓐ break off　　　ⓑ break in on　　　ⓒ break out　　　ⓓ break away

4. _____ the instructions without making any changes.

   ⓐ Elevate　　　ⓑ Proceed　　　ⓒ Carry out　　　ⓓ Explode

5. Have you _____ all the items on your list?

   ⓐ detected　　　ⓑ triggered　　　ⓒ equipped　　　ⓓ checked off

6. Could you _____ this report? It's too lengthy.

   ⓐ condense　　　ⓑ cross-check　　　ⓒ consume　　　ⓓ concentrate

7. My office _____ sharply with my new senior's in size and location.

   ⓐ suspends　　　ⓑ contrasts　　　ⓒ compels　　　ⓓ conspires

8. Who'd like to _______ this box of apples to the customer's apartment?

    ⓐ deliver   ⓑ delight   ⓒ deceive   ⓓ delight

9. _______ the button on the coffee table if you need service.

    ⓐ Depress   ⓑ Demonstrate   ⓒ Depress   ⓓ Distinguish

10. Policemen are very busy _______ traffic in the busiest areas downtown.

    ⓐ arranging   ⓑ directing   ⓒ converging   ⓓ distributing

11. Please remember to _______ the check, so I can cash it right now.

    ⓐ exchange   ⓑ direct   ⓒ endorse   ⓓ sign

12. Before we buy more supplies, we must use up what we have.

    ⓐ exercise   ⓑ exhaust   ⓒ expel   ⓓ expand

13. The production goal of the company was _______ by 27%.

    ⓐ excessive   ⓑ exceeded   ⓒ executed   ⓓ expanded

14. Before leaving for work, Steven _______ at himself in the mirror to make sure he is well dressed.

    ⓐ glimmered   ⓑ glittered   ⓒ glanced   ⓓ gloried

15. Excuse me. Am I _______ to park my car here?

    ⓐ permitted   ⓑ permitting   ⓒ permanent   ⓓ permissive

16. The boss _______ me to go to James' retirement party.

    ⓐ shared   ⓑ collected   ⓒ persuaded   ⓓ blamed

17. The course was plotted. It was _____ .
    ⓐ planned   ⓑ optional   ⓒ changed   ⓓ lengthened

18. If you need some legal advice, I can _____ you to a famous lawyer.
    ⓐ defer   ⓑ prefer   ⓒ refer   ⓓ confer

19. Bill puts aside some money each week.
    ⓐ delves   ⓑ transforms   ⓒ saves   ⓓ spends

20. The Robinsons live outside of town, so they're not _____ city taxes.
    ⓐ beyond   ⓑ subject to   ⓒ in touch with   ⓓ related to

21. I'm sorry, but I had better not _____ this red jacket for that green one.
    ⓐ substitute   ⓑ activate   ⓒ transfer   ⓓ deny

22. I'd like to _____ these two baseballs for a box of golf balls.
    ⓐ distribute   ⓑ trade   ⓒ trail   ⓓ trend

23. Tina got a new basketball for his birthday. Can we _____ ?
    ⓐ try it out   ⓑ purchase on   ⓒ take part in it   ⓓ cut down on it

24. Up to now they didn't _____ all of the supplies we sent them last year.
    ⓐ utilize   ⓑ useful   ⓒ access   ⓓ useless

25. Prices can _____ a lot from one supermarket to another.
    ⓐ repair   ⓑ fix   ⓒ vary   ⓓ drift

26. Mr. Allen remarked that he enjoyed last night's meeting a lot.

    ⓐ noticed   ⓑ commented   ⓒ claimed   ⓓ insisted

27. We have enough money to get a new car. We can _____ it.

    ⓐ believe in   ⓑ sell   ⓒ exchange   ⓓ afford

28. Thank you for coming. I really _____ all the help you have given me.

    ⓐ appreciate   ⓑ think   ⓒ satisfy   ⓓ throw away

29. Frank: Do all your bills _____ a lot of money?

    Greg: They sure do. $3,500 is a lot of money for me.

    ⓐ percent   ⓑ amount to   ⓒ enough   ⓓ make up

30. The troops aren't here because Captain Donald _____ them permission to come to the get-together.

    ⓐ fired   ⓑ trusted   ⓒ denied   ⓓ demanded

31. I wasn't invited to the party. Why was I _____ ?

    ⓐ argued   ⓑ included   ⓒ expected   ⓓ excluded

32. Our country _____ digital TVs, chemical fertilizer and technologically advanced cellular phones to other countries.

    ⓐ expels   ⓑ expand   ⓒ exports   ⓓ expend

33. Never resist a police officer. You'll get into trouble.

    ⓐ relate   ⓑ define   ⓒ implement   ⓓ defy

34. We _______ our goal by 8% because all of us worked hard.

   ⓐ excess   ⓑ extinguished   ⓒ exceeded   ⓓ exaggerated

35. They're going to _______ the new schedule after the first of the year.

   ⓐ postpone   ⓑ distinguish   ⓒ take action   ⓓ implement

36. The government is going to _______ a new kind of driver's license this year.

   ⓐ measure   ⓑ give in   ⓒ calibrate   ⓓ issue

37. Don't disregard that warning.

   ⓐ worry about   ⓑ disguise   ⓒ ignore   ⓓ be concerned about

38. The President of the United States has the authority to _______ people to certain government positions.

   ⓐ lead   ⓑ name   ⓒ research   ⓓ reach

39. How should we _______ the time and location of the meeting?

   ⓐ publicize   ⓑ public   ⓒ publicly   ⓓ publicist

40. The new tax law will _______ from next year.

   ⓐ go through   ⓑ take effect   ⓒ take place   ⓓ make efforts

41. The sergeant was told to keep the material for future use. He _______ it.

   ⓐ stored   ⓑ united   ⓒ issued   ⓓ shaped

42. To get downtown from the train station, you have to _______ from but 36 to bus 78.

   ⓐ transfer   ⓑ refer   ⓒ confer   ⓓ transform

43. Do you know how much this apartment is ______ ?

    ⓐ value   ⓑ worth   ⓒ cost   ⓓ afford

44. The mail I received yesterday was in reference to my new credit account at Lotte Department Store.

    ⓐ was perceived   ⓑ pertained

    ⓒ transferred   ⓓ was reduced to

45. The long flight left us ______ .

    ⓐ wearing out   ⓑ worn out   ⓒ wear out   ⓓ to wear out

46. The express mail is ______ by truck and by plane.

    ⓐ transported   ⓑ folded   ⓒ directed   ⓓ driven

47. They found a ______ package on the table.

    ⓐ wrap   ⓑ wrapped   ⓒ wrapping   ⓓ to wrap

48. The Johns ______ their guests at the door when they arrived.

    ⓐ escaped   ⓑ praised   ⓒ welcomed   ⓓ appreciated

49. Weary foreigners, documents in hand, line up for inspection by the U.S. Immigration and Naturalization Service.

    ⓐ are tied up   ⓑ pull the line up   ⓒ bring up   ⓓ stand in a row

50. As soon as there are more people than chairs, someone will make an excuse to get up to fetch a drink for anyone whose glass might be empty.

    ⓐ go get and bring back   ⓑ put ice in a drink

    ⓒ remove the empty glasses.   ⓓ buy a drink

51. Julia bought an expensive new car but now realized that on her salary she can't afford the payments. She doesn't intend to give up the car, though, so she'll need to moonlight in order to meet her car payments over the next few years.

ⓐ She's planning to save a lot of money.
ⓑ She's planning to ask a friend for the money.
ⓒ She's planning to get a second job in addition to her regular job.
ⓓ She's planning to rob a bank after dark.

52. By 2015, European train traffic will quadruple.

ⓐ become four times as great ⓑ become four times less
ⓒ become five times as great ⓓ become five times less

53. The government is worried that rail lines slated to run east from Brussels won't make a profit at first – or ever.

ⓐ scheduled ⓑ destroyed ⓒ moved ⓓ sloped

54. German industry has developed the Inter–City Express as a direct competitor to the French TGV, and so far has shunned invitations to collaborate on a Franco–German model.

ⓐ deliberated ⓑ agreed to ⓒ created ⓓ rejected

정답 / 해석

1. ⓐ 칼빈은 항공기 조종사가 되고자 많은 관심을 기울인다. 그는 이미 개인용 항공기 조종 면허를 땄다.
2. ⓓ 톰의 보스는 그에게 직원들을 위한 저녁파티를 준비하라고 요구했다.

3. ⓑ 식사를 방해해서 미안하지만, 장거리 전화가 왔습니다.

4. ⓒ 지시를 변경하지 말고 이행하여라.

5. ⓓ 목록에 있는 모든 품목을 대조확인 하였느냐?

6. ⓐ 이 보고서를 요약해 주세요. 너무 장황합니다.

7. ⓑ 내 사무실은 크기와 위치에서 내 상관의 사무실과 아주 대조가 된다.

8. ⓐ 고객의 아파트에 이 사과 상자를 누가 배달하겠느냐?

9. ⓐ 서비스가 필요하면 커피 테이블의 버튼을 누르세요.

10. ⓑ 경찰관들은 시내 번잡한 지역에서 교통정리 하느라 매우 바쁘다.

11. ⓒ 수표에 배서하는 것을 명심해라. 그러면 나는 지금 즉시 현금으로 바꾸어 줄 수 있다.

12. ⓑ 더 많은 물품을 사기전에 가진 것을 다 사용해야 합니다.

13. ⓑ 그 회사의 생산목표가 27% 초과되었다.

14. ⓒ 직장에 가기 전에 스티븐은 거울을 보고 자신의 옷차림을 확인하였다.

15. ⓐ 실례합니다. 여기에 차를 주차해도 됩니까?

16. ⓒ 그 사장은 내가 제임스의 퇴임 파티에 가도록 설득하였다.

17. ⓐ 방향이 정해졌다. 그것은 계획된 것이었다.

18. ⓒ 법적인 조언이 필요하면, 너에게 유명 변호사에게 소개해 줄 수 있다.

19. ⓒ 빌은 매주 일정 액수의 돈을 저금한다.

20. ⓑ 로빈손 가족은 시외에 거주하므로, 도시세를 내지 않는다.

21. ⓐ 실례지만, 나는 이 녹색 윗옷을 저 빨간 옷과 바꾸고 싶지 않습니다.

22. ⓑ 나는 이 야구공 두개를 골프볼 한 박스와 교환하고 싶다.

23. ⓐ 티나는 생일에 새 농구공을 샀다. 우리 한번 시구해 보지 않을래?

24. ⓐ 지금까지 그들은 우리가 지난 해 보낸 모든 보급품을 사용하지 않았다.

25. ⓒ 슈퍼마켓마다 가격이 매우 다르다

26. ⓑ 알렌씨는 어제 밤의 모임을 매우 즐겼다고 말했다.

27. ⓓ 우리는 새 차를 장만할 충분한 돈이 있다. 우리는 차를 살 여유가 있다.

28. ⓐ 와 주셔서 감사합니다. 저에게 베풀어 주신 도움에 진심으로 감사드립니다.

29. ⓑ 프랭크: 계산을 모두 합하면 많은 돈인데?

그레그: 그래요. 3,500불은 나에게 많은 돈입니다.

30. ⓒ 그 부대원들은 여기 없다. 왜냐하면 도널드 대령이 그 모임에 가는 것을 허락하지 않았기 때문이다.

31. ⓓ 나는 그 파티에 초대받지 않았다. 왜 빠졌지요?

32. ⓒ 우리나라는 TV, 화학비료, 첨단 휴대폰을 외국으로 수출한다.

33. ⓓ 경찰들에게 반항하지 마세요. 곤경에 빠지게 될 것입니다.

34. ⓒ 우리 모두는 열심히 일했기 때문에 목표를 8% 초과하였다.

35. ⓓ 그들은 첫 해가 끝난 후 새로운 계획을 집행하려고 한다.

36. ⓓ 그 정부는 올해 새로운 운전면허증을 교부하려고 한다.

37. ⓒ 그 경고를 무시하지 마라.

38. ⓑ 미국의 대통령은 어떤 사람을 정부 직위에 임명할 수 있는 권한을 갖고 있다.

39. ⓐ 그 모임 시간과 장소를 어떻게 알려야 할까요?

40. ⓑ 새 세법은 내년에 효력을 발휘할 것이다.

41. ⓐ 그 부사관은 향후 사용할 재료를 보관하도록 지시 받았다. 그는 그 재료를 보관했다.

42. ⓐ 기차역에서 시내에 도착하기 위해서는 36번에서 78번 버스로 환승해야 한다.

43. ⓑ 이 아파트의 가치가 얼마인지 아느냐?

44. ⓑ 내가 어제 받은 메일은 롯데 백화점의 새 신용카드에 대한 것이다.

45. ⓑ 장거리 비행으로 우리는 지쳤다.

46. ⓐ 특급우편은 트럭과 비행기로 수송된다.

47. ⓑ 그들은 포장된 소포가 탁자 위에 있는 것을 발견했다.

48. ⓒ 존의 가족은 손님들이 도착할 때 문에서 그들을 환영하였다.

49. ⓓ 피곤한 외국인들은 손에 서류를 들고, 미국 이민국의 조사를 받기 위해 줄을 섰다.

50. ⓐ 의자보다 사람이 더 많으면, 누군가가 실례하고 일어선 뒤에 잔이 빈 사람을 위해 음료수를 가져온다.

51. ⓒ 줄리아는 새 차를 샀지만, 그녀의 월급으로 비용을 지불할 수 없다는 것을 깨달았다. 그러나 그녀는 그 차를 포기하지 않을 생각이다. 그래서 그녀는 다음 몇 년간의 차량비용을 맞추기 위해 부업을 할 필요가 있다.

52. ⓐ 2015년이면 유럽의 철도교통이 4배로 많아질 것이다.

53. ⓐ 정부는 브뤼셀에서 동쪽으로 다리도록 예정된 철로는 처음에는 또는 영원히 이익을 내지 못할까 걱정한다.

54. ⓓ 독일산업계는 프랑스의 TGV와 직접 경쟁, Inter-City 고속철을 개발하여, 지금까지 프랑스 독일 모델을 합자 개발하지 않도록 하였다.

형용사

기본어휘 / 연습 문제

C

1. 기본어휘 — 형용사

actual / 실제의, 현실의 (existing in reality or in fact, true)

He asked me to leave. Well, her actual words were "Shit, get out of here."
(그는 나에게 떠나라고 말했다. 아마 그녀가 실제로 한 말은 "제길, 나가"였다.)

abundant / 충분한, 넉넉한 (ample, more than sufficient)

We must take an abundant supply of food with us when we go hiking.
(하이킹을 갈 때는 충분한 식품을 가지고 가야 한다.)

benign / 온화한, 인자한 (good-natured, beneficial, doing little or no harm)

After years of suffering at the hands of the cruel dictator, the people were grateful to finally have a benign, gentle leader
(잔인한 독재자의 손에서 몇 년간 고통을 겪은 뒤에 사람들은 상냥하고 점잖은 지도자를 둥 것에 대해 감사하였다.)

competent / 유능한 (capable of doing something in a satisfactory or effective way)

She is very competent at communicating.
(그녀는 의사소통에 아주 능하다.)

compulsory / 강제된, 의무적인 (mandatory, obligatory, required)

Wearing a life jacket in the boat is compulsory.
(배에서 구명조끼를 입는 것은 의무사항이다.)

dire / 비참한, 절박한 (desperate, urgent)

Because of his dire financial circumstances, Issac was forced to sell the farm which had been in his family for generations.

(그의 처참한 재정환경 때문에, 이삭은 수 세대 동안 그의 가족 소유였던 농장을 팔지 않을 수 없었다.)

disgruntled / 불만을 품은, 기분이 상한 (discontented, displeased)

When the company cut back on its benefits, several disgruntled employeesquit in anger.

(회사가 보조금을 삭감하자, 몇몇 불만을 품은 고용자들은 화가 치밀어 사직하였다.)

due / 만기가 된, 지급 기일이 된 (having reached the date for payment or submitting)

This bill is due next week. (이 수표는 다음 주가 만기다.)

economic / 경제의, 경제에 관한 (having to do with economics)

The economic situation in the eastern part of the country has not improved in the last six months.

(그 나라 동부의 경제상황은 지난 6개월 동안 개선되지 않았다.)

elastic / 유연한, 융통성 있는 (flexible, adaptable)

We should make elastic rules and regulations.

(우리는 유연한 규칙과 규정을 만들어야 한다.)

equivalent / 대등한, 일치하는 (equal)

A wish is often equivalent to a command in the navy.

(해군에서의 기대는 종종 명령과 일치한다.)

excess / 과잉, 지나침 (extra, surplus)

An excess of enthusiasm is not good. (열정이 지나치면 좋지 않다.)

forgery-proof / 위조방지 처리된 (preventing counterfeiting documents or signatures)

The three identifiers – the picture of the newcomer's face showing earlobe, a print of the right index finger, the person's signature – are printed on a computer-generated and forgery-proof permanent alien registration card.
(3가지 식별도구-새 입국자의 귀볼이 보이는 사진, 오른쪽 집게 손가락의 채취, 개인의 서명-이 컴퓨터로 생성되어 위조방지 처리된 영주 외국인 등록카드에 인쇄된다.)

genuine / 진정한, 진짜의 (real, sincere and honest)

Our government has a genuine interest in the human rights condition of NorthKorea.
(우리 정부는 북한의 인권상태에 대해 진정으로 관심을 가지고 있다.)

illegal / 불법의, 위법의 (unlawful, illicit)

It is illegal to drive a car that is not taxed or insured.
(세금을 안내거나 보험이 안된 차를 운전하는 것은 불법이다.)

industrial / 산업의 산업과 연관된 (connected with industry)

The world is being led by industrially advanced countries.
(세계는 산업 선진국들에 의해 인도되고 있다.)

inferior / 저질의, 낮은(lower in quality, value, order, rank, or status)

An inferior good is a good that decreases in demand when consumer income rises.
(저질품은 소비자의 소득이 증가할 때 수요가 감소하는 물품이다.)

informal / 비공식적인, 완화된(relaxed)

They cooperate with other groups on an informal basis.
(그들은 격의없이 다른 그룹들과 협력하였다.)

irregular / 평평하지 않은, 불규칙적인(not even, smooth, or straight in shape or appearance)

There were irregular surfaces around the museum.

(박물관 주위의 바닥은 고르지 않았다.)

legal / 합법적인(permitted or authorized by law)

Officers should act in a legal manner or with legal authority.

(경관들은 법에 따라 또는 법적 권위를 가지고 행동해야 한다.)

moderate / 합리적인, 온건한(reasonable and avoiding extreme opinions or actions)

She was in the moderate wing of the party.

(그녀는 그 당의 온건파에 속해 있었다.)

numerous / 수많은 (many, lots of)

There are numerous islands in the south of Korea.

(한국의 남쪽에는 많은 섬들이 있다.)

objective / 객관적인, 독립적인 (independent, without bias or prejudice)

We need your objective opinion on this issue.

(우리는 이 문제에 대해 당신이 객관적인 의견을 가져 주기를 바란다.)

practical / 시용적인, 유용한 (right, sensible, useful)

This book offers you practical vocabulary to improve your English.

(이 책은 영어능력 향상을 위한 실용적인 어휘를 제공하고 있다.)

personal / 개인적인 (private and not known or available to most people)

This is a personal matter and does not concern all of you.

(이는 개인적 문제로서 모든 사람들에게 해당되지는 않는다.)

pragmatic / 실용적인, 현실적인 (practical, useful)

Rather than relying on theory and philosophy, Col Torres takes a very pragmatic approach to leadership.

(토레스 대령은 이론과 철학에 의지하기보다는 리더쉽에 대해 매우 실용적으로 접근한다.)

vague / 막연한, 애매한 (not clearly or fully explained)

Some aspects of the law were somewhat vague and ill-defined.

(그 법의 어떤 내용은 다소 애매하고 제대로 정의되지 않았다.)

worth / 가치가 있는 (equal in worth or value to)

The house is worth one million dollars.

(그 집은 100만 달러의 가치를 지닌다.)

2. 연습문제

1. The painting was a gift for my birthday; I don't know its ______ cost.

   ⓐ relative   ⓑ active   ⓒ actual   ⓓ practicable

2. According to the police, the man who was shot has broken the law several times. He has a long ______ record.

   ⓐ innocent   ⓑ criminal   ⓒ judicial   ⓓ auditory

3. The price of beef is ______ expensive this year.

   ⓐ occasionally   ⓑ comparatively   ⓒ absolutely   ⓓ comprehensible

4. The trip is over difficult area, so you'd better send the most ______ driver you have.

   ⓐ competent   ⓑ strict   ⓒ distinct   ⓓ direct

5. In order to drive a car you must take the driver's license. It's ______ .

   ⓐ compulsory   ⓑ optional   ⓒ temporary   ⓓ conceptive

6. The store is only two blocks away. It's really ______ .

   ⓐ unnecessary   ⓑ possible   ⓒ convenient   ⓓ stern

7. All of us hear some ______ accidents on the TV everyday.

   ⓐ to disturb   ⓑ disturbing
   ⓒ disturbed   ⓓ disturbance

8. Their plane was late leaving Chicago. It's _____ they'll arrive at the scheduled time.

    ⓐ proper   ⓑ doubtful   ⓒ unnecessary   ⓓ certain

9. These socks will fit all sizes from small to large because it's so _____ .

    ⓐ inflexible   ⓑ elastic   ⓒ original   ⓓ rigid

10. Is a quarter _____ to two dimes and a nickel?

    ⓐ equable   ⓑ equivalent   ⓒ equally   ⓓ equatorial

11. I had to pay for my _____ baggage before I went aboard.

    ⓐ abnormal   ⓑ excess   ⓒ external   ⓓ extreme

12. Chuck: How much did you pay for that T-thirt?

    Nindo: Nothing. It was _____ . I won the race on Tuesday, and they gave it to me.

    ⓐ less   ⓑ discounted   ⓒ expensive   ⓓ free

13. Please don't park in front of my mailbox, and _____ , don't let your dog into my yard anymore.

    ⓐ would rather   ⓑ nevertheless   ⓒ furthermore   ⓓ rather than

14. The diamond she wore at the party is _____ .

    ⓐ precise   ⓑ mechanical   ⓒ genuine   ⓓ generous

15. It is _____ to use someone's car without his permission.

    ⓐ innocent   ⓑ unfair   ⓒ illegal   ⓓ ignorant

16. The city of Changwon manufactures many small automobiles. It's an _____ area.

    ⓐ toxic   ⓑ industrious   ⓒ industrial   ⓓ indulgent

17. The blue T-shirt Paul chose was _______ to what Kevin chose.

   ⓐ countless   ⓑ colony   ⓒ inferior   ⓓ ordinary

18. Herman's party is very _______ . He said we could wear jeans.

   ⓐ formal   ⓑ official   ⓒ informal   ⓓ perfect

19. There are several discount stores that sell only _______ clothes. There may be something wrong with them, but they're usually cheap.

   ⓐ irregular   ⓑ perfect   ⓒ free   ⓓ expensive

20. To fail to stop at a red light is against the law. but turning right after stopping is usually _______ .

   ⓐ fair   ⓑ legal   ⓒ reasonable   ⓓ innocent

21. That small store sells clothes at _______ prices.

   ⓐ similar   ⓑ moderate   ⓒ obsolete   ⓓ minute

22. That manager has _______ contacts in the banking business.

   ⓐ numerous   ⓑ orderly   ⓒ independent   ⓓ comfortable

23. The anchor-person who reports the news should have a(n) _______ viewpoint.

   ⓐ objective   ⓑ subjective   ⓒ directive   ⓓ ridiculous

24. The vending machines was _______ . No one could buy anything.

   ⓐ on   ⓑ in   ⓒ off   ⓓ aside

25. A set of glasses is a _______ gift for a newly married couple.

   ⓐ practical   ⓑ abrupt   ⓒ theoretical   ⓓ plump

2. 사회와 경제

26. The owner of the hotel doesn't use the airlines when he flies. He has his own airplane and his own _____ pilot to take him any spot he wants to go.
    ⓐ definite   ⓑ public   ⓒ personal   ⓓ indefinite

27. Many people are standing in line to buy tickets for the new film. It's extremely _____ .
    ⓐ succinct   ⓑ successful   ⓒ sufficient   ⓓ successive

28. The interest rates on some bank loans can change; the rates are _____ .
    ⓐ fixed   ⓑ obsolete   ⓒ variable   ⓓ moderate

29. Brian's first attempt to drive a brand-new car was not successful.
    ⓐ final   ⓑ initial   ⓒ real   ⓓ top

30. We must have abundant supplies to last for at least 10 days.
    ⓐ scanty   ⓑ practical   ⓒ ample   ⓓ overall

31. This blue jacket is inferior to the other red one.
    ⓐ worse than   ⓑ superior to   ⓒ better than   ⓓ incomparable to

32. They were asking an equitable price for the house. At least it seemed to be a fair price.
    ⓐ high   ⓑ steady   ⓒ low   ⓓ reasonable

33. Over forty million persons left their ancestral homes in order to begin a new life in a new world across the sed.
    ⓐ descendant's   ⓑ forefathers'   ⓒ traditional   ⓓ relative's

34. The immigrants' abject fears of living in the new country were brought on by feelings of loss and uncertainty.

ⓐ unimaginable   ⓑ real   ⓒ of the worst kind   ⓓ typical

35. The immigrants were subjected to a bewildering series of tests which sometimes left them feeling insecure and confused.

   ⓐ confusing   ⓑ reasonable   ⓒ rare   ⓓ severe

36. Every art and industry in the U. S. bears the indelible immigrant stamp which time cannot remove.

   ⓐ temporary   ⓑ irrecoverable   ⓒ permanent   ⓓ erasable

37. Tyler, the used car salesman, is notorious for cheating his customers by overcharging for poor quality cars. Luckily, we all know his reputation.

   ⓐ He is unfavorably known by many people.

   ⓑ He is known and admired for his good deeds.

   ⓒ He is totally unknown.

   ⓓ He treats his customers very well

38. Samuel strives to be ethical in all his business affairs by treating his customers fairly and honestly.

   ⓐ He treats his customers partially.

   ⓑ He has a bad reputation for his business practices.

   ⓒ He conforms to a moral standard in his business conduct.

   ⓓ He does business only with people who have similar customs and background to his.

39. When the network is completed sometime in the 21st century, it will bind peripheral counties like Greece and Portugal closer to the rest of Europe.

   ⓐ surrounding   ⓑ critical   ⓒ larger   ⓓ developing

정답 / 해석

1. ⓒ 그 그림은 내 생일 선물이다. 실제 가격은 모른다.

2. ⓑ 경찰에 따르면, 저격당한 사람은 여러 번 법을 어겼다. 그는 오랜 전과기록이 있다.

3. ⓑ 소고기 가격은 올해 비교적 비싸다.

4. ⓐ 그 여행에서 어려운 지역을 지나가야 한다. 그러므로 당신들 가운데 가장 유능한 운전기사를 보내는 것이 낫다.

5. ⓐ 차를 운전하기 위해서는 운전면허를 취득해야 한다. 그것은 의무다.

6. ⓒ 그 가게는 단지 두 블럭 떨어져 있다. 정말 편리하다.

7. ⓑ 우리는 매일 TV에서 불쾌한 사건을 듣는다.

8. ⓑ 그들의 비행기는 시카고 출발이 늦었다. 계획대로 도착할 지 의문이다.

9. ⓑ 이 양말은 신축성이 있으므로 발이 크건 작건 모든 사이즈에 맞다.

10. ⓑ 25센트는 다임 두 개 및 니켈 한 개와 같은 액수인가?

11. ⓑ 나는 탑승하기 전에 초과 수화물에 대해 지불해야 한다.

12. ⓓ 척: 그 티셔츠 얼마 주고 샀어요?

　　　닌도: 한 푼도 안냈어요. 공짜죠. 화요일 경주에서 이겨서 받았답니다.

13. ⓒ 내 우편함 앞에 주차하지 마세요. 또한 당신 개가 내 집마당에 들어오지 않도록 해 주세요.

14. ⓒ 그녀가 파티에서 낀 다이아몬드는 진짜다.

15. ⓒ 남의 차를 허락 없이 사용하는 것은 불법이다.

16. ⓒ 창원시는 소형자동차를 많이 생산한다. 창원시는 산업지역이다.

17. ⓒ 폴이 선택한 푸른 티셔츠는 캐빈이 선택한 것보다 못하다.

18. ⓒ 헐만의 파티는 비공식 파티이다. 그는 우리가 일상용 바지를 입어도 된다고 말했다.

19. ⓐ 흠이 있는 옷만 할인 판매하는 가게들이 있다. 어딘지 잘못 만들어진 옷들이겠지만 대부분은 싸다.

20. ⓑ 붉은 신호등에 멈추지 않으면 불법이지만, 멈춘 뒤에 우측으로 가는 것은 대개 합법적이다.

21. ⓑ 그 작은 가게에서는 옷을 싸게 판다.

22. ⓐ 그 관리인은 은행계에 많은 연줄이 있다.

23. ⓐ 뉴스를 보고하는 종합 사회자는 객관적인 관점을 가져야 한다.

24. ⓒ 그 자동판매기는 고장 났다. 아무 것도 살 수 없다.

25. ⓐ 유리 기구 한 벌은 신혼부부에게 실용적인 선물이다.

26. ⓒ 그 호텔 사장은 비행기로 여행할 때 항공사의 비행기를 타지 않는다. 그가 가고 싶은 지점에 바로 갈 수 있는 개인 항공기와 개인 조종사가 있다.

27. ⓑ 많은 사람들이 새로 나온 영화표를 사기 위해 줄서 있다. 그 영화는 아주 성공적이다.

28. ⓒ 은행의 대출 이자율은 달라질 수 있다. 그 이자율은 변화가능하다.

29. ⓑ 새 차를 운전하려는 브라이언의 최초 시도는 성공적이지 못하였다.

30. ⓒ 우리는 적어도 10일 동안 유지할 수 있는 충분한 물자를 가지고 있어야 한다.

31. ⓐ 이 푸른 자켓은 다른 붉은 자켓보다 못하다.

32. ⓓ 그들은 그 집에 대해 공정한 가격을 요구하고 있다. 요구 가격은 정당한 것 같다.

33. ⓑ 4백만 이상의 사람들이 조상의 고향을 버리고 바다 건너 신세계에서 새 삶을 시작하였다.

34. ⓒ 이민자들의 삶에 대한 절망적 두려움은 상실감과 불확실한 기분에 기인한다.

35. ⓐ 이민자들은 당혹스러운 시험을 받으며, 그로인해 때때로 그들은 불안하고 혼란스러워진다.

36. ⓒ 미국의 모든 예술과 산업은 시간으로 지울 수 없는 이민자의 영원한 흔적을 지니고 있다.

37. ⓐ 중고차 판매원인 타일러는 고객을 속여 질이 좋지 않는 차에 대해 비용을 많이 부과하는 것으로 악명이 높다. 다행히, 우리 모두는 그의 평판을 알고 있다.

38. ⓒ 사무엘은 자신의 고객을 공정하고 정직하게 대우하여 업무상 윤리적이 되려고 노력한다.

39. ⓐ 통신망이 21세기 언젠가 완성되면, 그리스와 포르투갈 같은 주변국을 나머지 유럽국가에 보다 가까이 묶게 될 것이다.

어휘, 관용구, 문형 종합

기본어휘 / 연습 문제

D

New American Language Course

furthermore / 더군다나, 그 위에 (in addition, besides)

Mr. Brown has earned the respect of farmers everywhere. Furthermore, they know they can trust him.

(브라운 씨는 어디서든 농부들의 존경을 받고 있다. 게다가 사람들은 그를 믿을 수 있는 사람으로 알고 있다.)

break in on / 끼어들다, 방해하다 (to interrupt, to intrude on)

The newcomer broke in on our private conference.

(신입자가 우리의 사적인 회의에 끼어들었다.)

by virtue of / ~에 의해, 때문에 (on the grounds of, because of)

By virtue of the fact that the president is head of the government, he is also commander-in-chief of the military.

(대통령은 정부의 수장이기 때문에, 군대의 최고 지휘관이 된다.)

carry out / 수행하다, 완수하다 (to perform or complete)

I am carrying out research on pragmatics.

(나는 화용론에 대한 연구를 수행하고 있다.)

check off / 대조확인하다 (to put a mark beside)

He wrote down the names of all the students and then he checked them off against the list.

(그는 모든 학생들의 이름을 적고, 목록을 대조 확인하였다.)

check out... on / ~에 대해 확인시켜주다 (to make one familiar with the operation of)

Before you fly the helicopter, the instructor must check you out on the instrument panel.
(헬리콥터를 몰기 전에 교관은 계기판에 대해 확인시켜 주어야 한다.)

chip in / 추렴하다, 갹출하다 (to share in giving money or help)

We each should chip in 3000 won and buy a cake for her.
(우리 각자 3천원씩 내어 그녀에게 케익을 사주자.)

come across / 우연히 만나다 (to find by chance, to meet by accident)

I came across the book that I forgot in the closet.
(나는 벽장 속에서 잃어버린 책을 우연히 찾았다.)

come along / 좋아지다 (to improve or proceed)

He is coming along well after the operation.
(그는 수술 후에 나아지고 있다.)

cross out [off] / 삭제하다, 지우다 (to cancel by drawing lines across)

They crossed the meat off their shopping list.
(그들은 쇼핑목록에서 육고기를 삭제했다.)

drop by / 잠깐 들르다 (to make a short visit somewhere)

Why don't you drop by for coffee some time?
(잠깐 커피 한잔 하러 오시지 않겠어요?)

in reference to / ~에 대해 (with reference to, in regard to)

Our superintendent spoke in reference to the graduation ceremony.
(우리 교장님은 졸업식에 대해 언급하였다.)

subject (to) / ~하게 되는, 지배받는 (being under domination or control)

All beings are subject to death.

(모든 존재하는 것은 죽기 마련이다.)

substitute A for B / A로 B를 대체하다 (to use A instead of B, to replace B with[by] A)

The mechanic substituted a new tire for the old one.

(그 기술자는 헌 타이어를 새 타이어로 교체하였다.)

take effect / 효력을 발휘하다 (to become operative, to begin to apply)

International sanctions on North Korea were beginning to take effect.

(북한에 대한 국제적인 제제가 효력을 발휘하기 시작하였다.)

fix up / 수리하다 (to repair, mend, remedy)

The whole block is being fixed up.

(전 구역이 수리 중이다.)

in the vicinity of / 가까이, 근처에 (near, close to)

There are two stores in the close vicinity of my house.

(내 집 아주 가까이에 두 개의 상점이 있다.)

in place of / 대신에 (instead of, in lieu of)

The grown-up usually have coffee instead of milk.

(어른들은 대개 우유 대신 커피를 마신다.)

make a speech / 연설하다 (talk formally)

I'm nervous about making a speech at the wedding.

(나는 결혼식 주례를 하기가 불안하다.)

on top of / 위에, 뿐만 아니라 (at the top of, besides)

Put the letter on top of the T.V. where it can be seen easily.

(편지를 쉽게 볼 수 있도록 텔레비전 위에 두어라.)

part with / 내어놓다, 내어주다 (to give something to somebody else)

You must read the contract before parting with any money.

(대금을 지불하기 전에 계약서를 읽어야 합니다.)

pay back / 갚다 (to give money back)

Jill finally paid me back twenty dollars last week.

(마침내 지난 주, 질은 나에게서 빌려갔던 20달러를 갚았다.)

pick up / 사귀다 (to get acquainted with, to make friends with)

He often goes to clubs to pick up girls.

(그는 여자를 사귀려고 종종 술집에 간다.)

set out / 배치하다 (to arrange or display things)

We need to set out the tables for the meeting. (우리는 모임을 위해 테이블을 배치하였다.)

set aside / 저축하다, 비축하다 (to keep or save something from a larger amount or supply in order to use

Have you set aside some money for your kid's education?

(아이들의 교육비를 위해 약간의 돈을 저축해 두었습니까?)

take effect / 발효하다 (to become operative, to begin to apply)

The new regulation will take effect by the first of January.

(새 규정은 내년 1월 1일 발효될 것이다.)

tear down / 파괴하다, 헐다 (demolish, pull or knock down)

They tore down the old building to put up a new church.

(그들은 헐고 새 교회를 짓기 위해 오래된 건물을 헐었다.)

try out / 시험해보다 (to test someone or something to see what they are like orwhether they are appropriate or effective)

The idea seems to be good but it needs to be tried out.

(좋은 생각인 듯 보이나 실지로 실험해 볼 필요가 있다.)

wear out / 지치게 하다, 피곤하게 하다 (to be weary, fatigue, exhaust)

Hard toil and much care can wear the spirit.

(심한 고난과 지나친 근심은 정신을 쇠잔하게 한다.)

2. 연습문제

1. All the customers _____ smoke only in designated areas in this department store.

   ⓐ are forced to   ⓑ are delighted with ⓒ are permitted to   ⓓ are guaranteed to

2. A: Can I borrow your new digital camera?

   B: Sure, but I want to _____ you _____ on it first.

   ⓐ set / out   ⓑ check / out   ⓒ check / up

3. If all of us _____ we can afford to give her a birthday present.

   ⓐ chip away   ⓑ chip in   ⓒ subscribe   ⓓ submit

4. Did anyone happen to _____ the earring I left at the washstand?

   ⓐ come down on   ⓑ chip in   ⓒ come across   ⓓ come about

5. Linda is new here. Let's ask her to _____ us at the party tonight.

   ⓐ be up to   ⓑ part with   ⓒ come along with   ⓓ get through with

6. You must _____ from your grocery list the items you have already bought at the supermarket.

   ⓐ cross over   ⓑ cross out   ⓒ cross up   ⓓ crosscheck

7. Can I _____ tonight? I'd like to see you.

   ⓐ blow out   ⓑ drop by   ⓒ keep on   ⓓ cast away

8. The vote to adopt the plan were ______ affirmative, with 120 for adoption and only 50 against.

    ⓐ previously   ⓑ hardly   ⓒ approximately   ⓓ extensively

9. Mike: Do they have dictionaries ______ at the BX?
   Dan: Yes, I bought mine there.

    ⓐ bargain   ⓑ for sale   ⓒ free   ⓓ cost

10. Could you give me a bag of potato ______ this bag of corn, please?

    ⓐ in exchange of   ⓑ is spite of   ⓒ in favor of   ⓓ in memory of

11. Can we have pizza ______ bread for lunch?

    ⓐ in regard to   ⓑ in place of
    ⓒ in consequence of   ⓓ in the face of

12. Alex parked his car ______ mine.

    ⓐ under   ⓑ besides   ⓒ aside   ⓓ next to

13. I am too busy to talk to anyone on the phone ______ it is.

    ⓐ no matter who   ⓑ no matter which
    ⓒ no matter how   ⓒ no matter what

14. At this time of the day the parking lot gets completely full. There is ______ to park.

    ⓐ no place   ⓑ anyplace   ⓒ someplace   ⓓ every place

15. The bread is in a box ______ the refrigerator.

    ⓐ forward   ⓑ on top of   ⓒ throughout   ⓓ into

16. My brother didn't want to _____ those gloves, but they were just too small for him.

ⓐ stand by   ⓑ put on   ⓒ part with   ⓓ keep

17. Margaret owns many _____ shoes.

ⓐ pieces of   ⓑ pairs of   ⓒ sales   ⓓ bucks

18. Nina: When are you going to _____ the five dollars I lent you?

Mars: The day after tomorrow.

ⓐ wake up   ⓑ cast away   ⓒ throw away   ⓓ pay back

19. The robber is stealing clothes from the store. He's trying to take them without _____ .

ⓐ trying them on   ⓑ paying for them   ⓒ wearing them   ⓓ asking the price

20. Tom _____ some Japanese while he was stationed in Hawaii.

ⓐ picked up   ⓑ took after   ⓒ called off   ⓓ picked out

21. Gerry and I have some money _____ for a vacation to Europe next summer.

ⓐ set aside   ⓑ corrected   ⓒ shared   ⓓ carried

22. In order to have dinner we must _____ the dishes.

ⓐ set out   ⓑ set back   ⓒ set aside   ⓓ set apart

23. It _____ dinner is almost ready.

ⓐ smells like   ⓑ to smell like   ⓒ smells   ⓓ like a smell

24. The new traffic law to raise the speed limit will _____ next year.

ⓐ take effect   ⓑ make effort

ⓒ have an effect   ⓓ carry out

25. The old library building downtown was ______ . A parking lot is being built there now.

   ⓐ rebuilt   ⓑ rubbed

   ⓒ malfunctioned   ⓓ torn down

26. There are ______ dogs on the other side of that gate.

   ⓐ black two guard   ⓑ two black guard

   ⓒ guard black two   ⓓ two guard black

27. Jeff's car is in the garage; ______ , he needs a ride to work this morning.

   ⓐ however   ⓑ thus   ⓒ because   ⓓ if

28. When I arrive at the airport, you will be gone.

   ⓐ Until   ⓑ By the time   ⓒ What time   ⓓ Since

29. Lots of people arrived late on account of the icy streets.

   ⓐ due to   ⓑ without regard to

   ⓒ according to   ⓓ regardless of

30. Flight 123 is approaching the San Francisco at 7 p.m.

   ⓐ going away from   ⓑ departing for

   ⓒ coming near to   ⓓ on the ground at

31. you are a stranger at a party someone will take you under his wing and introduce you to other guests to help ease your discomfort.

   ⓐ escort you around   ⓑ put his arm around you

   ⓒ take you to his flight division   ⓓ guide someone into the guest room

32. After an informal introduction and a short conversation, the topic of children came up. This struck common ground and the couple automatically felt more at ease with each other.

ⓐ brought up a new subject   ⓑ brought up a familiar subject

ⓒ brought up a touchy subject   ⓓ brought up current affairs

33. Doug: Do you think the jury will believe his story?

Mike: He doesn't have a leg to stand on.

ⓐ He's never done anything wrong.   ⓑ He has no defence.

ⓒ He's in a wheelchair.   ⓓ He made great mistake

34. Pat: Tim, did you tell David you were wrong after your argument?

Tim: No, but I'll have to swallow my pride and do it.

ⓐ Tim and David were wrong to argue.

ⓑ Tim is proud that they ended the argument.

ⓒ Tim is right but doesn't want to argue with David

ⓓ Tim is wrong and hates to have to admit it.

35. The motion was unanimously approved by the committee. All the members voted in favor of it.

ⓐ comparatively speaking   ⓑ actually in some cases

ⓒ based on competent authority   ⓓ agreeably to all concerned

36. He worked for a bank for a few years, but it didn't pan out.

ⓐ work out   ⓑ carry out   ⓒ hold out   ⓓ put out

37. He usually puts in about 60 hours a week at the office.

ⓐ runs   ⓑ works   ⓒ gives   ⓓ saves

ECL시험 대비 New ALC 필수어휘 완성

38. Capt Roberts ran up expenses of over $600 at the conference.

ⓐ incurred　　ⓑ saved　　ⓒ brought up　　ⓓ collected

39. At first he insisted that the building be constructed as planned, but he had to back down when he saw the cost projections.

ⓐ cooperate　　ⓑ counteract　　ⓒ yield　　ⓓ cancel

40. The deal wrapped up before bedtime.

ⓐ completed　　ⓑ discussed　　ⓒ began　　ⓓ quit

41. The French and West German railway companies have offered to make up some Belgian losses, and the European Community's executive commission is looking for ways to help.

ⓐ add to　　ⓑ pay for　　ⓒ create　　ⓓ constitute

정답 / 해석

1. ⓒ 이 백화점에서는 모든 고객은 단지 지정된 지역에서만 흡연이 허용된다.

2. ⓑ A: 디지털카메라 빌릴 수 있니?

   B: 그래, 그런데 먼저 작동법에 대해 확인시켜 주어야겠다.

3. ⓑ 우리 모두가 조금씩 내면 그녀에게 생일선물을 사줄 수 있다.

4. ⓒ 누가 세면대에 놓아 둔 귀걸이 보았니?

5. ⓒ 린다는 여기 새로 왔다. 그녀에게 오늘밤 파티에 우리와 함께 가자고 말해라.

6. ⓑ 슈퍼마켓에서 이미 구입한 물품은 구매목록에서 지워야 한다.

7. ⓑ 오늘 밤에 들러도 될까요? 만났으면 합니다.

8. ⓓ 그 계획을 채택하려는 선거는 찬성 120, 반대 50으로 압도적인 찬성이었다.

9. ⓑ 마이크: BX에는 사전도 있나요?

   덴: 예, 내 사전도 그곳에서 샀어요.

10. ⓐ 이 옥수수 한 푸대와 감자 한 푸대를 바꿀 수 있니?

11. ⓑ 점심으로 빵 대신 피자를 먹을 수 있습니까?

12. ⓓ 알렉스는 자기 차를 내차 옆에 주차하였다.

13. ⓐ 나는 너무 바빠서 누구든 상관없이 전화건 사람과 이야기 할 수 없다.

14. ⓐ 이 때 쯤에는 주차장이 완전히 가득 찬다. 주차할 공간이 없다.

15. ⓑ 빵은 냉장고 위의 상자에 있다.

16. ⓒ 내 동생은 이 장갑을 버리기를 싫어한다. 그러나 그것은 그에게 너무 작다.

17. ⓑ 마가레트는 신발이 많다.

18. ⓓ 니나: 내가 빌려준 5달러를 언제쯤 갚아주시겠어요?

    마즈: 모레 돌려 드리겠습니다.

19. ⓑ 그 도둑이 상점에서 옷을 훔치고 있다. 그는 대금을 지불하지 않고 옷을 가져가려 하고 있다.

20. ⓐ 톰은 하와이에 주둔하고 있는 동안 일본인 몇 명을 사귀었다.

21. ⓐ 제리와 나는 다음 여름 유럽 여행을 가기 위해 약간의 돈을 저축했다.

22. ⓐ 저녁을 먹기 위해서는 음식을 차려야 한다.

23. ⓐ 저녁 준비가 다 되어가는 냄새가 난다.

24. ⓐ 속도제한 시속을 올리려는 새로운 교통법이 내년에 발효될 것이다.

25. ⓓ 시내에 있는 오래된 도서관 건물이 헐리고, 주차장이 만들어지고 있다.

26. ⓑ 대문 반대편에 두 마리 검은 경비견이 있다.

27. ⓑ 제프의 차는 정비소에 있다. 오늘 아침 직장에 가기 위해서는 누군가가 태워 주어야 한다.

28. ⓑ 내가 공항에 도착할 때는, 너는 떠나고 없을 것이다.

29. ⓐ 많은 사람들이 얼음길 때문에 늦게 도착하였다.

30. ⓒ 항공기123기가 오후 7시에 센프란시스코에 도착할 것이다.

31. ⓐ 그 파티에 처음 온 사람이면, 누군가가 당신을 다른 손님에게 소개하여 불편을 덜어 줄 것이다.

32. ⓑ 비공식적으로 소개하고 짧은 대화를 나눈 뒤에, 자녀들에 대해 이야기 하기 시작했다. 공통된 화제를 내놓아서 그 부부는 자연히 더욱 더 서로에게 편안하게 느꼈다.

33. ⓑ 도거: 배심원이 그의 이야기를 믿을 것이라고 생각하니?

　　　마이크: 그는 어쩔 줄 몰라하고 있다.

34. ⓓ 팻: 팀, 다툰 뒤에 데이비드에게 너가 잘못했다고 말했느냐?

　　　팀: 아니, 그렇지만 나는 자존심을 억누르고 그렇게 해야 할 것이다.

35. ⓓ 위원회는 그 발의를 만장일치로 승인했다. 모든 위원들이 그것에 찬성했다.

36. ⓐ 그는 어떤 은행에 몇년 동안 근무하였지만, 일은 잘 되지 않았다.

37. ⓑ 그는 대개 사무실에서 일 주일에 약 60시간을 보낸다.

38. ⓐ 로버트 대령은 회의에서 600달러 이상의 비용을 사용했다.

39. ⓒ 처음에는 건물이 예정대로 건설되어야 한다고 주장했지만, 비용 견적을 보자 이를 철회했다.

40. ⓐ 그 거래는 취침시간 전에 끝났다.

41. ⓑ 프랑스와 독일의 철도회사는 벨기에의 손실을 보상하려고 제의했으며, EC 집행위원회는 도와 줄 방법을 찾고 있다.

New American Language Course

New American
Language Course

교육과 직업 3

A. 명사   B. 동사   C. 형용사   D. 어휘, 관용구, 문형 종합

ECL시험 대비 NEW ALC 必 필수어휘 완성

명사

기본어휘 / 연습 문제

A

New American
Language Course

1. 기본어휘 　　　명사

abbreviation / 축소, 생략 (a shortened form of a word or phrase)
I've only read an abbreviated version of the novel. (나는 그 소설의 축약본만 읽었다.)

abundance / 풍부, 충분 (plentiful or sufficient quantity or supply)
There was an abundance of wine at the wedding.
(결혼식에는 충분한 포도주가 있었다.)

astronomer / 천문학자 (an expert in astronomy)
Astronomers have a knowledge of the laws of the heavenly orbs.
(천문학자들은 천체의 궤도 법칙에 대한 지식을 가지고 있다.)

attendance / 참석, 출석 (being present at a place)
Teachers must keep a record of students' attendance.
(선생님은 학생들의 출석기록을 유지해야 한다.)

background / 배경 (the whole of one's study, training, and experience)
The Twin Tower of New York City's World Trade Center stood against a background of crisp blue sky.
(뉴욕 세계 무역센터의 쌍둥이 탑은 맑고 푸른 하늘을 배경으로 서 있었다.)

column / 칼럼, 난 (a part of a newspaper dealing with a particular subject)
He is writing a regular column for the newspaper.
(그는 신문에 규칙적으로 한 칼럼을 쓰고 있다.)

context / 문맥, 전후관계 (the whole situation, background)

Idioms and slangs are meaningless until you hear them in the context of everyday use.
(관용구와 속어는 일상적으로 사용되는 맥락에서 듣지 않으면 의미가 없다.)

correlation / 상관관계 (a shared relationship)

There is some correlation between the ability to think conceptually and theability to use the language. The two cannot be thought of as totally separate entities.
(개념적으로 생각할 능력과 언어를 사용할 능력 사이에는 상관관계가 있다. 그 둘은 전혀 별개의 대상으로 생각되어서는 안 된다.)

coworker / 동료, 협력자 (a fellow worker)

Coworker is a person who work as a partner or helper.
(동업자는 협력자 또는 조력자로 일하는 사람이다.)

decade / 10년 (a group of ten, a period of ten years)

The researcher spent two decades working on various assignments.
(그 연구원은 여러 가지 임무를 수행하는 데 20년을 보냈다.)

digit / 한자리 숫자, 아라비아 숫자 (any numeral from 0 to 9)

Her phone number is different from mine by one digit.
(그녀의 전화번호는 나의 번호와 한 자리가 다르다.)

dimensions / 치수 (measurement s in length, width, and often depth)

The dimensions for the photograph is 8" wide by 7" high.
(그 사진의 치수는 가로 8인치 세로 7인치이다.)

discrepancy / 불일치, 차이 (lack of agreement, inconsistency)

There are some discrepancies between the original estimates of the cost and the actual bills.

(비용에 대한 최초 평가와 실제 계산서는 약간의 차이가 있다.)

district / 구역, 지역 (an area of town or country)

They live in one of the most exclusive districts of Paris.

(그들은 파리의 가장 상류지역에서 살고 있다.)

editor / 편집자 (a person who is in charge of publishing a book or a newspaper)

He is the sports editor of a national newspaper.

(그는 전국지의 스포츠 편집자이다.)

engineering / 공학 (the activity if designing things such as roads, bridges, or machines)

Engineering majors are popular these days.

(공학 전공학도들은 요즘 인기가 높다.)

expert / 전문가 (a person with special knowledge, skill or training)

He is an expert in driving.

(그는 운전 전문가이다.)

failure / 실패, 쇠약 (failing or proving unsuccessful)

The failure of our health can make retirement necessary.

(건강이 악화되면 은퇴할 수도 있다.)

foundation / 기초, 기반 (the most basic part of something)

The first two years of study provide a solid foundation in computing.

(첫 2년간의 학습은 계산에 대한 확고한 기초를 다진다.)

formula / 공식, 처방 (a rule or method for doing something)

Socialism can't offer a formula for prosperity and well-being.
(사회주의는 번영과 행복을 위한 공식을 제공하지 못한다.)

glare / 노려봄, 섬광 (a fierce angry stare, strong light)

Although his boss never reprimanded him, Jack knew how he felt from hisglare.
(그의 상관은 그를 비난하지 않았지만, 잭은 그가 노려보는 데서 그가 어떻게 느끼는지 알았다.)

graduate / 졸업생 (someone who has finished their studies at a school)

The 63rd class graduates of the naval academy will be commissioned next Friday.
(다음 주 금요일에는 해군사관학교 63기 졸업생들의 임관식이 있다.)

interference / 방해, 참견 (intervening or meddling)

He regards any help or advice from me as interference.
(그는 나의 도움이나 충고를 방해로 생각한다.)

interval / 간격, 사이 (a space or gap)

In the event of fire, the alarm will sound at intervals of 10 seconds.
(화재시 경보는 10초 간격으로 울린다.)

judge / 판사 (a public officer authorized to decide cases in a court of law)

The judge adjourned the hearing until next Monday.
(그 판사는 청문회를 다음 월요일로 연기하였다.)

myriad / 무수, 많은 수 (a large and varied number)

When Ms. Lee was studying Russian in college, because of the complexities of the grammar, she had a myriad of difficulties,
(이양은 대학에서 러시아어를 공부할 때 복잡한 문법으로 인해 갖은 어려움을 겪었다.)

obstacle / 장애물, 방해 (hinderance, obstruction)

We should cross some obstacles to foreign investment in Korea.
(한국에서의 외국인 투자에 대한 장애물을 넘어야 한다.)

obligation / 의무, 책무 (a social, legal, moral requirement)

If you have not signed a contract, you are under no obligation to pay anymoney.
(계약서에 서명을 하지 않았기 때문에 돈을 지불할 필요가 없다.)

phase / 단계, 국면 (a stage in a progress of change or development)

Each phase of life brings its own joys.
(인생의 모든 단계는 그 나름의 즐거움이 있다.)

posture / 입장, 자세 (an official stand or position)

At the top we should consider the public posture of the particular organization.
(지휘부에서는 특정기관의 공적인 지위를 고려해야 한다.)

procedure / 절차, 과정 (a way of doing something)

There's a complicated procedure for setting up the copy machine.
(복사기를 설치하기 위한 복잡한 절차가 있다.)

pressure / 압력, 압박 (the force or weight, difficulties or feelings of anxiety)

She has been under great pressure lately because her boss expects her to getthe job done in three months.
(그녀는 사장이 석 달 안에 그 일을 처리하기를 바라고 있으므로 최근에 심한 압박을 받고 있디.)

principle / 원리, 법칙 (a law, a rule, or a theory)

Our country is run on Democratic principles.
(우리나라는 민주주의의 원칙 아래 운영된다.)

process / 과정 (a series of things or activities in order to achieve a result)

To make things changed is a long process.
(상황을 변화시키는 데는 긴 과정이 필요하다.)

progress / 진전, 진보 (the process of improving or developing)

We didn't make any progress in controlling inflation.
(인플레이션을 통제하는 데 아무런 진전도 없었다.)

promotion / 승진, 진급 (a move to a higher level in a company, institution, or sport)

His number one objective is to get a promotion.
(그의 최우선 목표는 진급하는 일이다.)

psyche / 정신, 영혼 (the mind, soul, or spirit)

During her recent psychology course, Martina learned about the human psyche and the
basic motives behind human behaviour.
(그녀는 최근 심리학 과정을 이수하는 동안 마르티나는 인간의 마음과 인간 행동의 저변에 있는 기본
적인 동기에 대해 배웠다.)

purpose / 목적, 의도 (intention, aim)

I suppose that she is weak of purpose.
(나는 그녀가 목적의식이 약하다고 생각한다.)

reference / 언급, 참조 (resource, citation, mention)

He made frequent references to economic problems.
(그는 종종 경제 문제를 언급하였다.)

retirement / 은퇴(시기) (the time when you stop working)

I am now approaching retirement. (이제 나는 퇴직할 때가 다 되어간다.)

security / 안전 (freedom care, anxiety, or doubt)

The insurance policy gave our family security.

(보험은 우리 가족을 안전하게 해 주었다.)

section / 구역, 코너 (area within place)

The frozen-food section is in the rear of the store.

(냉동 음식 코너는 그 가게의 끝부분에 있다.)

status / 신분, 지위 (the social or professional position)

In most societies doctors and lawyers enjoy a very high status.

(대부분의 사회에서 의사와 변호사는 매우 높은 지위를 누린다.)

tactic / 전술 (a particular plan or method for achieving something)

She often used the tactic of threatening to quit.

(그녀는 그만 두겠다고 위협하는 전술을 종종 사용하였다.)

tenure / 정년 재직권 (length of time a position is held)

Near the end of his tenure at the university, the aging Professor Wilson published his most brilliant work.

(그 대학에서 그의 정녕이 끝날 때 쯤, 그 나이들은 윌슨 교수는 그의 가장 뛰어난 작 품을 출판했다.)

tray / 식판, 쟁반 (a shallow, boxlike, removable compartment or container or receptacle)

The guest ordered a breakfast tray from room service.

(손님은 룸 안내자에게 아침 식판을 주문했다.)

trash / 쓰레기 (waste material such as paper, plastic bags, etc.)

Did you put the newspaper in the trash?

(신문을 쓰레기통에 버렸나요?)

tip / 정보, 조언 (a useful information)

She gave me a useful practical tip about growing persimmon.

(그녀는 감 재배에 대한 유용하고 실용적인 정보를 주었다.)

unemployment / 실업, 실직 (a situation in which people do not have work)

The community here has been devastated by poverty and unemployment.

(이곳 공동체는 가난과 실직으로 황폐화되었다.)

veteran / 노병, 퇴역군인 (an experienced soldier)

The hardy veteran will resign today.

(그 강건한 노병은 오늘 사임할 것이다.)

want ads / 광고란 (classified advertisements for people who wants a job or a rent)

If you look for an apartment to rent, you must look at the want ad in thenewspaper.

(아파트를 전세 내려면, 신문의 광고란을 보아야 한다.)

2. 연습문제

1. Do you know why lb is the ______ for pound?
   ⓐ abbreviation   ⓑ department   ⓒ advantage   ⓓ branch

2. At first we were worried that we wouldn't get enough volunteers. In fact, we had ______ .
   ⓐ a jury   ⓑ an amount   ⓒ a number   ⓓ an abundance

3. John never missed a day of school for 3 years. He was the only student who graduated
   with a perfect ______ record.
   ⓐ confidence   ⓑ capability   ⓒ attendant   ⓓ attendance

4. Turn to page 87 and look at the top right-hand ______ .
   ⓐ column   ⓑ volume   ⓒ colony   ⓓ shelf

5. The ______ in the newspaper today aren't as funny and instructive as some of the ones
   from years ago.
   ⓐ comics   ⓑ editors   ⓒ chapters   ⓓ tailors

6. There is a ______ machine in the other building.
   ⓐ copied   ⓑ copying   ⓒ copies   ⓓ copy's

7. To explain its sentence structure, the teacher drew a ______ of the sentence on the white
   board.
   ⓐ picture   ⓑ outline   ⓒ diagram   ⓓ composition

8. A birth certificate is a ______ .

   ⓐ date   ⓑ history   ⓒ graduate   ⓓ document

9. The ______ decided not to print the fantastic story that John wrote.

   ⓐ author   ⓑ editor   ⓒ governor   ⓓ insomnia

10. Nick's interested in designing and building machines. He'll probably get a degree in

   ______ .

   ⓐ mathematics   ⓑ chemistry   ⓒ engineering   ⓓ biology

11. If we want to be an ______ on every subject or topic, we have to read everything about it

   first of all.

   ⓐ accuracy   ⓑ expert   ⓒ export   ⓓ experience

12. We drew a ______ of all the information so we could visualize it better.

   ⓐ telephone   ⓑ balance   ⓒ graph   ⓓ disk

13. Hillman attended two years of college, but he didn't receive a degree. He's not a college

   ______ .

   ⓐ passenger   ⓑ leader   ⓒ candidate   ⓓ graduate

14. There is a ______ every year to discuss the newest medical technology.

   ⓐ consequence   ⓑ conference   ⓒ criticism   ⓓ contest

15. The word ______ refers to men and women.

   ⓐ neighborhood   ⓑ human

   ⓒ digest   ⓓ sex

16. I like Harman's sense of _____ . He's always telling funny stories.

    ⓐ humor   ⓑ horror   ⓒ drama   ⓓ rock music

17. Jackson's clothes are dirty and worn out, and also he needs a haircut. What kind of _____ is he going to make to his seniors?

    ⓐ impression   ⓑ expression   ⓒ compression   ⓓ depression

18. Since he is an expert, we'd like to have his _____ before we start the big project.

    ⓐ ignorance   ⓑ storage   ⓒ code   ⓓ input

19. Steven: Jeff always interferes with my presentation.

Williams: Tell him you don't like his _____ .

    ⓐ interfere   ⓑ interfered   ⓒ interference   ⓓ interfering

20. Taking advantage of a short _____ before the commander called back, I could corrected the report.

    ⓐ interval   ⓑ impact   ⓒ instinct   ⓓ intention

21. Be careful not to make _____ on the table when you write.

    ⓐ marks   ⓑ course   ⓒ coats   ⓑ piles

22. This _____ is used in the classroom to teach students about flying.

    ⓐ poison   ⓑ brand   ⓒ model   ⓓ fashion

23. What are some _____ you have in the Navy?

    ⓐ brands   ⓑ obligations   ⓒ discharges   ⓓ extensions

24. Money is no ______ to many Korean parents because they would pay whatever it costs to give his children a good education.

ⓐ vitality   ⓑ solution   ⓒ obstacle   ⓓ importance

25. Ann has too many things to do. She's under a lot of ______ .

ⓐ process   ⓑ purpose   ⓒ progress   ⓓ pressure

26. John made ______ rather quickly and moved on to the next level.

ⓐ presentation   ⓑ progress   ⓒ effort   ⓓ propose

27. Last month Bob was a lieutenant; now he's a captain. He received a ______ .

ⓐ retirement   ⓑ position   ⓒ promotion   ⓓ degrade

28. People who have a ______ of duty always try to do their job as well as possible.

ⓐ sense   ⓑ respect   ⓒ seniority   ⓓ responsibility

29. The ______ in the procedure were quite easy to follow.

ⓐ distances   ⓑ bandage   ⓒ steps   ⓓ safety

30. If that method doesn't work, why don't you try a different ______ ?

ⓐ research   ⓑ contingency   ⓒ tactic   ⓓ task

31. This book is no good. I think I'll throw it in ______ .

ⓐ the trash   ⓑ stock   ⓒ booklet   ⓓ a bundle

32. The ______ of this pencil gets very dull. You have to sharpen it.

ⓐ top   ⓑ hole   ⓒ nut   ⓓ tip

33. The _______ rate is very high right now. There are many people without work.
    ⓐ unemployment   ⓑ employment   ⓒ chief   ⓓ boss

34. My uncle retired from the Navy last month. Now, he's a _______ .
    ⓐ recruit   ⓑ employee   ⓒ discharge   ⓓ veteran

35. You should check the _______ in the newspaper if you're looking for a job .
    ⓐ cartoons   ⓑ articles   ⓒ want ads   ⓓ wanted man

36. David reads many books. He _______ two every week.
    ⓐ estimates   ⓑ averages   ⓑ occurs   ⓒ arranges

37. Do you know how many _______ are in the number 80?
    ⓐ dimensions   ⓑ angles   ⓒ digits   ⓓ digital

38. You must get the _______ of the windows before you buy the blind.
    ⓐ dimensions   ⓑ formulas   ⓒ numbers   ⓓ space

39. Victor keys _______ into the computer before he prints out the charts.
    ⓐ copy   ⓑ data   ⓒ drums   ⓓ print

40. The schools in this _______ of the city are excellent.
    ⓐ transportation   ⓑ district   ⓒ temporal   ⓓ central

41. Your report didn't balance. There were many _______ in it.
    ⓐ experiments   ⓑ interruptions
    ⓒ discrepancies   ⓓ criticism

42. Daniel is a very good _____ . He always gets to the office early, he works hard, and he gets his job done.
ⓐ employee ⓑ employ ⓒ service ⓓ employment

43. The _____ in this immersion program will be on speaking and reading comprehension.
ⓐ emphasis ⓑ character ⓒ amusement ⓓ criticism

44. We didn't hire that man because he had no __ in economics.
ⓐ foundation ⓑ expert ⓒ traits ⓓ integrity

45. Jennifer's _____ in math prevented her from being an engineer.
ⓐ expert ⓑ failure ⓒ protest ⓓ faculty

46. You must memorize a lot of mathematical _____ when studying algebra and function.
ⓐ digital ⓑ formulas ⓒ deductions ⓓ forms

47. Completing your application is only the _____ to enter the company.
ⓐ initial step ⓑ first of all ⓒ at first series ⓓ final stage

48. Twelve _____ equals one foot.
ⓐ fingers ⓑ inches ⓒ meter ⓓ yards

49. A _____ occupies a position of authority, so he is addressed as "Your Honor."
ⓐ court ⓑ judge ⓒ lawyer ⓓ justice

50. The books on the shelf are not in the right _____ .
ⓐ authority ⓑ procedure ⓒ order ⓓ load

51. What's the _______ of this word?

    ⓐ ore   ⓑ original   ⓒ origin   ⓓ originality

52. Mr. Evans has been assigned to work on a new _______ .

    ⓐ service   ⓑ station   ⓒ project   ⓓ safety

53. Michael got hurt because he didn't follow the proper _______ .

    ⓐ progress   ⓑ safety   ⓒ procedure   ⓓ precede

54. Is Mr. Riggs a teacher or the _______ in your school?

    ⓐ principle   ⓑ principal   ⓒ province   ⓓ privilege

55. Three-year-old children are in a difficult _______ of development.

    ⓐ phenomena   ⓑ pharynx   ⓒ phase   ⓓ phrase

56. Where'd you get that information? My _______ was Wikipedia.

    ⓐ reference   ⓑ deference   ⓒ conference   ⓓ inference

57. They need to _______ their office procedures so they don't waste so much time.

    ⓐ systemic   ⓑ systematist

    ⓒ systematize   ⓓ systemization

58. There was no way they could have completed that _______ in the time given them.

    ⓐ mercury   ⓑ instrument   ⓒ task   ⓓ opponent

59. Put the paper for the copy machine in this _______ .

    ⓐ space   ⓑ tray   ⓒ area   ⓓ room

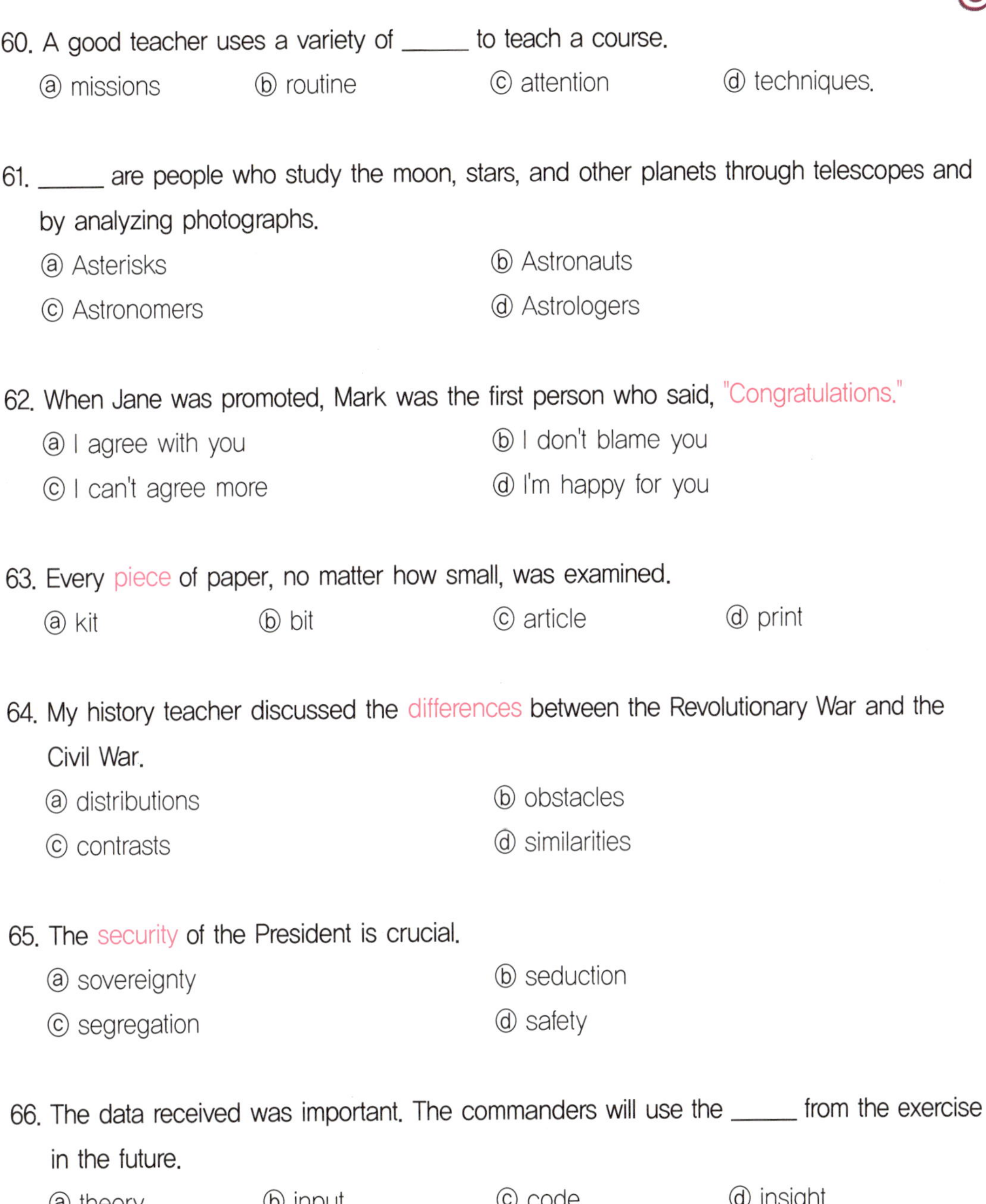

60. A good teacher uses a variety of _____ to teach a course.

    ⓐ missions   ⓑ routine   ⓒ attention   ⓓ techniques.

61. _____ are people who study the moon, stars, and other planets through telescopes and by analyzing photographs.

    ⓐ Asterisks   ⓑ Astronauts

    ⓒ Astronomers   ⓓ Astrologers

62. When Jane was promoted, Mark was the first person who said, "Congratulations."

    ⓐ I agree with you   ⓑ I don't blame you

    ⓒ I can't agree more   ⓓ I'm happy for you

63. Every piece of paper, no matter how small, was examined.

    ⓐ kit   ⓑ bit   ⓒ article   ⓓ print

64. My history teacher discussed the differences between the Revolutionary War and the Civil War.

    ⓐ distributions   ⓑ obstacles

    ⓒ contrasts   ⓓ similarities

65. The security of the President is crucial.

    ⓐ sovereignty   ⓑ seduction

    ⓒ segregation   ⓓ safety

66. The data received was important. The commanders will use the _____ from the exercise in the future.

    ⓐ theory   ⓑ input   ⓒ code   ⓓ insight

67. When each student gave his interpretation of the reading, the nuances between each interpretation were so slight that we suspected the students of doing the work as a group rather than individually.

ⓐ merchandise　　ⓑ new method　　ⓒ mistakes　　ⓓ differences

68. Some of the best minds on the fringes of the business have attempted to define and deal with the subject of advertising.

ⓐ center　　ⓑ marginal areas　　ⓒ decoration　　ⓓ core

69. Professor Brooks, always very demanding of and impatient with his students, had no rapport with them because he was such a martinet in the classroom.

ⓐ generous person　　　　　　　ⓑ person who suffers for his beliefs
ⓒ a very strict disciplinarian　　　ⓓ troublesome person

70. A good leader has integrity towards his men and country. He is honest and ethical in all his endeavors.

ⓐ skill and cleverness in making or arranging things

ⓑ strength and firmness of character or principle

ⓒ lack of stability of character

ⓓ the ability to feel rather than to reason

71. Although Lucy had nothing to base her feelings on, her intuition told her that she was about to be fired.

ⓐ Lucy's next door neighbor said she was getting fired.

ⓑ Lucy used tea leaves to look into the future.

ⓒ Without apparent reason, Lucy somehow knew she would be fired.

ⓓ Luchy thought that it will be better for her to quit the job soon.

72. The professor felt secure when his tenure was granted after a period of probation. His position was no longer temporary.

ⓐ permanent position
ⓑ valuable time
ⓒ terminal leave
ⓓ scholarship

73. The friction between the two men, stemming from their opposing views on the issue, created tension in the office.

ⓐ fraction
ⓑ conflict
ⓒ distortion
ⓓ creativity

74. There was a lot of dissension among the members of the committee before a decision could be reached. They quarreled a great deal.

ⓐ precaution
ⓑ disappointment
ⓒ discrimination
ⓓ disagreement

1. ⓐ lb가 왜 파운드의 약자인지 아십니까?

2. ⓓ 처음에는 지원자가 충분하지 않을까 우려했다. 사실은 충분히 많았다.

3. ⓓ 존은 3년 동안 하루도 결석하지 않았다. 그는 완벽한 출석기록으로 졸업한 유일한 학생이다.

4. ⓐ 87페이지를 펴고, 오른편 상단을 보아라.

5. ⓐ 오늘 날 신문의 코믹은 몇 년 전 만큼 재미있거나 교훈적이지 않다.

6. ⓑ 다른 건물에 복사기가 있다.

7. ⓒ 문장구조를 설명하기 위해서 선생님은 화이트보드에 문장구조를 그렸다.

8. ⓓ 출생증명서는 기록물이다.

9. ⓑ 편집자는 존이 쓴 환상적인 이야기를 출판하지 않기로 결정하였다.

10. ⓒ 닉은 기계를 고안하고 만드는 데 관심이 있다. 그는 아마 공학부문에서 학위를 취득할 것이다.

11. ⓑ 어떤 주제나 화제에 대한 전문가가 되려면 먼저 그것에 대한 모든 것을 읽어야 한다.

12. ⓒ 우리는 그 정보를 좀 더 시각적으로 보기 위하여 그래프를 만들었다.

13. ⓓ 힐먼은 2년 간 대학을 다녔으나 학위를 받지 못했다. 그는 대학 졸업자가 아니다.

14. ⓑ 최신 의학기술 관련 토론을 위해 매년 회의가 열린다.

15. ⓑ 인간이라는 단어는 남과 여를 지칭한다.

16. ⓐ 나는 할만의 유머 감각을 좋아한다. 그는 항상 재미있는 이야기를 한다.

17. ⓐ 잭슨의 옷은 더럽고 낡았다. 또한 머리를 깎을 필요가 있다. 상급자에게 어떤 인상을 줄까?

18. ⓓ 그는 전문가이기 때문에 그 큰 사업을 시작하기 전에 도움을 받기를 바란다.

19. ⓒ 스티븐: 제프가 항상 나의 시연을 방해한다.

　　위리엄: 그가 방해하는 것을 싫어한다고 말해라.

20. ⓐ 지휘관이 전화를 도로 걸기 전의 짧은 틈을 이용하여 나는 보고서를 수정했다.

21. ⓐ 글을 쓸 때에는 테이블 위에 자국이 남지 않도록 조심하세요.

22. ⓒ 그 모형은 학생들에게 비행에 대해 가르치기 위해서 교실에서 사용된다.

23. ⓑ 해군에서의 너의 임무는 무엇이냐?

24. ⓒ 한국의 부모들에게는 돈이 문제가 아니다. 그들은 자녀들에게 좋은 교육을 시키기 위해서 무엇이든 지불하기 때문이다.

25. ⓓ 앤은 해야 할 일이 많다. 그녀는 압박을 받고 있다.

26. ⓑ 존은 다소 빠르게 진행하여 다음 단계로 넘어갔다.

27. ⓒ 밥은 지난 달에 중위였다. 지금은 대위이다. 그는 진급하였다.

28. ⓐ 사명감이 있는 사람은 가능한 자신의 임무를 수행하려고 노력한다.

29. ⓒ 그 절차는 단계별로 따라하기 매우 쉽다.

30. ⓒ 만약 그 방법이 좋지 않다면 다른 전술을 사용함이 어떨까요?

31. ⓐ 이 책은 좋지 않다. 나는 이 책을 쓰레기통에 집어던질 것이다.

32. ⓐ 이 연필의 끝이 무디게 되었다. 깎을 필요가 있다.

33. ⓐ 현재 실업률은 매우 높다. 직장이 없는 사람들이 많다.

34. ⓓ 내 삼촌은 지난 달 해군에서 은퇴하였다. 이제 그는 퇴역군인이다.

35. ⓒ 직업을 찾으려면 신문의 구인광고를 확인해야 한다.

36. ⓑ 데이비드는 다독을 한다. 그는 매주 평균 두 권을 읽는다.

37. ⓒ 숫자 80에는 얼마나 많은 숫자가 있느냐?

38. ⓐ 창문 가리개를 사기 전에 창문 치수를 알아야 한다.

39. ⓑ 빅터는 도표를 프린터하기 전에 컴퓨터에 데이터를 입력한다.

40. ⓑ 이 도시 지역의 학교들은 아주 훌륭하다.

41. ⓒ 너의 보고서는 균형이 맞지 않다. 많은 모순이 있다.

42. ⓐ 다니엘은 아주 훌륭한 고용원이다. 그는 항상 일찍 출근해서 열심히 근무하며 그의 일을 완수한다.

43. ⓐ 이 집중교육의 주안점은 말하기와 읽기 이해에 있다.

44. ⓐ 우리는 그 사람을 채용하지 않았다. 그는 경제학에 대한 기본이 없었다.

45. ⓑ 제니스는 수학과목에 낙제하여 기술자가 되지 못했다.

46. ⓑ 대수학과 함수를 배울 때에는 많은 수학 공식을 암기해야 한다.

47. ⓐ 지원서를 작성하는 것은 회사에 들어가는 첫 번째 단계일 뿐이다.

48. ⓑ 12인치는 1피트와 같다.

49. ⓑ 판사는 권위 있는 직위에 있으므로, "선생님" 이라고 불린다.

50. ⓒ 선반 위에 책이 잘 정돈되어 있지 않다.

51. ⓒ 이 단어의 유래는 무엇입니까?

52. ⓒ 에반스씨는 새 임무에 임하도록 배치되었다.

53. ⓒ 마이클은 적합한 절차를 따르지 않았기 때문에 상처를 입었다.

54. ⓑ 리거씨는 당신 학교의 선생님입니까? 교장선생님입니까?

55. ⓒ 3살 된 어린이들은 어려운 발달단계에 처해있다.

56. ⓐ 너는 그 정보를 어디서 얻었느냐? 나는 인터넷사전을 참고했다.

57. ⓒ 너무 많은 시간을 허비하지 않도록 그들의 행정절차를 체계화할 필요가 있다.

58. ⓒ 그들은 주어진 시간 안에 과업을 완수하기는 불가능하였다.

59. ⓑ 복사용 종이를 이 받침대에 넣어라.

60 ⓓ 훌륭한 선생님은 한 과정을 가르치기 위해 다양한 기법을 구사한다.

61. ⓒ 천문학자는 망원경이나 사진을 분석하여 달, 별 그리고 다른 위성을 연구하는 사람들이다.

62. ⓓ 제인이 승진하자, 마크는 "축하한다"고 말했다.

63. ⓑ 모든 종이 조각은 아무리 작더라도 검사해야 한다.

64. ⓒ 우리 역사 선생님은 혁명과 내전의 차이를 이야기 하였다.

65. ⓓ 대통령의 안전은 매우 중요하다.

66. ⓑ 접수받은 자료는 중요한 것이었다. 사령관은 향후 훈련에서 도출된 자료를 사용할 것이다.

67. ⓓ 학생들이 해석을 했을 때, 각자의 해석 차이가 거의 없어서 우리는 학생들이 숙제를 개인이 아닌 단체로 했다고 의심했다.

68. ⓑ 그 분야 주변의 몇몇 뛰어난 지성들이 광고의 주제를 정의하고 다루려고 했다.

69. ⓒ 항상 학생들에게 강요를 하고, 성급한 브룩스 교수는 엄격한 사람이었기 때문에 학생들과 교감을 가지지 못했다.

70. ⓑ 훌륭한 지도자는 자신의 부하와 조국에 대해 성실해야 한다. 그는 매사에 정직하고 윤리적이다.

71. ⓒ 루시는 느낌의 근거는 없었지만, 해고될 것이라고 직감했다.

72. ⓐ 검정 기간을 거친 뒤에 자신의 종신재직권이 허용되자 그 교수는 안도감을 느꼈다. 그의 직위는 더 이상 임시적인 것이 아니다.

73. ⓑ 대립적 견해에서 나온 그 두 사람 간의 마찰은 사무실에 긴장감을 형성했다.

74. ⓓ 결정을 내리기 전에 그 위원회의 위원들 간에는 많은 불화가 있었다. 그들은 심하게 다투었다.

동사

기본어휘 / 연습 문제

B

New American Language Course

1. 기본어휘   동사

alternate / 교체하다, 번갈아 일어나다 (occurring by turns, succeeding each other)

Wet days alternated with dry ones.

(궂은 날과 맑은 날은 번갈아 가며 반복된다.)

anticipate / 예상하다, 예기하다 (to take care of in advance)

Problem-finding skills require that somebody anticipate future problems, so that they may be solved before they become major.

(문제 발견 기술에는 누군가가 미래의 문제를 예측할 수 있어야 한다. 그래야만 그 문제가 커지기 전에 해결될 수 있는 것이다.)

attach / 걸다, 결합하다 (to fasten or join one thing to another)

Attach the rope to the branch of a tree. (나무 가지에 로프를 걸어라.)

authorize / 허가하다, 허용하다 (to give permission)

The invasion was authorized by the president. (대통령이 공격을 허락하였다.)

average / 평균...이다 (to do or take on an average)

Many employees average 50 hours a week.

(많은 노동자들은 일주일에 평균 50시간 일한다.)

brief / 요약하다 (to make a summary of)

We brief all the agents before assigning the task.

(우리는 그 일을 부과하기 전에 모든 관계관에게 브리핑할 것이다.)

construct / 건설하다 (to build or make)

The company has won the contract to construct a new highway.

(그 회사는 새로운 고속도로의 건설 계약을 따내었다.)

coordinate / 조정하다, 통합하다 (adjust, organize)

They coordinated the relief effort at the earthquake zone.

(그들은 지진지역에서 구제 직업을 조정했다.)

demonstrate / 증명하다, 논증하다 (to show clearly by giving proof or evidence)

He demonstrated some of the difficulties we faced.

(그는 우리가 당면한 몇 가지 어려움을 제시하였다.)

distribute / 분배하다, 나누다 (to divide and give out)

The world's wealth is not fairly distributed between the rich and the poor.

(세상의 부는 부자와 가난한 자에게 공정하게 분배되어 있지 않다.)

intersect / 가로지르다, 교차하다 (to cut or divide by passing through)

The highway intersects the village.

(고속도로가 마을을 가로지른다.)

interrupt / 방해하다, 막다 (to stop a person, to break off)

May I interrupt you to comment on your last remark?

(잠시 당신의 마지막 말에 논평해도 좋습니까?)

interpret / 해석하다 (to translate orally)

We should interpret the hidden meaning of a parable.

(우리는 우화의 숨은 의미를 해석해야 한다.)

blame / 비난하다 (to say or think that someone or something is responsible for an accident)
If all goes wrong, don't blame me. (만약 모든 것이 잘못 되더라도 나를 비난하지는 마라.)

claim / 주장하다, 요구하다 (to say that something is true, even though there is no definite proof)
The report claimed that hundreds of civilians has crossed the border.
(그 보고서는 수백 명의 시민들이 그 경계선을 넘었다고 주장하였다.)

classify / 구분하다, 분류하다 (to arrange or divide in groups, to designate to be secret or confidential)
The books in the library are classified by subject. (도서관의 책들은 주제별로 구분된다.)

distort / 왜곡하다, 곡해하다(to change an information so that it is no longer true or accurate)
The paper was accused of the distorting the truth.
(그 논문은 진실을 왜곡하여 비난받고 있다.)

deserve / ...할 만하다, 받을 가치가 있다(to be worth)
After five hours on your feet, you deserve a break.
(당신 발 위에 다섯 시간 있으면, 발이 부러질 것이다.)

embed / 깊숙이 박다, 새기다 (fix deeply, implant)
The day of his promotion has been embedded into his memory forever.
(그가 승진한 날은 그의 기억 속에 영원히 남아있다.)

encompasses / 포함하다, 둘러싸다 (to contain or include)
The American Language Course encompasses all levels of instruction, from beginning to advanced. (미국영어 과정은 초급부터 고급까지 전 단계의 교육을 포함한다.)

encourage / 격려하다, 용기를 북돋우다 (to suggest that someone does something that you believe would be good)

Mom always encouraged us discuss our problems.
(엄마는 항상 우리들의 문제에 관해 이야기하고 격려해 주었다.)

expel / 내쫓다, 몰아내다 (to drive out, to dismiss or send away by authority)

Some students were expelled from school for bad behaviour.
(몇몇 학생들이 비행으로 인해 학교에서 퇴학당했다.)

evaluate / 평가하다, 사정하다(to think carefully before making a judgement)

The performance of each employee is evaluated once a year.
(모든 고용인들은 1년에 한 번씩 그들의 실적을 평가 받는다.)

foster / 조성하다, 육성하다 (to promote or help to grow)

It's up to the boss to foster the climate that allows you and me to feel free to make decisions.
(여러분과 내가 자유롭게 결정을 내리도록 하는 분위기를 민드는 일은 상관에게 달려 있다.)

glance / 힐끗 보다, 일별하다 (to look suddenly and briefly, to take a quick look)

I never glance at the political page of a daily newspaper.
(나는 일간지의 정치면을 결코 보지 않는다.)

guide / 안내하다, 이끌다 (to direct the course or motion to move in a particular direction)

She guided us through the busy streets to the museum.
(그녀는 우리를 번잡한 길을 가로질러 박물관으로 안내하였다.)

incorporate / 합동시키다, 혼합하다 (to add or include something)

The course incorporates a strong German language elements.
(그 코스는 기본적인 독일어 요소들을 넣을 것이다.)

motivate / 동기를 부여하다, 자극하다 (incite, impel)

A good manager can motivate his employees to set higher goals for themselves.
(훌륭한 경영자는 고용인이 스스로 높은 목표를 설정하도록 동기를 부여한다.)

recruit / 신병(을 보충하다) (to supply with new men, to enroll or to engage persons for military service)

The raw recruits were trained for three months and then sent to the war front.
(신병들은 3달 동안 훈련을 받은 후, 전선으로 보내졌다.)

relate / 연관시키다, 관계가 있다 (to show or make a connection)

We offer courses that relate English literature to other subjects.
(우리는 영문학과 연관되는 여러 가지 교과들을 가르칩니다.)

remind / 상기하게하다, 생각나게 하다 (to tell someone again about an event)

I can't think of her name. Can you remind me?
(그녀의 이름이 생각나지 않는다. 기억해 낼 수 있겠니?)

resign / 사임하다 (to give up a position)

The chairman resigned because he misappropriated funds.
(의장은 자금을 유용했기 때문에 사임했다.)

retell / 다른 형식으로 표현하다 (to tell again or in a different form)

The Aesop fable is often retold within Western literature.
(이솝 우화는 서양문학에서 종종 재음미 된다.)

settle / 해결하다, 놓다 (put an end to, decide, arrange)

There is pressure on the union to settle the dispute.
(그 논쟁을 해결하기 위해 조합에 압력이 가해졌다.)

sustain / 떠받치다, 유지하다 (to maintain, to supply, to suffer)

He found it difficult to sustain relationships with the woman.

(그는 그 여자와의 관계를 지속하기 어렵다는 것을 알았다.)

subscribe (to) / 기부하다, 구독하다 (to agree to receive and pay for a periodical or service for a specified period)

I subscribe to a newspaper and a linguistic periodical.

(나는 신문과 언어학의 정기간행물을 구독하고 있다.)

substitute / 대체하다, 대용하다 (to act or serve in place of another, to take the place of)

Some people substitute regular milk by fat-free milk.

(어떤 사람들은 일반 우유 대신 무지방 우유를 대체한다.)

systematize / 조직화하다, 체계화하다 (to organize something according to a system)

We need to systematize this strange procedure.

(우리는 이 이상한 절차를 체계화 시키도록 해야 한다.)

transfer / 옮기다, 갈아타다 (to move from one place to another)

I need to transfer some money to the account of my daughter.

(내 딸의 계좌에 송금해야겠다.)

yell / 고함치다, 소리지르다 (to say something in a loud voice)

We heard someone yelling for help.

(우리는 어떤 사람이 살려달라고 외치는 소리를 들었다.)

2. 연습문제

1. A thesaurus will ______ you in completing this assignment.

   ⓐ need   ⓑ aid   ⓒ interpret   ⓓ represent

2. The new employees have just reported to work. Will you please ______ them on their assignments?

   ⓐ brief   ⓑ contact   ⓒ command   ⓓ contend

3. Harry needs to ______ three books from the library.

   ⓐ take part in   ⓑ check out   ⓒ put off   ⓓ try out

4. The new high school will be ______ at the corner of Kensington and Queens.

   ⓐ destructed   ⓑ instructed   ⓒ constructed   ⓓ considered

5. If we're going to work together, first of all we had better ______ our schedule and work.

   ⓐ coordinate   ⓑ cooperate   ⓒ correspond   ⓓ corrode

6. The instructor ______ to us how to handle a handgun.

   ⓐ indicated   ⓑ demonstrated   ⓒ inspected   ⓓ illuminated

7. The teacher usually ______ the answer sheets before handing out the test.

   ⓐ disperses   ⓑ contributes

   ⓒ corresponds   ⓓ distributes

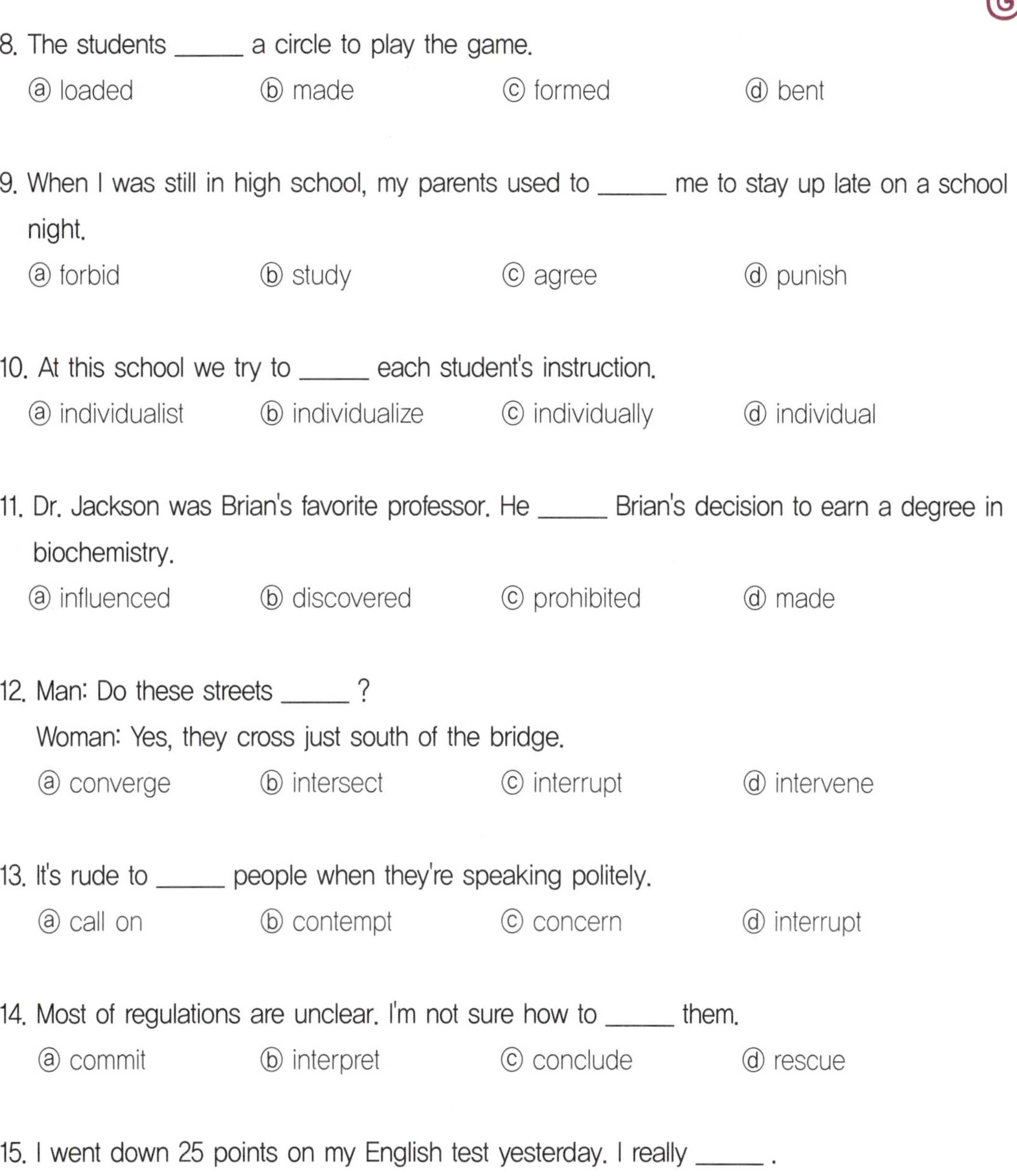

8. The students _______ a circle to play the game.

   ⓐ loaded   ⓑ made   ⓒ formed   ⓓ bent

9. When I was still in high school, my parents used to _______ me to stay up late on a school night.

   ⓐ forbid   ⓑ study   ⓒ agree   ⓓ punish

10. At this school we try to _______ each student's instruction.

    ⓐ individualist   ⓑ individualize   ⓒ individually   ⓓ individual

11. Dr. Jackson was Brian's favorite professor. He _______ Brian's decision to earn a degree in biochemistry.

    ⓐ influenced   ⓑ discovered   ⓒ prohibited   ⓓ made

12. Man: Do these streets _______ ?
    Woman: Yes, they cross just south of the bridge.

    ⓐ converge   ⓑ intersect   ⓒ interrupt   ⓓ intervene

13. It's rude to _______ people when they're speaking politely.

    ⓐ call on   ⓑ contempt   ⓒ concern   ⓓ interrupt

14. Most of regulations are unclear. I'm not sure how to _______ them.

    ⓐ commit   ⓑ interpret   ⓒ conclude   ⓓ rescue

15. I went down 25 points on my English test yesterday. I really _______ .

    ⓐ calculate   ⓑ computed   ⓒ messed up   ⓓ missed

16. The people who apply for the job will be told they would be _______ of the manager's decision in two weeks.

    ⓐ alerted   ⓑ engaged   ⓒ notified   ⓓ noticed

17. Some students often _______ the idea of going to school everyday.

    ⓐ object to   ⓑ make sense   ⓒ adjust to   ⓓ account for

18. Supervisors must be able to clearly _______ their ideas to the clerks.

    ⓐ put on   ⓑ put across   ⓒ put out   ⓓ put up with

19. I was confused because the subject of the speech didn't ____ to what we're learning in class.

    ⓐ give   ⓑ encourage   ⓒ relate   ⓓ exhibit

20. My secretary forgot to _______ me about the 3:00 meeting.

    ⓐ order   ⓑ persuade   ⓒ accuse   ⓓ remind

21. Brian _______ from his job at the plant last week because he was worn-out.

    ⓐ consigned   ⓑ assigned   ⓒ resigned   ⓓ regained

22. George quit his job yesterday, and the manager is already trying to _______ someone to fill George's position.

    ⓐ inform   ⓑ extend   ⓒ recruit   ⓓ orient

23. The English teacher tried to explain the meaning of the word to the students, but he only _______ in confusing them.

    ⓐ obtained   ⓑ assume   ⓒ achieved   ⓓ succeeded

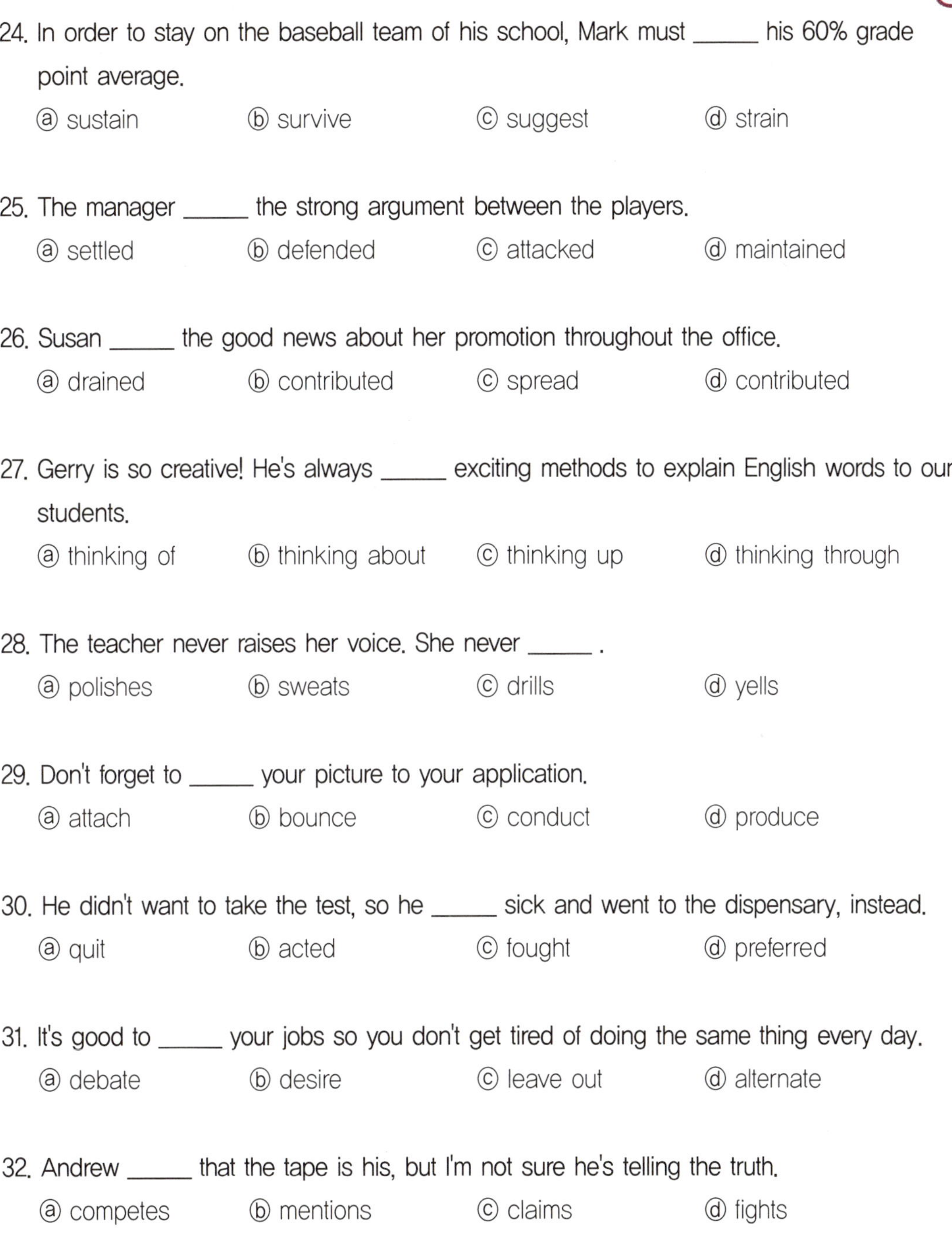

24. In order to stay on the baseball team of his school, Mark must _____ his 60% grade point average.

  ⓐ sustain   ⓑ survive   ⓒ suggest   ⓓ strain

25. The manager _____ the strong argument between the players.

  ⓐ settled   ⓑ defended   ⓒ attacked   ⓓ maintained

26. Susan _____ the good news about her promotion throughout the office.

  ⓐ drained   ⓑ contributed   ⓒ spread   ⓓ contributed

27. Gerry is so creative! He's always _____ exciting methods to explain English words to our students.

  ⓐ thinking of   ⓑ thinking about   ⓒ thinking up   ⓓ thinking through

28. The teacher never raises her voice. She never _____ .

  ⓐ polishes   ⓑ sweats   ⓒ drills   ⓓ yells

29. Don't forget to _____ your picture to your application.

  ⓐ attach   ⓑ bounce   ⓒ conduct   ⓓ produce

30. He didn't want to take the test, so he _____ sick and went to the dispensary, instead.

  ⓐ quit   ⓑ acted   ⓒ fought   ⓓ preferred

31. It's good to _____ your jobs so you don't get tired of doing the same thing every day.

  ⓐ debate   ⓑ desire   ⓒ leave out   ⓓ alternate

32. Andrew _____ that the tape is his, but I'm not sure he's telling the truth.

  ⓐ competes   ⓑ mentions   ⓒ claims   ⓓ fights

33. College students are usually ______ as freshmen, sophomores, juniors, or seniors.
    ⓐ clasped   ⓑ classified   ⓒ classic   ⓓ clashed

34. That story is false; the author has ______ the truth.
    ⓐ illustrated   ⓑ amplified   ⓒ distorted   ⓓ radiated

35. Ted's a good student. He ______ the honor he was given at school.
    ⓐ relieved   ⓑ passed   ⓒ deserves   ⓓ commits

36. Sometimes we have a hard time finding the right words to ______ our feelings.
    ⓐ insist   ⓑ express   ⓒ mention   ⓓ claim

37. We took a test to ______ our proficiency in Italian.
    ⓐ recover   ⓑ incorporate   ⓒ evaluate   ⓓ admire

38. The officer couldn't find the report because it wasn't ______ properly.
    ⓐ distinguished   ⓑ revealed   ⓒ showed   ⓓ filed

39. Cindy: Do you think Murphy's intelligent?
    Kara: Well, he's able to ______ difficult puzzles.
    ⓐ replace   ⓑ copy   ⓒ shut down   ⓓ figure out

40. The students will ______ in room 225 at 1600 hrs for a meeting with Maj Richards.
    ⓐ govern   ⓑ gather   ⓒ complete   ⓓ display

41. Smith doesn't want to remain a clerk with the company. He wants to be promoted to a
    supervisor soon. He wants to ______ .
    ⓐ get ahead   ⓑ catch on   ⓒ get together   ⓓ make up

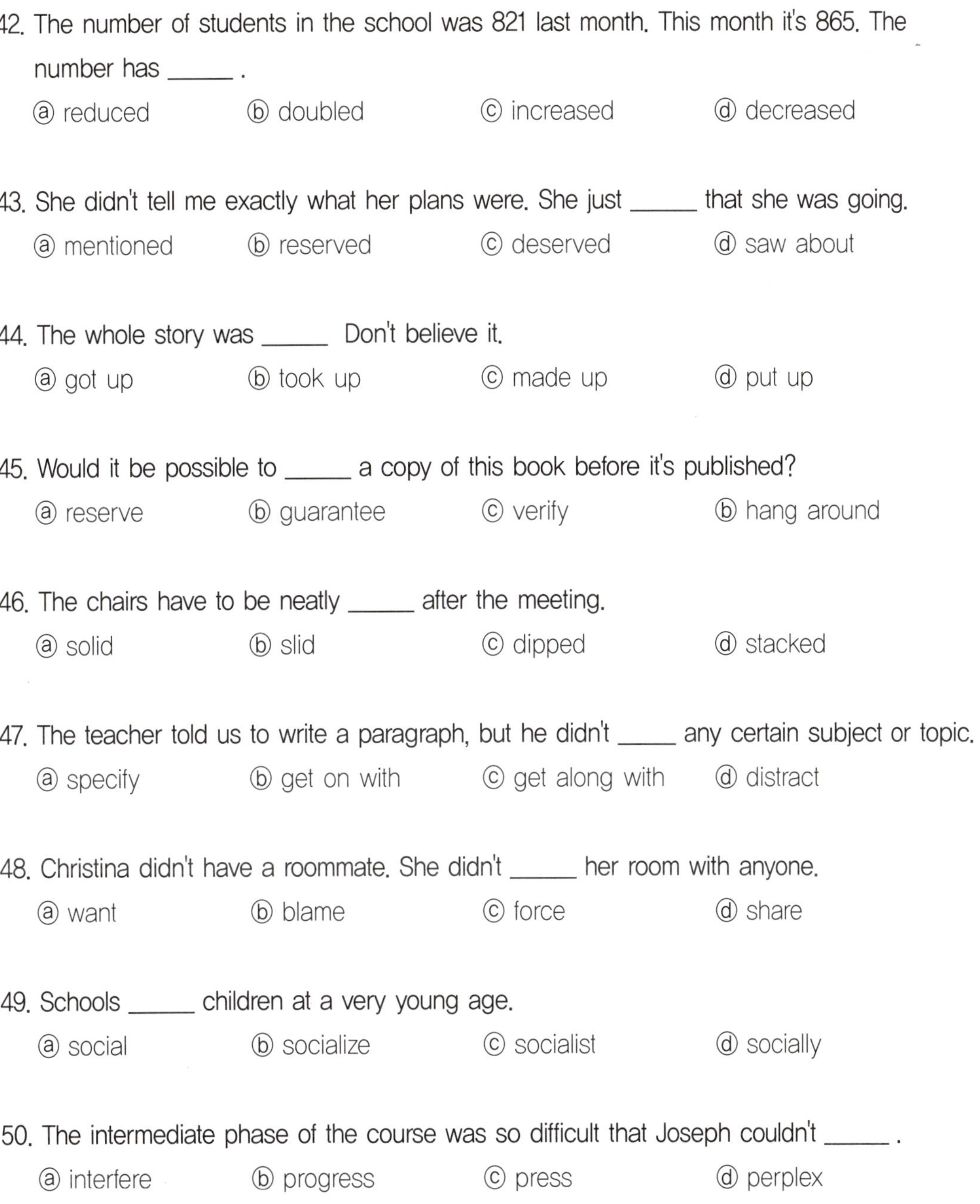

42. The number of students in the school was 821 last month. This month it's 865. The number has _____ .
    ⓐ reduced   ⓑ doubled   ⓒ increased   ⓓ decreased

43. She didn't tell me exactly what her plans were. She just _____ that she was going.
    ⓐ mentioned   ⓑ reserved   ⓒ deserved   ⓓ saw about

44. The whole story was _____ Don't believe it.
    ⓐ got up   ⓑ took up   ⓒ made up   ⓓ put up

45. Would it be possible to _____ a copy of this book before it's published?
    ⓐ reserve   ⓑ guarantee   ⓒ verify   ⓑ hang around

46. The chairs have to be neatly _____ after the meeting.
    ⓐ solid   ⓑ slid   ⓒ dipped   ⓓ stacked

47. The teacher told us to write a paragraph, but he didn't _____ any certain subject or topic.
    ⓐ specify   ⓑ get on with   ⓒ get along with ⓓ distract

48. Christina didn't have a roommate. She didn't _____ her room with anyone.
    ⓐ want   ⓑ blame   ⓒ force   ⓓ share

49. Schools _____ children at a very young age.
    ⓐ social   ⓑ socialize   ⓒ socialist   ⓓ socially

50. The intermediate phase of the course was so difficult that Joseph couldn't _____ .
    ⓐ interfere   ⓑ progress   ⓒ press   ⓓ perplex

51. David's sister _____ five years in the Army.
  ⓐ deserved   ⓑ waited   ⓒ served   ⓓ promoted

52. Are you going to _____ to any magazine now?
  ⓐ contrive   ⓑ subscribe   ⓒ propose   ⓓ describe

53. I can hear you perfectly. You don't have to _____ .
  ⓐ sink   ⓑ shout   ⓒ speak   ⓓ swallow

54. She's going to _____ for Donald for class president.
  ⓐ vote   ⓑ drop   ⓒ spot   ⓓ nominate

55. Were you able to work out this math problem?
  ⓐ solve   ⓑ research   ⓒ explain   ⓓ illustrate

56. Our teacher was sick, so a part-time teacher _____ for him.
  ⓐ substituted   ⓑ replaced   ⓒ overcame   ⓓ suppressed

57. A good teacher gives confidence to learners so they won't give up trying.
  ⓐ distinguishes   ⓑ sways   ⓒ incorporates   ⓓ encourages

58. We're going to include more technical words in our textbooks next month.
  ⓐ distinguish   ⓑ outfit   ⓒ incorporate   ⓓ admire

59. In the article I mentioned my experience in the U.K.
  ⓐ referred (to)   ⓑ transcribed   ⓒ replaced   ⓓ researched

60. We need someone to guide the motorboat because none of us know how to operate the
    equipment.

  ⓐ steer   ⓑ abuse   ⓒ persist   ⓓ skim

61. The manager tried integrating all their work assignments into one major project.

  ⓐ giving notice to   ⓑ taking apart
  ⓒ bringing together   ⓓ setting apart

62. The manager of this company underwrites educational programs in order to give young
    people the chance to attend college.

  ⓐ gives notice to   ⓑ speak favorably of
  ⓒ emphasize   ⓓ agrees to finance a project

63. While testing, Wyatt frittered away too much time on the questions he didn't understand,
    and then found himself short of time at the end of the test.

  ⓐ solved in a creative way   ⓑ was worried and anxious
  ⓒ caused his hair to go into short wiry curls   ⓓ wasted

64. Good teachers inculcate their students with a love of knowledge and learning by
    impressing them with the need and urgency to know.

  ⓐ maintain an even temperature   ⓑ feel guilty about their teaching
  ⓒ influence someone to accept an idea   ⓓ punish severely

65. He hedged each time that he was questioned about his whereabouts. No matter how
    hard they tried, the police could never get a straight answer out of him.

  ⓐ refused to answer directly   ⓑ told a lie
  ⓒ pulled and lifted with effort
  ⓓ interrupted with confusing or unfriendly remarks

66. While everyone else is working hard, trying to get the job finished, Brody always finds a way to shirk his duties.

ⓐ avoids his work because of laziness

ⓑ carry out quickly

ⓒ speak or say something very kindly

ⓓ keep a record of his duties

67. The instructor extolled the student for achieving a perfect test score because it was a great accomplishment.

ⓐ doubted

ⓑ asked the reason

ⓒ praised very much

ⓓ investigated

68. Arriving late for work on just one occasion isn't serious enough to warrant being fired.

ⓐ Arriving late for work occasionally is encouraged.

ⓑ Arriving late for work on one occasion is a good reason for being fired.

ⓒ Arriving late for work occasionally will be a good reason you are fired.

ⓓ Arriving late for work on one occasion doesn't justify being fired.

69. The man's job with the company was terminated after only one month, and he had to look for other employment.

ⓐ started   ⓑ ended   ⓒ forgotten   ⓓ changed

70. The experienced teacher is contending that the selection was unfair. He feels that the school district hired the inexperienced, first-year teacher in an attempt to save money.

ⓐ enduring   ⓑ wishing   ⓒ arguing   ⓓ agreeing

정답 / 해석

1. ⓑ 동의어 사전은 이 숙제를 끝내는 데 도움을 줄 것이다.

2. ⓐ 신입사원들이 방금 출근하였다. 그들의 임무에 대해 간단히 설명해 주어라.

3. ⓑ 해리는 도서관에서 세 권의 책을 빌려야 한다.

4. ⓒ 새로운 고등학교가 캔싱톤과 퀸즈가의 모퉁이에 건설될 것이다.

5. ⓐ 우리가 함께 일하려면 우선 우리의 계획표와 업무를 조정하는 것이 좋다.

6. ⓑ 교관은 우리에게 권총을 다루는 방법을 보여주었다.

7. ⓓ 선생님은 대개 문제지를 나누어 주기 전에 답안지를 나누어 준다.

8. ⓒ 학생들은 놀이를 하기 위해 원을 만들었다.

9. ⓐ 내가 아직 고등학교에 다닐 때, 나의 부모님은 등교 전날 밤에 늦게까지 자지 않는 것을 금지하곤 했다.

10. ⓑ 이 학교에서 우리는 각 학생들의 교육을 개별적으로 하고자 한다.

11. ⓐ 잭슨박사는 브라이언이 좋아하는 교수다. 그는 브라이언이 생화학 학위를 취득함에 있어 영향을 미쳤다.

12. ⓑ 남자: 이 거리는 교차합니까?

　　여자: 예, 다리 바로 남쪽에서 교차합니다.

13. ⓓ 공손하게 말 할 때 이를 방해하는 것은 무례하다.

14. ⓑ 대부분의 규정이 명확하지 않다. 그것들을 어떻게 해석해야 할지 확실하지 않다.

15. ⓒ 나는 어제 영어시험에서 25점 내려갔다. 나는 정말로 망쳤다.

16. ⓒ 그 직업에 지원한 사람들은 2주 후에 메니저의 결정을 통보 받게 될 것이다.

17. ⓐ 몇몇 학생들은 매일 학교에 가야 하는 것에 반대한다.

18. ⓑ 감독관은 자신의 견해를 점원들에게 분명히 전달할 수 있어야 한다.

19. ⓒ 나는 그 연설의 주제가 교실에서 배우는 것과 관련이 없어 다소 당황스러웠다.

20. ⓓ 나의 비서는 3시에 내가 회의에 참석해야 한다는 것을 상기시켜주지 않았다.

21. ⓒ 브라이언은 지쳤기 때문에 지난 주 그 공장의 자신의 직무를 사직했다.

22. ⓒ 조지는 어제 직장을 그만 두었으며, 매니저는 이미 조지의 자리를 채울 다른 사람을 모집하려 하고 있다.

23. ⓓ 영어선생님은 단어의 의미를 학생들에게 설명하려고 하였지만, 오히려 그들을 혼란하게 하였다.

24. ⓐ 마크가 학교 야구부에 남기 위해서는 평균성적 60%를 유지해야 한다.

25. ⓐ 그 메니저는 두 선수 간의 심한 논쟁을 해결하였다.

26. ⓒ 수잔은 자신의 승진에 대한 소식을 모든 사무실에 알렸다.

27. ⓒ 제리는 매우 창의적이다. 그는 학생들에게 영어단어를 설명할 때 항상 재미있는 방법을 생각해 낸다.

28. ⓓ 선생님은 목소리를 높이지 않는다 그녀는 결코 소리치지 않는다.

29. ⓐ 당신 신청서에 사진 붙이는 일을 잊지 마세요.

30. ⓑ 그는 시험을 치르고 싶지 않았다. 그래서 시험 대신 아픈 것처럼 행동하고 의무실로 갔다.

31. ⓓ 하는 일을 바꾸는 것이 좋다. 그러면 매일 반복되는 똑같은 작업으로 인한 피로감을 없앨 수 있다.

32. ⓒ 앤드류는 이 테이프가 자신의 것이라고 주장한다. 그러나 나는 그가 진실을 말하고 있는지 확신이 서지 않는다.

33. ⓑ 대학생들은 대개 신입생, 2학년, 3학년, 또는 4학년으로 구분된다.

34. ⓒ 그 이야기는 엉터리다. 작가가 진실을 왜곡했다.

35. ⓒ 테드는 좋은 학생이다. 그는 학교에서 명예상을 받을 만하다.

36. ⓑ 가끔 우리는 우리의 감정을 표현하는 적합한 단어를 찾기 어려울 때가 있다.

37. ⓒ 우리는 이태리어 성취도 시험을 보았습니다.

38. ⓓ 그 장교는 보고서를 볼 수 없었다. 파일에 정리되어 있지 않았기 때문이다.

39. ⓓ 신디: 머피의 지능에 대해 생각해 보았습니까?

　　카라: 아마도 그는 어려운 수수께끼를 풀 수 있을 것입니다.

40. ⓐ 학생들은 리차드 소령과 만나기 위해 1600시에 225호실에 모일 것이다.

41. ⓐ 스미스는 그 회사 직원으로 남기를 원하지 않는다. 그는 곧 감독관으로 승진하기를 원한다. 그는 성공하기를 원한다.

42. ⓒ 지난 달 그 학교의 학생은 821명이었다. 이번 달에는 865명이다.

43. ⓐ 그녀는 자신의 계획을 정확하게 일러 주지 않았다. 그녀는 자신이 떠난다고만 말했다.

44. ⓒ 이야기 전부가 조작되었다. 그것을 믿지 마라.

45. ⓐ 책이 출판되기 전에 예매 신청을 할 수 있나요?

46. ⓓ 그 의자들은 회의가 끝난 후 단정하게 쌓아두어야 한다.

47. ⓐ 그 선생님은 글을 쓰도록 지시했다. 그러나 그는 글의 주제나 제목에 대하여는 자세히 말하지 않았다.

48. ⓓ 크리스티나는 방을 같이 사용하는 친구가 없다. 그녀는 누구하고도 방을 같이 사용하지 않는다.

49. ⓑ 학교는 아주 어린 아이들에게 사회성을 길러준다.

50. ⓑ 그 과정의 중간단계가 너무 어려워 조셉은 진전이 없었다.

51. ⓒ 데이비드의 여동생은 육군에서 5년간 복무하였다.

52. ⓑ 너는 지금 잡지를 구독할 예정이냐?

53. ⓑ 나는 너의 말을 잘 들을 수 있다. 소리칠 필요가 없다.

54. ⓐ 그녀는 반장으로 도널드에게 투표할 예정이다.

55. ⓐ 이 수학문제를 풀 수 있었습니까?

56. ⓐ 우리 선생님이 편찮아서, 강사 선생님이 대체하였다.

57. ⓓ 훌륭한 선생님은 학습자들이 포기하지 않도록 자신감을 불어넣어 준다.

58. ⓒ 우리는 다음 달에 교과서에 좀 더 전문적인 단어들을 포함시키고자 한다.

59. ⓐ 그 기사에서 나는 영국에서의 나의 경험을 언급하였다.

60. ⓐ 우리는 모터보트를 운전할 사람이 필요하다. 우리 중 아무도 그 장비를 작동하는 방법을 모른다.

61. ⓒ 경영자는 그들의 모든 과업을 하나의 큰 업무로 통합하려고 하였다.

62. ⓓ 이 회사의 경영자는 젊은이들에게 대학에 갈 기회를 주기 위해서 교육 프로그램에 비용을 지원하기로 동의 하고 있다.

63. ⓓ 시험 중에, 와이어트는 자기가 이해하지 못하는 문제에 너무 많은 시간을 낭비하여, 시험이 끝날 때에는 시 간이 모자랐다.

64. ⓒ 훌륭한 선생님은 학생들에게 알아야 할 필요성과 절박함을 명심하게 함으로, 그들에게 지식과 학습에 대한 사랑을 주입한다.

65. ⓐ 그는 주소를 물을 때마다 매번 애매한 태도를 취했다. 아무리 노력해도, 경찰은 그에게서 솔직한 답을 얻을 수 없었다.

66. ⓐ 모두가 열심히 일해서, 일을 끝마치려고 노력하는 반면, 브로디는 항상 자신의 임무를 회피할 방법을 찾는다.

67. ⓒ 교관은 시험성적이 만점이었기 때문에 그 학생을 크게 칭찬하였다. 왜냐하면 그것은 대단한 성취이기 때문 이었다.

68. ⓓ 직장에 단 한번 지각했다는 것은 해고를 정당화할 정도로 심각한 것은 아니다.

69. ⓑ 그 회사에서의 그가 맡은 일은 단지 한 달 후에 종료되었다. 그는 다른 직업을 찾아야 했다.

70. ⓒ 경험있는 교사는 그 선발이 부당하다고 주장하고 있다. 그는 학교 당국이 경비를 절약하기 위해서 경험없 는 1년차 선생님을 고용했다고 느낀다.

형용사

기본어휘 / 연습 문제

C

New American Language Course

1. 기본어휘　　　형용사

absolute / 절대적인, 완전한 (perfect, positive, definite)

It is impossible to find out an absolute proof of fraud.

(사기에 대한 절대적인 증거를 찾기는 불가능하다.)

advanced / 진보한, 고급의 (base on the most recent methods or ideas)

An advanced society uses the most recent technology or ideas.

(선진화된 사회에서는 최신 기술과 아이디어를 사용한다.)

comic / 희극의, 익살스런 (comic strip, comic books, amusing, humorous)

I can't forget the comic an exciting moments during my trip.

(나는 여행하는 동안의 우습고 재미있는 순간을 잊을 수 없다.)

considerable / 중요한, 꽤 많은 (noteworthy, large, great in amount)

Our shopping habits may have considerable effects on our environment.

(우리의 구매습관은 환경에 상당한 영향을 미친다.)

demanding / 지나친, 너무 많은 (needing a lot of time, ability, and energy)

The work from the department head was so demanding these days.

(요즘 과장이 요구하는 일은 아주 힘 든다.)

diagonal / 대갓선의, 비스듬한 (oblique, slanting)

The capital letter, X is formed by two diagonal lines.

(대문자 X는 두개의 사선으로 구성된다.)

distinguished / 뛰어난, 저명한 (noted, famous, celebrated, eminent)

White hair makes him look very distinguished.

(흰머리는 그를 매우 뛰어나게 보이게 한다.)

feasible / 실행할 수 있는 (possible or likely to succeed)

It is finally feasible to use coal as an energy.

이제는 석탄을 에너지로 사용할 수 있게 되었다.

fundamental / 기본적인, 근본적인 (most important, primary, original)

Our foreign minister expressed a fundamental objection to Japan's membership on the U.N. Security Council.

(외무부장관은 일본이 유엔 안보위원회 회원이 되는 것을 근본적으로 반대하였다.)

initial / 처음의, 최초의 (first, occurring at the beginning)

His initial reaction was to decline the offer.

(그의 첫 번째 반응은 그 제의를 거절한 것이었다.)

intermediate / 중급의, 중간의 (situated between two stages)

This novel is too difficult for intermediate students of English.

(이 소설은 중급 영어능력의 학생들에게는 너무 어렵다.)

judicial / 사법의, 재판상의 (of or pertaining to a judge)

He would like to go through proper judicial procedures.

(그는 적절한 법적 절차를 거치기를 원한다.)

justice / 정의, 공정 (fairness, impartiality)

The winner has been disqualified for cheating, so justice has been done.

(승자가 속였기 때문에 자격이 박탈되었다. 정의가 이긴 것이다.)

manageable / 다루기 [처리하기] 쉬운 (that can be managed or controlled)

Olivia has reduced her work load so that it is now at a manageable level.
(올리비아는 그녀의 업무량을 줄여서, 이제는 처리할 만한 수준이다.)

mandatory / 강제적인, 의무적인(ordered by a law or rule)

A new accounting system will soon become mandatory for all departments.
(새로운 회계 시스템은 조만간 모든 과에 의무적으로 적용될 것이다.)

negative / 부정적인, 마이너스의 (expressing a denial or refusal)

The media often define a recession as six months of negative economic growth.
(미디어는 종종 경기침체를 6달 간의 마이너스 경제성장이라고 정의한다.)

orderly / 질서있는 정연한 (neat or tidy in arrangement, in regular or proper order)

The clerk guided the guests in orderly fashion out of the building.
(직원은 건물 밖으로 질서있게 손님들을 안내하였다.)

ordinary / 일상적인, 보통의 (common, usual)

He ended the speech with the ordinary expressions of thanks.
(그는 연설을 평범한 감사의 말로 끝내었다.)

overall / 통틀어서, 종합적인 (generally, in general rather than in particular)

The company will invest one million dollars overall in new equipment
(그 회사는 새 장비에 총 백만 달러를 투자할 것이다.)

primary / 일차적인, 가장 중요한 (most important)

Dealing with crime is our primary concern.
(위범행위를 다루는 일이 우리들의 일차적 임무이다.)

principal / 가장 중요한 (most important, main)

Export is our principal source of foreign exchange earnings.
(수출은 외국환을 획득하기 위한 주요 원천이다.)

private / 개인적인, 사적인 (used only by a particular person or group, or available only to them)

They found a private spot where they could talk.
(그들은 자신들이 이야기 할 수 있는 은밀한 장소를 발견했다.)

proficient / 능숙한, 숙달된 (competent, skilled, adept)

A lot of Arabians are proficient in foreign languages.
(많은 아랍인들은 외국어에 능숙하다.)

responsible / 책임있는, 신뢰할 수 있는 (sensible, reliable)

The prime minister and his ministers are all responsible to parliament.
(수상과 각료들은 모두 국회에 대하여 책임을 진다.)

sleepy / 졸린, 활기없는 (drowsy, sluggish from sleep)

The heat and alcohol made me sleepy.
(열도 나고 술도 마셔서 졸립다.)

(be) through / 관계가 끊어진, 끝난 (finished)

I've told Larry I'm through with him, but he keeps bothering me.
(나는 레리에게 그와의 관계를 끊겠다고 말했다. 그러나 그는 나를 계속 괴롭힌다.)

tiny / 아주 작은, 미세한 (extremely small, minute)

Though he is tiny, he has a very loud voice.
(그의 체구는 작지만, 목소리는 크다.)

tough / 엄격한, 단호한 (very strict, severe)

We must take a tough stance against terrorism.

(우리는 테러리즘에 대하여 단호한 자세를 취해야 한다.)

vital / 절대 필요한, 생생한 (necessary or essential to life or existence)

The defense of the port is vital to the allies.

(항만 방어는 연합군에게는 매우 중요하다.)

2. 연습문제

1. I have _______ confidence in your ability to carry out the project successfully.
   ⓐ absurd　　　　ⓑ abundant　　　　ⓒ fundamental　　　　ⓓ absolute

2. Deter tried to be very exact in his work. Hir reports are usually _______ .
   ⓐ accurate　　　　ⓑ level　　　　ⓒ strict　　　　ⓓ biased

3. Lt Runk: What will you do after you finish your basic English course?
   Lt. Cho: I'll take an _______ English course.
   ⓐ enlisted　　　　ⓑ advanced　　　　ⓒ assignment　　　　ⓓ promotion

4. Capt Campbell said he didn't have much to tell us, so that meeting would be _______ .
   ⓐ useful　　　　ⓑ flexible　　　　ⓒ brief　　　　ⓓ unfair

5. Readers want more stories about _______ people and less stories about the rich and famous.
   ⓐ common　　　　ⓑ unusual　　　　ⓒ wonderful　　　　ⓓ contradictory

6. A _______ amount of work went into the new project.
   ⓐ mechanical　　　　ⓑ considerable　　　　ⓒ dependent　　　　ⓓ considerate

7. Mr. Heiman made us work very hard in his class. He's a _______ instructor.
   ⓐ reliable　　　　ⓑ demanding　　　　ⓒ neat　　　　ⓓ suitable

ECL시험 대비 New ALC 필수어휘 완성

8. If you want to learn much more about teeth, you should go to a _____ school.
   ⓐ surgery   ⓑ dental   ⓒ optical   ⓓ physical

9. Are the stripes supposed to be straight or _____ ?
   ⓐ dimension   ⓑ diagonal   ⓒ even   ⓓ delicate

10. The man is a _____ scientist, known around the world.
   ⓐ disappointed   ⓑ disciplined   ⓒ distinguished   ⓓ discriminated

11. The basic courses make up the _____ level.
   ⓐ elementary   ⓑ intermediate   ⓒ advanced   ⓓ ignorant

12. I have so much work to do right now that a vacation is not really _____ .
   ⓐ global   ⓑ feasible   ⓒ unavailable   ⓓ joint

13. What was the basic cause of their discontent?
   ⓐ instantaneous   ⓑ fundamental   ⓒ absolute   ⓓ foolish

14. Professor Carter was quite disappointed because her student's assignment was _____ .
   ⓐ understandable   ⓑ convincing   ⓒ attractive   ⓓ incomplete

15. Before the advanced level comes the _____ level.
   ⓐ elementary   ⓑ intermediate   ⓒ advanced   ⓓ highly advanced

16. Because he has years of _____ experience, William will be chosen to serve as a judge
    in the country's highest court.
   ⓐ just   ⓑ judicial   ⓒ efficient   ⓓ judicious

17. In _______ to all the applicants, everyone will have the same amount of time to complete the test.

ⓐ aid   ⓑ justice   ⓒ case   ⓓ abundance

18. Col Jackson said the meeting was _______ . We all have to go.

ⓐ mandatory   ⓑ discipline   ⓒ regular   ⓓ national

19. Most people work 8 hours a day, 5 days a week. That's their _______ work schedule.

ⓐ recent   ⓑ minimum   ⓒ normal   ⓓ regulated

20. His typing isn't so good, but he does a good job _______ .

ⓐ original   ⓑ overall   ⓒ above all   ⓓ at all

21. Maria occasionally writes magazine articles, but her _______ occupation is managing a travel agency.

ⓐ social   ⓑ primary   ⓒ academic   ⓓ outside

22. This office is _______ ; only employees may enter.

ⓐ old   ⓑ public   ⓒ private   ⓓ open

23. The _______ qualification for that job is physical strength.

ⓐ principal   ⓑ priority   ⓒ property   ⓓ prosperous

24. I am not very _______ at keying in data, so I spend much time completing a report.

ⓐ practical   ⓑ pragmatic

ⓒ proficient   ⓓ profitable

25. Chuck has completed all of the required training in automobile repair. Now he's a _____ mechanic.

    ⓐ primary   ⓑ interested   ⓒ qualified   ⓓ eligible

26. Maria always completes her work. She is _____ .

    ⓐ messy   ⓑ responsible   ⓒ honest   ⓓ humorous

27. The student was _____ during class today; consequently, he didn't understand the lesson.

    ⓐ sleeping around   ⓑ to sleep
    ⓒ sleep   ⓓ sleepy

28. Sam: Are you finished with your work?
    Max: No, I'm not _____ yet.

    ⓐ running   ⓑ through   ⓒ charging   ⓓ powerful

29. You'll learn a lot in Mr. Daniel's class, but he is very _____ .

    ⓐ strong   ⓑ correct   ⓒ tough   ⓓ physical

30. The test was really _____ ! Only three students passed.

    ⓐ easy   ⓑ sweat   ⓒ terrific   ⓓ tough

31. Our deadline for the presentation is Thursday, so it's _____ that all our work be finished by Wednesday.

    ⓐ vital   ⓑ proficient   ⓒ mortal   ⓓ awesome

32. Doctors have jobs that require careful attention. Their work is _____ .

    ⓐ free   ⓑ dishonest   ⓒ demanding   ⓓ irresponsible

33. Mrs. Handel has two jobs, one in the morning and one at night.

    She is ______ .

    ⓐ hardworking
    ⓑ easy going
    ⓒ unfriendly
    ⓓ demanding

34. Once Judge Foster revokes a motorist's license, he will not change his decision. His decisions are irrevocable.

    ⓐ changed abruptly
    ⓑ can't be changed
    ⓒ can't be repaired
    ⓓ can't be agreed on

35. The student was straightforward and honest in what he had to say. His story was unvarnished, and we understood it clearly.

    ⓐ neat and clean
    ⓑ straight and narrow
    ⓒ plain and simple
    ⓓ technical and learned

36. Both car companies have merged. They are now a corporate business.

    ⓐ joint
    ⓑ separate
    ⓒ modest
    ⓓ massive

37. His idea was too elusive to express in words. He had to show it in a diagram before we could understand it.

    ⓐ speaking aggressively
    ⓑ speaking or reading clearly
    ⓒ easy to define or describe
    ⓓ difficult to define or describe

38. A recent study showed that Japan has fewer illiterate adults than the United States.

    ⓐ unmarried
    ⓑ unable to read and write
    ⓒ talented in drawing pictures
    ⓓ using or having imagination

3. 교육과 직업

39. He was selected as the Flight Training Instructor because he was so adept in flying and aircraft maintenance.

   ⓐ able to move quickly and easily   ⓑ dependent on others

   ⓒ able to change easily   ⓓ highly skilled or experienced

40. We require that all teachers pass a test before being certified to teach, to reduce the number of incompetents who hold teaching certificates illegally.

   ⓐ individuals who don't consider other people's feelings

   ⓑ people unable to be comforted because of great sorrow

   ⓒ senior citizens who are over the age of 60

   ⓓ unskilled individuals, unable to do their jobs

41. It is incumbent upon a police officer to inform the accused of his rights under the law. If an officer fails to do so, the accused cannot be held over for questioning.

   ⓐ It's not convenient for a police officer to inform the accused of his rights.

   ⓑ A police officer's income depends on his informing the accused of their rights.

   ⓒ It's a police officer's obligation to inform the accused.

   ⓓ It depends on a police officer whether he informs the accused.

42. At first, Mr. Lopez didn't like the hours of his new job, but once he became oriented to the new schedule, he enjoyed working the long hours.

   ⓐ interested   ⓑ adjusted   ⓒ relaxed   ⓓ devoted

43. The information contained in the memo related directly to the matter at hand, and therefore had a direct bearing on the issue. It was pertinent information.

   ⓐ permanent   ⓑ relevant   ⓒ opposite   ⓓ considerable

정답 / 해석

1. ⓓ 나는 그 계획을 성공적으로 수행하기 위한 당신의 능력을 절대적으로 신뢰합니다.

2. ⓐ 디터는 그의 일에서 매우 정확하려고 노력했다. 그의 보고서는 대개 정확하다.

3. ⓑ 룬트 대위: 기본 영어 과정을 끝내면 무엇을 할 겁니까?

   조 대위: 고급 영어 과정에 들어갈 것입니다.

4. ⓑ 켐벨 대령[대위]가 우리에게 할 말이 별로 없다고 하니, 그 모임은 간단히 끝날 것이다.

5. ⓐ 독자들은 평범한 사람들에 대한 이야기를 많이 원하며, 부유하고 유명한 사람들의 이야기는 별로 원하지 않는다.

6. ⓑ 새 업무에 상당한 노력이 투자되었다.

7. ⓑ 하이만씨는 그 수업에서 우리를 열심히 공부하게 만든다. 그는 많은 것을 요구하는 교수다.

8. ⓑ 이빨에 대해 더 많이 배우고 싶다면, 치과학교에 가야 한다.

9. ⓑ 줄무늬는 직선이냐 사선이냐?

10. ⓒ 그 사람은 세계적으로 알려진 유명한 과학자이다.

11. ⓐ 기본과정은 초보단계로 구성되어 있다.

12. ⓑ 나는 지금 너무나 많은 일을 해야 하기 때문에 휴가를 정말 갈 수 있을 것 같지 않다.

13. ⓑ 그들의 불만의 근본적인 원인은 무엇이냐?

14. ⓓ 카트 교수는 학생들의 과제가 미비하여 매우 실망했다.

15. ⓑ 고급과정 전에 중급과정이 있다.

16. ⓑ 윌리엄은 수년 간 법에 대한 경험이 있기 때문에, 그 나라의 최고법원에서 판사로 근무하도록 선출될 것이다.

17. ⓒ 모든 지원자들에게 공평하게, 모두가 시험을 치기 위해 꼭 같은 시간이 주어질 것이다.

18. ⓐ 잭슨 대령은 회의에 모두 참석하라고 했다. 우리는 모두 가야 한다.

19. ⓒ 대부분의 사람들은 하루 8시간, 매주 5일 일한다. 그것이 그들의 정상적인 업무 일과이다.

20. ⓑ 그의 타이핑은 좋지 않지만 전반적으로 일을 잘한다.

21. ⓑ 마리아는 종종 잡지 기사를 쓴다. 그러나 그녀의 주 직업은 여행사를 경영하는 일이다.

22. ⓒ 이 공실은 사적인 공간이다. 직원들만 들어올 수 있다.

23. ⓐ 그 일에 주요한 자격요건은 신체적인 강인함이다.

24. ⓒ 나는 자료를 입력하는 데 능숙하지 못하다. 그래서 나는 보고서를 완성하는 데 많은 시간이 걸린다.

25. ⓒ 척은 자동차 수리와 관련한 연습을 모두 마쳤다. 지금은 자격증 있는 기사다.

26. ⓑ 마리아는 항상 그녀의 일을 완수한다. 그녀는 책임감이 있다.

27. ⓓ 그 학생은 오늘 수업 중에 졸았다. 그래서 그 학과 내용을 이해하지 못했다.

28. ⓑ 샘 : 당신에게 맡겨진 일을 끝냈나요?.

   맥스: 아니오 아직 끝내지 못했습니다.

29. ⓒ 당신은 다니엘의 수업에서 많이 배울 것입니다. 하지만 그는 매우 엄한 사람입니다.

30. ⓓ 그 시험은 정말 어려웠다. 단지 3명만이 합격하였다.

31. ⓐ 발표마감일이 목요일이다, 그래서 우리 일은 수요일까지 반드시 마쳐야 한다.

32. ⓒ 의사들의 직업은 세심한 주의가 요구된다. 그들의 일은 힘든다.

33. ⓐ 헨델 부인의 직업은 두 개다. 하나는 아침에, 다른 하나는 저녁에 실시한다.

34. ⓑ 포리스트 판사가 운전자의 면허를 취소하면, 그는 결정을 바꾸지 않을 것이다. 그의 결정은 취소할 수 없다.

35. ⓒ 그 학생은 자기가 해야 할 말을 할 때 직설적이고 정직하였다. 그의 이야기는 꾸밈이 없어서 우리는 그것을 명백하게 이해했다.

36. ⓐ 두개의 자동차 회사가 합병하였다. 그것들은 이제 합작회사이다.

37. ⓓ 그의 생각은 말로 표현하기가 어려웠다. 그가 그것을 도표로 보여주었을 때 우리는 그것을 이해할 수 있었다.

38. ⓑ 최근 조사에 의하면 일본이 미국보다 문맹 성인이 적다.

39. ⓓ 그는 조종과 비행기 정비에 아주 능숙했기 때문에 항공훈련 교관으로 선발되었다.

40. ⓓ 불법으로 교사자격을 소지하는 부적격자의 수를 줄이기 위해, 우리는 교사자격증을 받기 전에 모든 선생님들이 시험에 통과하기를 요구한다.

41. ⓒ 피고에게 법적 권리를 알리는 것은 경찰관의 의무이다. 경찰이 그렇게 하지 않으면, 피고는 심문을 위해 유치할 수가 없다.

42. ⓑ 처음에 로페즈씨는 그의 새 직업의 근무를 좋아하지 않았다. 그러나 일단 새 일과에 적응하게 되자, 그는 오랫동안 일하는 것을 즐겼다.

43. ⓑ 그 쪽지 속의 정보는 현안에 직접 연관가 있었으며, 그러므로 그 문제에 직접 관계가 있었다. 그것은 관련성이 있는 정보였다.

어휘, 관용구, 문형 종합

기본어휘 / 연습 문제

D

New American Language Course

as long as / ~하는 한, 조건으로 (only if, provided that)

You may go to the meeting as long as you promise to come home by 10 p.m.
(오후 10시까지 돌아 온다고 약속하면 모임에 가도 좋다.)

be behind in / 밀리다, 늦다 (delay, to do more slowly)

We are two months behind in our work.
(우리는 두달치 업무가 뒤쳐져 있다.)

be in on / 참여하다, 관여하다 (to have a share or part of, to join together for)

I'd like to be in on the project.
(나는 그 계획에 참여하고 싶다.)

bring up / 내놓다, 언급하다 (to introduce into discussion, to mention a subject)

He brought up a very critical topic in the conference.
(그는 회의에서 매우 중대한 화제를 꺼내었다.)

call down / 심하게 야단치다 (to scold sharply)

I was often called down by my teacher for being late to class.
(나는 종종 수업에 늦는다고 선생님에게 심하게 꾸중 들었다.)

check out / 대출하다 (to borrow a book from a library)

You can check out twenty books from the village library.
(너는 읍내 도서관에서 20권의 책을 빌릴 수 있다.)

check up on / 조사하다, 검토하다 (to investigate, to examine the record, character, etc of)

His father used to visit him twice a term at college to check up on him.

(그의 아버지는 한 학기에 두 번 대학에 방문하여 그를 확인한다.)

catch up on / (진도를) 만회하다, 따라잡다 (to come up by extra work, overtake)

I stayed up late to catch up on some reports.

(나는 몇 가지 보고서를 맞추기 위해 늦게까지 자지 못했다.)

count on / 믿다, 의지하다 (to depend on, rely on, trust)

A regiment counts on the commander's making the right decision.

(연대는 지휘관의 정확한 결정에 따라 좌우된다.)

even so / 그렇다 하더라도 (in spite of that)

There are lots of grammatical errors in his essays; even so, it is quite a good essay.

(그의 글에는 많은 문법적인 오류가 있다. 그럼에도 불구하고 아주 좋은 글이다.)

end up / 끝나다 (be finished, come to an end)

How did the story end up?

(그 이야기는 어떻게 끝났니?)

figure out / 이해하다, 계산하다 (to understand something or solve a problem)

We had to figure out the connection between the two events.

(우리는 그 두 사건 간의 관계를 이해해야 했다.)

furthermore / 뿐만 아니라 (besides, moreover)

The restaurant is very good and furthermore it's very cheap.

(식당은 매우 좋고 더구나 값도 아주 싸다.)

get across / 이해시키다, 알게 하다 (to clarify and explain easily)

His point of view was not getting across to his subordinates.
(그의 가치관이 부하들에게 전달되지 않고 있다.)

get ahead / 성공하다 (to become successful)

The person with a good character is easier to get ahead.
(성격이 좋은 사람은 성공하기가 더 쉽다.)

get by / 꾸려나가다, 빠져나가다 (to succeed without being punished, to survive or manage)

He must get by on such a small salary.
(그는 작은 봉급으로 살아가야 한다.)

give out / 배부하다 (to distribute, to give something to people)

The teacher gave out the exam papers.
(선생님이 시험지를 나누어 주었다.)

go over / 검토하다, 복습하다 (to examine thoroughly, review)

I went over the events of the day in my mind.
(나는 그 날의 사건을 마음 속으로 되새겨 보았다.)

in accordance with / 일치하여 (in agreement with)

We must behave in strict accordance with the law.
(우리는 엄격히 법에 따라 행동해야 한다.)

look down on / 멸시하다(to think of a person or thing as less good or important)

He likes tennis but he looks down on golf as too slow.
(그는 테니스를 좋아하지만, 골프는 너무 느린 운동이라고 깔본다.)

make a mark / 족적을 남기다, 큰 영향을 발휘하다 (to have a very strong and noticeable effect)

He's just been here four days but he's already made his mark.
(그는 이제 4일 동안 여기 있었다. 하지만 벌써 그의 족적을 남겼다.)

make sense / 논리적이다 (to be logical)

These sentences don't make sense.
(이 문장은 의미가 통하지 않는다.)

meanwhile / 그 동안에 (at the same time)

The court is deliberating; meanwhile, we must be patient.
(법정이 심의하고 있다. 그 동안 우리는 인내해야 한다.)

mess up / 엉망으로 만들다, 혼란시키다 (make a mistake, botch things up)

The company fires anyone who messes up.
(그 회사는 업무를 망치는 사람을 해고한다.)

once and for all / 단호히, 최종적으로 (finally, decisively, completely)

Our intention is to destroy their defensive capability once and for all.
(우리의 의도는 그들의 방어능력을 한 번에 파괴시키는 것이다.)

put across 쉽게 설명하다 (to explain clearly, to do successfully)

The teacher knows well how to put his ideas across.
(선생님은 자신의 생각을 전달하는 방법을 잘 안다.)

providing / 만약 ~하면 (provided, on condition (that))

Providing that there is no objection we will go to the next agenda.
(이의가 없으면 다음 안건으로 넘어가겠습니다.)

run into / 충돌하다, 빠지다 (to be affected by, to get into)

I ran into trouble on the last question on the test.
(나는 시험의 마지막 문제에서 난관에 부딪혔다.)

self-confident / 자신있는 (have confidence in one's ability)

He blossomed into a self-confident young statesman.
(그는 자신에 찬 젊은 정치가로 출세하였다.)

talk back to / 말대꾸하다, 무례하게 반응하다 (to answer or reply rudely)

The captain never allows his followers to talk back.
(그 함장은 부하들이 말대꾸하는 것을 허락하지 않는다.)

think up / 고안하다, 구상하다 (to invent to contrive)

Could you think up an arrangement of tables for this office?
(이 사무실에 맞도록 테이블을 배치할 수 있겠니?)

throw out / 버리다 (throw away)

I've thrown out my old boots.
(나는 오래 된 부츠를 버렸다.)

work out / 해결하다, 트레이닝하다 (to find an answer to, to plan, develop, or arrange)

The engineers worked out a system for getting electricity to the factory.
(기술자들은 공장에 전기를 끌어들이는 시스템을 해결했다.)

wind up / 마무리 짓다, 끝내다 (to finish or stop, to arrange or settle)

Smith wound up his business and personal affairs before retiring.
(스미스는 은퇴 전에 그의 사업과 개인적인 문제를 마무리지었다.)

2. 연습문제

1. I was absent last week, so I ______ my assignment.

   ⓐ substitute   ⓑ dispose of   ⓒ am behind in   ⓓ made up

2. The students left the building in ______ .

   ⓐ a muscular manner   ⓑ an orderly manner

   ⓒ a mechanical way   ⓓ a friendly way

3. Prof. Obama is self-confident.

   ⓐ has a lot of ability.   ⓑ doubts his own abilities.

   ⓒ believes in his own abilities   ⓓ have no concern

4. John should ______ the planning for the new office.

   ⓐ be in with   ⓑ get down on   ⓒ be in on   ⓓ take after

5. Would you like to ______ a new topic to talk about?

   ⓐ bring up   ⓑ bring back   ⓒ bring down   ⓓ bring along

6. Paul was behind all the other student in math, but he could ______ by studying hard during the winter vacation.

   ⓐ catch up   ⓒ get up   ⓒ sum up   ⓓ take up

7. Laura worked after hours to ______ her work.

   ⓐ catch up   ⓑ catch hold of   ⓒ catch up on   ⓓ be caught in

8. The recruit was not reliable so the instructor ______ him frequently.

    ⓐ checked out   ⓑ checked into   ⓒ checked up on   ⓓ checked off

9. The airman was ______ for his awful mistake.

    ⓐ called down   ⓑ calmed down   ⓒ talked back to   ⓓ called off

10. Since Jason is very dependable. his seniors ______ him to solve some complicated matters.

    ⓐ count on   ⓑ look down on   ⓒ take on   ⓓ get on

11. Who do you ______ for a promotion?

    ⓐ be considered to the best candidate   ⓑ consider to be the best candidate

    ⓒ the best candidate is considered   ⓓ consider the best candidate be

12. He ______ immediately and showed he understood.

    ⓐ caught on   ⓑ got on   ⓒ put on   ⓓ took on

13. Lora needs to lose weight. She's decided to ______ her eating.

    ⓐ cut out   ⓑ take up   ⓒ cut down on   ⓓ add to

14. I can't figure out this problem. ______ , I must try because it's on the test.

    ⓐ Even so   ⓑ In addition   ⓒ Despite   ⓓ Moreover

15. You can ______ take care of the problem now while it's small and insignificant, ______ wait until it's very complicated and serious.

    ⓐ not only/but also   ⓑ either/or

    ⓒ neither/ nor   ⓓ both /and

16. How did the discussion _____ ?
    ⓐ come together ⓑ inquire   ⓒ end up   ⓓ neglect

17. Margaret retired from the teaching profession last year. Now she sells real estate _____ .
    ⓐ of no use   ⓑ in general   ⓒ for a living   ⓓ on purpose

18. The mother gave up her job _____ her children.
    ⓐ in the form of ⓑ with respect to ⓒ for lack of   ⓓ for the sake of

19. Our teacher is excellent. He finds just the right way to _____ what his students need to
    remember.
    ⓐ get across   ⓑ mess up   ⓒ get down to   ⓓ get off

20. Our superintendent _____ by generousness and perseverance.
    ⓐ got ahead   ⓑ made up   ⓒ stuck out   ⓓ caught on

21. He just barely _____ in that course. He almost didn't make it.
    ⓐ got ahead   ⓑ got by   ⓒ made up   ⓓ caught on

22. After the instructor _____ the test papers, you can begin the test.
    ⓐ gives out   ⓑ gives up   ⓒ gives in   ⓓ give away

23. Don't let a failure force you to _____ ; keep on trying, you can make it.
    ⓐ give up   ⓑ give in   ⓒ give off   ⓓ give away

24. _____ the test before you hand it in.
    ⓐ Run short of   ⓑ Go over   ⓒ Run across   ⓓ Fool around

25. _____ the regulations, they examined all vehicles in the base.

    ⓐ In behalf of   ⓑ In accordance with

    ⓒ In the event of   ⓓ In case of

26. They both learn the new words and share their notes. They study _____ .

    ⓐ in a different way   ⓑ in the same way

    ⓒ altogether   ⓓ in another way

27. Charles was considered inferior by the rest of the classmates. He was _____ .

    ⓐ looked up to   ⓑ looked forward to

    ⓒ looked in on   ⓓ looked down on

28. The report doesn't _____ . Could you explain it to me?

    ⓐ assume responsibility   ⓑ stay away

    ⓒ make sense   ⓓ get along

29. Our team listened to tapes in the lab _____ , the other teams checked their homework in the classroom.

    ⓐ Meanwhile   ⓑ Means   ⓒ By means of   ⓓ By all means

30. I want to go to graduate school after finishing college, and _____ , I want to get a part-time job on the weekend.

    ⓐ otherwise   ⓑ compulsory   ⓒ moreover   ⓓ on the contrary

31. A : Is there anything new I can add to what I've already told you?

    B: No, _____ else. Sorry.

    ⓐ something   ⓑ nothing   ⓒ anything   ⓓ everything

32. Jill: Why isn't Mary at work today?

    Fred: She's _______ this week.

    ⓐ on leave   ⓑ put out   ⓒ fond of   ⓓ put on

33. I'm fed up with all of the argument! _______ , please be quiet.

    ⓐ Once and for all   ⓑ Once more
    ⓒ Once up a time   ⓓ More than once

34. That doesn't _______ a true story to me.

    ⓐ like to sound   ⓑ sound to   ⓒ sound like it   ⓓ sound like

35. Because some people didn't understand, she retold the story.

    ⓐ She told another story   ⓑ She told the story again
    ⓒ She couldn't remember the story ⓓ She told a different story.

36. Most teachers don't like it when their students _______ them.

    ⓐ talk back to   ⓑ look up to   ⓒ count on   ⓓ think much of

37. Commander Martin didn't have time to write the report, so he told Lt. Evans to _______ .

    ⓐ take to it   ⓑ take after it
    ⓒ take care of it   ⓓ take along with it

38. The private knew he didn't dare _______ the sergeant.

    ⓐ look up to   ⓑ talk back to
    ⓒ take sides in   ⓓ get down with

39. Who on earth _______ this ridiculous and dangerous idea?

    ⓐ woke up   ⓑ thought up   ⓒ put up with   ⓓ got on

40. Moore got a promotion; _______ , he won't work in this office any longer.

    ⓐ but   ⓑ therefore   ⓒ whether   ⓓ result

41. Mrs. Greg: Do you still need these papers?

    Mr. Greg: No, you can _______ .

    ⓐ do them over   ⓑ put them out   ⓒ put off   ⓓ throw them out

42. Mr. Williams is the captain of this ship. It is _______ him to see that everything runs smoothly.

    ⓐ up against   ⓑ along with   ⓑ up for   ⓒ up to

43. They couldn't leave the classroom when the bell rang; they _______ the test.

    ⓐ went on with   ⓑ gave up   ⓒ gave out

44. The players _______ the plans from the beginning.

    ⓐ were in on   ⓑ were cut off   ⓒ were stuck to

45. Push the print button on the computer. _______ it prints, you can begin a new work.

    ⓐ Meanwhile   ⓑ In the course of
    ⓒ While   ⓓ In the meantime

46. John _______ the math problem all by himself.

    ⓐ worked out   ⓑ took asides   ⓒ counted on   ⓓ got up to

47. The researchers _______ the project on time and started the next one.

    ⓐ put off   ⓑ checked out   ⓒ wound up   ⓓ laid over

48. Sindy is authorized by her boss to buy a new computer for the company.

    ⓐ given the duty   ⓑ given the power

    ⓒ given the money   ⓓ given instruction

49. When you read your instruction manual, look closely at Number 2. Before every other consideration, that is the most important step.

    ⓐ Above all   ⓑ In addition   ⓒ moreover   ⓓ At least

50. Because Mark was such a bad student, they forced him to leave the college.

    ⓐ exhausted him from   ⓑ emitted him from

    ⓒ expelled him from   ⓓ expected him to

51. I'll allow you to enter the university providing you pass the exam.

    ⓐ as long as   ⓑ in case   ⓒ unless   ⓓ before

52. Our office is being moved from Busan to Seoul next month.

    ⓐ preferred   ⓑ elevated

    ⓒ transferred   ⓓ transcribed

53. Prior to their deadlines, you'll see copywriters working vigorously and untiringly on last minute changes on the children's commercials.

    ⓐ energetically   ⓑ moderately

    ⓒ creatively   ⓓ hopefully

54. Tim: What did you think of the presentation yesterday?

    Pat: I could hardly keep a straight face until it was over.

    ⓐ keep myself from laughing   ⓑ stay awake

    ⓒ keep myself from looking around the room   ⓓ concentrate on it

55. COL Denny: Have you finished the report yet?

   MAJ Kenny: No. Some time this afternoon we need to put our heads together and come up with a conclusion.

   ⓐ to come to an agreement   ⓑ to work together
   ⓒ to stay close to each other   ⓓ to make a complaint

56. Tony: You know we're supposed to have this project finished by tomorrow, don't you?

   Mary: Yeah, we'd better shake a leg, huh?

   ⓐ hurry up and finish   ⓑ get some help
   ⓒ come up with a good excuse   ⓓ give up the project

57. Ashley: So how's work?

   Tracey: So far I've enjoyed teaching, but I've always got my hands full.

   ⓐ I have to carry a lot of things   ⓑ I have too many students in a small room
   ⓒ I am in trouble   ⓓ I am very busy

58. Ron: Has Miller finished his report?

   Ken: Not yet. He's been really busy.

   Ron: You'd better do it for him.

   Ken: He might say I'm stepping on his toes.

   ⓐ forcing him to do it   ⓑ trespassing in his area
   ⓒ trying to hurt him purposefully   ⓓ interfering with his work

59. Liz: I heard Mary took her old boss to court. Did she win?

   Ann: Yeah, she fought him tooth and nail.

   ⓐ used her speaking ability   ⓑ let her lawyers handle the case
   ⓒ fought by herself   ⓓ used all her strength

60. Gerald: How'd the exam go?

Harold: We just got our scores an hour ago – passed by the skin of my teeth!

ⓐ I passed with a high score

ⓑ I passed the exam by bribing the instructor

ⓒ I passed the exam by one point

ⓓ I got a perfect score

61. Ivan: How did your meeting with the Prime Minister go?

Hans: Not as well as I'd hoped We couldn't see eye to eye.

ⓐ talk personally   ⓑ speak our opinion

ⓒ agree on anything   ⓓ talk frankly

62. Barb: When is Dorothy going to retire?

Jean: I don't know. She looks like she's on her last leg to me.

ⓐ has severe pain in her leg.   ⓑ doesn't have enough money to retire

ⓒ retires soon   ⓓ slows down physically and mentally

63. We racked our brains for days trying to find a solution of the affairs, but it never came to us.

ⓐ competed in a speed contest

ⓑ worked in a group

ⓒ strived desperately to remember or think of something

ⓓ put clothing on hanger racks

64. Mr. Barnes is very depresseⓓ He can't seem to come to grips with the loss of his job.

ⓐ have emotional impact on   ⓑ have tight hold on

ⓒ cope with   ⓓ complain about

ECL시험 대비 New ALC 필수어휘 완성

65. Because it was critical that the project be finished by the end of the month, the manager urged the workers to get the job done as expeditiously as possible.

ⓐ The manager indicated that the workers could take all the time and money they wanted in order to do the job

ⓑ The manager stated that the quickest and most efficient methods should be used to complete the job

ⓒ The manager decided to postpone the project

ⓓ The manager said that the worker will be fired if they spend too much time and money

66. I hate to butt in, but are you sure that's the right code to use?

ⓐ change the subject　　　　　　ⓑ interrupt
ⓒ call the supervisor　　　　　　ⓓ participate

67. I think Airman Ryan would be great for this job; he really catches on fast.

ⓐ learns　　　　ⓑ responds　　　　ⓒ drives　　　　ⓓ cooperate

68. The firm has had to cut back on the amount of overtime the employees are putting in.

ⓐ increase　　　　ⓑ regulate　　　　ⓒ reduce　　　　ⓓ rearrange

69. Let's hold off on this decision for awhile; we need more data.

ⓐ move　　　　ⓑ delay　　　　ⓒ act　　　　ⓓ change

70. The students thought his lectures were above their heads. They left class not understanding anything the instructor said.

ⓐ not able to pay　　　　　　ⓑ sleepy all the time
ⓒ unable to respond　　　　　ⓓ difficult to understand

71. We knew the speaker was off to a good start; he had a good introduction and got the attention of the audience right away.

   ⓐ favorable condition   ⓑ specific order

   ⓒ unrelated start   ⓓ good beginning

72. The speaker had his subject down pat. He knew exactly what he should do.

   ⓐ gave words of encouragement   ⓑ wrote it in outline form

   ⓒ understood his subject thoroughly   ⓓ studies his subject by himself

73. John get so nervous before tests. The instructor told him he'd do better if he'd stay loose.

   ⓐ remember the facts   ⓑ stop talking

   ⓒ remain relaxed   ⓓ give up the test.

74. The speaker built rapport with his audience by talking at a level they could easily understand.

   ⓐ established a close relationship   ⓑ gave an excellent speech

   ⓒ explained everything well   ⓒ got together

75. He wanted to approach his employer aggressively, but in the interest of saving his job, he was advised to back off.

   ⓐ be more assertive   ⓑ refrain

   ⓒ change his opinion   ⓓ retire

정답 / 해석

1. ⓒ 나는 지난 주 결석하여 과제가 밀려 있다.

2. ⓑ 학생들은 건물을 질서있게 떠났다.

3. ⓒ 오바마 교수는 자신감이 있다.

4. ⓒ 존은 새 사무실을 위한 계획에 가담해야 한다.

5. ⓐ 토의할 새로운 주제를 내놓지 그래?

6. ⓐ 폴은 수학에서 다른 학생들에게 뒤졌지만, 겨울방학 동안 열심히 공부하여 이를 만회할 수 있었다.

7. ⓒ 로라는 그녀의 일을 만회하기 위해 근무 시간 후에 일하였다.

8. ⓒ 그 신병은 믿을만 하지 못하여 교관은 그를 종종 확인한다.

9. ⓐ 그 공군병사는 큰 실수 때문에 심하게 추궁당했다.

10. ⓐ 제임스는 매우 신뢰할 수 있기 때문에 그의 상관들은 복잡한 문제를 해결하기 위해서 그에게 의존한다.

11. ⓑ 승진에 가장 적격인 후보는 누구라고 생각하느냐?

12. ⓐ 그는 즉시 뜻을 이해하고, 이해했다는 표시를 했다.

13. ⓒ 로라는 체중을 줄여야 할 필요가 있다. 그녀는 음식을 줄이기로 결심했다.

14. ⓐ 나는 이 문제를 해결할 수 없다. 그렇더라도 그것은 시험에 나오기 때문에 풀어야 한다.

15. ⓑ 너는 그 문제가 사소하고 하찮은 지금 처리하거나, 매우 복잡하고 심각해 질 때까지 기다릴 수 있다.

16. ⓒ 그 토론은 어떻게 끝났니?

17. ⓒ 마가렛은 지난 해 교단에서 은퇴했다. 이제 그녀는 생계를 위해 부동산을 판다.

18. ⓓ 그 어머니는 아이들을 위해 직업을 포기했다.

19. ⓐ 우리 선생님은 뛰어나다. 그는 그의 제자들이 기억해야 할 필요가 있는 것을 이해시키는 데 적절한 방법을 찾아낸다.

20. ⓐ 우리 교장님은 관대함과 인내로 성공하였다.

21. ⓑ 그는 그 과정에서 가까스로 통과했다. 그는 거의 실패할 뻔 했다.

22. ⓐ 교관이 시험지를 나누어 준 뒤에 너는 시험을 시작 할 수 있다.

23. ⓐ 실패 때문에 포기하지 마라. 계속하면 성공할 수 있다.

24. ⓑ 시험지를 제출하기 전에 다시 한번 검토하시오.

25. ⓑ 규정에 따라 그들은 기지에 있는 모든 차량을 검사하였다.

26. ⓑ 그들 둘 다 새 단어를 배우고 공책을 함께 쓴다. 그들은 같은 방식으로 공부한다.

27. ⓑ 찰스는 나머지 급우들에게 열등한 것으로 평가받고 있다. 그는 멸시 당했다.

28. ⓒ 그 보고서는 논의에 맞지 않다. 설명해 볼래?

29. ⓐ 우리 팀은 실습실에서 테이프를 들었다. 반면에 다른 팀은 교실에서 숙제를 확인했다.

30. ⓒ 나는 대학을 마친 뒤에 대학원에 가고 싶다. 뿐만 아니라, 나는 주말에 부업을 하고 싶다.

31. ⓑ A: 내가 당신에게 말한 것에 덧붙일 것이 있습니까?

　　B: 아니, 그 밖에 아무것도 없습니다. 미안해요.

32. ⓐ 질: 메리는 왜 오늘 나오지 않았지?

　　프레드: 그녀는 이번 주 휴가입니다.

33. ⓐ 나는 모든 논쟁에 신물이 난다! 제발 조용히 해라.

34. ⓓ 그것은 진실한 이야기가 아닌 것처럼 보인다.

35. ⓑ 몇몇 사람들이 이해하지 못했기 때문에 그녀는 이야기를 다시 하였다.

36. ⓐ 대부분의 선생님들은 학생들이 말대꾸하면 싫어한다.

37. ⓒ 마틴 중령은 보고서를 쓸 시간이 없어서, 에반스 대위에게 처리하라고 했다.

38. ⓑ 그 병사는 부사관에게 대꾸할 용기가 없다는 것을 알았다.

39. ⓑ 도대체 누가 이 어리석고 위험한 생각을 하였느냐?

40. ⓑ 무어는 승진했다. 그래서 그는 더 이상 이 사무실에서 근무하지 않을 것이다.

41. ⓓ 그레그 부인: 아직도 이 서류가 필요하세요?

　　그레스: 아니요, 없애 버려도 됩니다.

42. ⓒ 윌리암씨는 이 배의 함장이다. 모든 것이 잘 진행되는 지 살펴보는 것은 그의 책임이다.

43. ⓐ 그들은 벨이 울릴 때까지 교실을 떠날 수 없었다. 그들은 시험을 계속 치뤘다.

44. ⓐ 그 선수들은 처음부터 그 계획에 개입되어 있다.

45. ⓒ 컴퓨터의 프린터 단추를 누르세요. 프린터 되는 동안에 다른 작업을 시작할 수 있습니다.

46. ⓐ 존은 혼자서 수학 문제를 모두 풀었다.

47. ⓒ 연구원들은 과제를 시간에 맞추어 마치고, 새 과제를 시작하였다.

48. ⓑ 신디는 상관으로부터 회사에 사용할 새 컴퓨터를 구매할 권한을 부여받았다.

49. ⓐ 지침서를 읽을 때는 2번을 잘 보세요. 무엇보다 그것이 가장 중요한 단계입니다.

50. ⓒ 마크는 나쁜 학생이었기 때문에 그들은 그를 퇴학시켰다.

51. ⓐ 너가 시험에 합격하면 대학 입학을 허락하겠다.

52. ⓒ 우리 사무실은 다음 달 부산에서 서울로 이전될 것이다.

53. ⓐ 마감시간 전에 광고방송 작성자들이 어린이용 상업광고에 대한 마지막 수정작업을 활기있게 지칠 줄 모르고 하는 것을 보게 될것이다.

54. ⓐ 팀: 어제 발표를 어떻게 생각하나?

   팻: 끝날 때까지 웃음을 참기가 힘들었어.

55. ⓑ 데니 대령: 보고서 이미 끝났니?

   케니 소령: 아니요. 오늘 오후 함께 머리를 맞대고 결론을 내릴 필요가 있습니다.

56. ⓐ 토니: 우리가 이 업무를 내일까지 끝내기로 되어 있는 것 알지?

   메어리: 예, 서둘러 끝마치는 것이 좋습니다.

57. ⓓ 애쉴리: 일이 잘 되니?

   트레이시: 지금까지는 가르치는 것이 즐거웠다. 그러나 나는 항상 바쁘다.

58. ⓑ 론: 밀러는 보고서를 완수했니?

   캔: 아니 아직. 그는 매우 바빴어.

   론: 너가 그를 대신에 주는게 좋겠다.

   캔: 그는 내가 그의 권리를 침해한다고 말할지도 몰라.

59. ⓓ 리즈: 메어리가 자신의 과거 상관을 고소했다고 들었다. 그녀가 이겼니?

   앤: 그래, 그녀는 전력으로 싸웠어.

60. ⓒ 제랄드: 시험은 어떻게 했니?

   헤랄드: 방금 전에 성적을 받았어. 가까스로 통과했어.

61. ⓒ 이반: 수상과의 회합은 어떻게 되었니?

   한스: 바라는 대로 되지는 않았어. 의견이 전혀 일치하지 않았어.

62. ⓒ 바브: 도로시는 언제 은퇴하지?

   진: 몰라. 그녀는 완전히 지친 것 같아.

63. ⓒ 우리는 그 사건의 해결책을 찾기 위해 며칠 간 머리를 짰지만, 생각이 떠오르지 않았다.

64. ⓒ 반즈씨는 매우 낙담해 있다. 그는 직업을 잃은 것에 대해 어떻게 할 수 없는 것 같았다.

65. ⓑ 그 업무를 월말에 끝내는 것이 매우 중요하기 때문에, 그 경영자는 직원들이 가능한 신속히 끝내도록 독려했다.

66. ⓑ 참견하고 싶지 않지만 그것이 사용하기에 맞는 코드니?

67. ⓐ 공군병사 라이언이 이 일을 잘할 것이다고 생각한다. 그는 실제로 빨리 업무를 익힌다.

68. ⓒ 그 회사는 고용인들이 투입되는 초과근무의 양을 줄여야 했다.

69. ⓑ 잠시 동안 이 결정에 대해 미룹시다. 우리는 더 많은 자료가 필요합니다.

70. ⓓ 그 학생들은 그의 강연이 너무 어렵다고 생각하였다. 그들은 그 교관이 말하는 것을 하나도 이해하지 못한 채 떠났다.

71. ⓓ 우리는 연설의 시작이 좋았다는 것을 알았다. 시작이 좋았고 즉시 청중의 주의를 끌었다.

72. ⓒ 연사는 그의 주제를 완벽히 알고 있었다. 그는 정확히 무엇을 해야 할 지 알았다.

73. ⓒ 존은 시험 전에는 초조해한다. 교관은 그에게 긴장을 풀면 더 잘할 것이라고 말했다.

74. ⓐ 연사는 그들이 쉽게 이해할 수 있는 수준으로 이야기하여 청중과 교감을 형성하였다.

75. ⓑ 그는 그의 고용주에게 공격적으로 대하려고 했지만, 자신의 직업을 지키기 위해서 이를 삼가 하라는 충고를 들었다.

New American
Language
Course

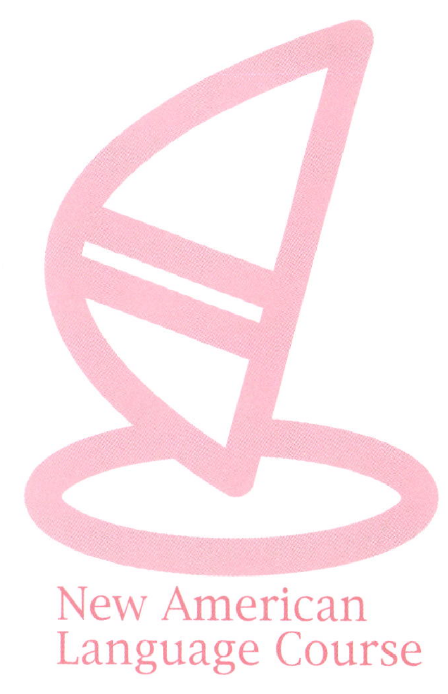

New American
Language Course

문화와 레저4

A. 명사   B. 동사   C. 형용사   D. 어휘, 관용구, 문형 종합

ECL시험 대비 NEW ALC 필수어휘 완성

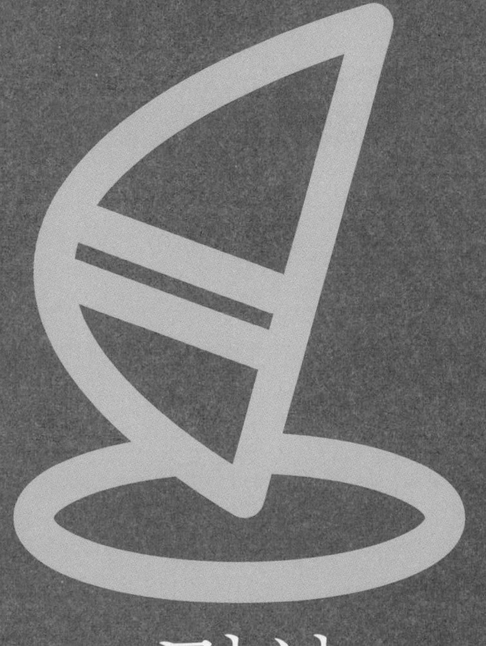

명사

기본어휘 / 연습 문제

A

New American
Language Course

1. 기본어휘 — 명사

advent / 출현, 도래 (the coming or arrival of)

With the advent of the printing press in the fifteenth century, knowledge and ideas were spread from country to country, and learning became available to more people.
(15세기 인쇄기가 도래하여, 지식과 사고가 국가에서 국가로 퍼졌으며, 더 많은 사람들이 학습을 할 수 있게 되었다.)

amusement 즐거움, 재미 (a game or an activity that provides entertainment or pleasure)

Students have few amusements to choose from. (학생들이 선택해서 즐길 만한 것들이 거의 없다.)

border / 경계, 가장자리 (a dividing line between two countries, fringe)

The dress was red with a delicate lace border.
(그 옷은 가장자리에 섬세한 레이스가 있는 붉은 옷이다.)

bronze / 청동 (an alloy consisting of copper and tin)

The bell of the temple is made of bronze. (그 절의 종은 청동으로 만들어져 있다.)

category / 범주, 계급 (a class or division in a system of classification)

There are three categories of accommodation in the hotel – standard, executive, de luxe.
(호텔에는 3가지 범주의 숙박 – 표준형, 귀빈용, 고급용 – 이 있다.)

challenge / 도전, 힘든 일 (a demand, an invitation, a suggestion)

The instruments with which we meet our challenge may be new but those values upon which our success depends – honesty, hard work, and courage – are old.

(우리가 다루는 도구는 새로울 지 모르지만, 우리의 성공을 좌우하는 가치 – 정직, 근면, 용기 – 는 오래 된 것이다.)

cliff / 절벽, 낭떠러지 (the steep side of an area of high land)

They pushed the car over the edge of the cliff. (그들은 낭떠러지 끝으로 차를 밀었다.)

compact / 소형의 (smaller than most things of the same kind)

There are compact apartments in the city. (그 도시에는 소형 아파트들이 있다.)

compartment / 칸막이, 구획 (a separate section for keeping things in)

We should keep a bottle of champagne in the freezer compartment.

(우리는 샴페인 병을 냉장 칸에 보관해야 한다.)

compass / 한계, 범위 (an instrument for finding direction, a particular range)

The discussion was beyond the compass of my brain.

(그 토론 내용은 내 머리의 범위 밖에 있다.)

confirmation / 인가, 승인 (ratification, verification)

Please wait in the lounge until confirmation of that flight has been received.

(그 비행에 대한 인정을 받을 때 까지 라운지에 기다리세요.)

contest / 경쟁, 논쟁 (a competition, especially one in which people's skill in a particular activity or sport is tested)

A contest between the two top–rated tennis players in the world will be held the end of this month. (세계 최상급 테니스 선수들 간의 경기가 이달 말에 개최될 것이다.)

destination / 목적지, 도착지 (the place where a person is going or a thing is being sent)

Jejudo is a popular tourist destination these days. (제주도는 요즈음 인기 있는 관광지이다.)

display / 전시, 진열 (an arrangement of things for people to look at)

The costumes were placed on display in the museum.

(그 의복들은 박물관에 전시되었다.)

distance / 거리 (the amount of space between two people or things)

They started to walk the short distance to the camp.

(그들은 부대까지의 짧은 거리를 걷기 시작하였다.)

dive / 뛰어들다 (to jump or swim underwater)

The submarine dived to avoid the enemy attack.

(잠수함은 적의 공격을 피하기 위해 물 속으로 갔다.)

emphasis / 강조 (special stress or attention)

His statement gave emphasis to the deficiency of budget. (그는 예산이 부족하다는 점을 강조했다.)

enthusiasm / 열정, 열의 (zeal, passion, intense or eager interest)

Greg never loses his enthusiasm for teaching. (그랙은 가르치는 데 결코 열정을 잃지 않는다.)

commercial / 광고방송 (an advertisement on television or radio)

There are so many interesting commercials these days. (요즈음에는 재미있는 광고들이 많다.)

fare / 요금, 운임 (the money you pay for a trip)

She had argued with a cab driver after refusing to pay her fare.

(그녀는 택시 요금지불을 거절한 후 기사와 다투었다.)

facility / 시설, 설비 (buildings, services, or equipments for a particular purpose)

The shopping center has special facilities for disabled people.

(그 쇼핑센터에는 지체부자유자를 위한 특별시설이 있다.)

fracture / 골절, 부수다 (the breaking of a bone, to disrupt or destroy as if by breaking)

He fractured the delicate balance of power. (그는 미묘한 힘의 균형을 깨뜨렸다.)

hindrance / 방해, 훼방 (impediment, something that makes it difficult to do something)

High inflation is a hindrance to economic recovery. (높은 인플레는 경제 회복에 장애가 된다.)

honeymoon / 밀월, 신혼여행 (a vacation that two people take after they get married)

Where are they going on their honeymoon? (그들은 신혼여행 때 어디로 갈 건가요?)

incarnation / 구체화, 상징 (embodiment, symbol)

The flag they created was the incarnation of the nation's political and religious history.
(그들이 만든 국기는 그 나라의 정치적 종교적 역사를 구체화한 것이다.)

landmark / 이정표, 경계표 (any object to mark the boundary, something you can see from a distance)

The 63 building is a famous landmark on the Seoul skyline.
(63빌딩은 서울 시내의 가장 뚜렷한 이정표이다.)

leisure / 여가, 한가한 (spare, free and unoccupied)

Many seamen have no leisure on weekends. (많은 수병들은 주말에 여가가 없다.)

orchestra / 관현악단 (a large group of musicians playing together)

The person in charge of an orchestra is conductor.
(오케스트라를 책임지는 사람은 지휘자이다.)

passenger / 승객 (someone who travels in a motor vehicle, aircraft, or ship)

Two other passengers in the car suffered serious injuries.
(그 차의 탑승자 2명이 심한 부상을 입었다.)

photography / 사진술 (the art or process of taking photographs or filming something)

She is teaching an evening class in photography.

(그녀는 사진에 대한 야간 강의를 하고 있다.)

pool / 웅덩이 (area of liquid)

The water collected in a little pool at the bottom of the cliff.

(그 물은 낭떠러지 바닥의 조그만 웅덩이에 고였다.)

precaution / 조심, 경계 (care taken beforehand, caution used in advance)

We must take all reasonable precautions to protect our family.

(우리는 가족을 보호하기 위해 모든 합리적인 예방책을 취해야 한다.)

prime / 첫째의, 가장 중요한 (most important)

Truman had been the prime architect of the NATO alliance.

(트루먼은 나토 동맹국들의 최고 기획자였다.)

quickness / 신속, 빠름 (rapidity)

He is a great tennis player because of his quickness at the net.

(그는 네트에서 민첩하기 때문에 훌륭한 테니스 선수이다.)

ratio / 비율 (a relationship between two things expressed by numbers or amounts)

We are aiming for a more equal sex ratio on our staff.

(우리는 참모진의 남녀 비율을 동일하게 하고자 한다.)

stadium / 경기장 (a large building where people watch sports events)

Most universities in the US have their own stadium.

(대부분의 미국대학들은 자체 경기장을 갖고 있다.)

surroundings / 환경, 주위상황 (conditions or influences that surround a person or a place)

Houses should fit in with their surroundings. (가옥은 주변 환경에 맞추어야 한다.)

tie / 동점 (equal point), 끈 (string, cord)

There was a tie for fourth place. (4회전에서는 동점이었다.)

track / 자국, 진로 (a type of path or road, a course of action or procedure)

You are on the right track to solve the problem.

(너는 문제 해결을 위한 올바른 방식을 취하고 있다.)

wilderness / 황야, 황무지 (an area of land where people do not live or grow crops)

The Senator spent several years in the political wilderness.

(그 상원의원은 정치적 불모지에서 몇 년간을 보냈다.)

2. 연습문제

1. They traveled to Africa by _______ .

    ⓐ air   ⓑ see   ⓒ ride   ⓓ direction

2. Our passports were checked twice by the guards at the _______ .

    ⓐ zone   ⓐ combat   ⓑ border   ⓒ defense

3. "The Thinker" is a famous _______ statue.

    ⓐ bronze   ⓑ access   ⓒ resource   ⓓ carbon

4. This is classical music while that's modern musiⓒ So they don't belong in the same _______ .

    ⓐ classification   ⓑ branch   ⓒ design   ⓓ category

5. The soccer team accepted the _______ of the losers to a rematch.

    ⓐ challenge   ⓑ reprimand   ⓒ change   ⓓ compromise

6. The climbers used ropes to reach the top of the _______ .

    ⓐ cliff   ⓑ scope   ⓒ echo   ⓓ valley

7. I saw a very funny _______ on television last night.

    ⓐ commercially   ⓑ commercial

    ⓒ commercialize   ⓑ commercialist

8. You need a(n) _____ suitcase that will fit under your seat on the airplane.

    ⓐ condo   ⓑ limited

    ⓒ compact   ⓓ occupied

9. The _____ tells you the direction where you should go.

    ⓐ altimeter   ⓑ compass   ⓒ attitude   ⓓ distinction

10. We arrived at our _____ tired and hungry.

    ⓐ destination   ⓑ interruption   ⓒ instruction   ⓓ destruction

11. The _____ of the flag of nations from all over the world was beautiful.

    ⓐ position   ⓑ fasting   ⓒ occasion   ⓓ display

12. Pvt West: What's the _____ between San Atonio and Austin?

    Pvt King: It's about 80 mi.

    ⓐ length   ⓑ height   ⓒ way   ⓓ distance

13. His favorite sport is _____ . He loves to go underwater even in winter.

    ⓐ diving   ⓑ navigating   ⓒ drifting   ⓓ driving

14. When we play games, the _____ should be on fair play and enjoyment, not winning the game or defeating the other team.

    ⓐ emphasis   ⓑ problem   ⓒ handicap   ⓓ construction

15. The audience showed a lot of _____ for the wonderful entertainer.

    ⓐ experience   ⓑ intention

    ⓒ enthusiasm   ⓓ reputation

16. What's the round-trip _____ to New York?

   ⓐ fare   ⓑ passenger   ⓒ guest   ⓓ honor

17. There's a _____ near the university. We can kick the ball there.

   ⓐ show   ⓑ field   ⓒ match   ⓓ system

18. Hank was a _____ in the swimming competition.

   ⓐ finalize   ⓑ finally   ⓒ final   ⓓ finalist

19. Nicholas and Olivia got married and went to Europe on their _____ .

   ⓐ honeymoon   ⓑ work   ⓒ leave   ⓓ holiday

20. What's the best _____ to help me find my way in a strange road?

   ⓐ landslide   ⓑ landmark   ⓒ landlord   ⓓ lane

21. What do you usually like to do in your _____ time?

   ⓐ leisurely   ⓑ intentional   ⓒ leisure   ⓓ mechanical

22. The soldier can travel in his _____ time now that he's retired.

   ⓐ leisure   ⓑ interest   ⓒ experience   ⓓ working

23. The plane was full. There were 250 _____ on it.

   ⓐ refreshments   ⓑ something   ⓒ passengers   ⓓ crimes

24. When you go hiking you're on the right _____ if you see a red piece of cloth hanging on the branch of a tree in the trail.

   ⓐ pass   ⓑ passage   ⓒ path   ⓓ passport

25. When David got his new camera, he took up _______ as a hobby.

   ⓐ photograph   ⓑ photography

   ⓒ photographic   ⓓ photosynthesis

26. I had one of the _______ seats at the performance. I could see and hear the performers extremely well.

   ⓐ poor   ⓑ prime   ⓒ distinguished   ⓓ competent

27. Your team outscored us by a _______ of 3 to 1 last year.

   ⓐ ratio   ⓑ link   ⓒ first   ⓓ priority

28. Let's take a _______ in the country. It's a lovely day!

   ⓐ ride   ⓑ visa   ⓒ life   ⓓ victory

29. The reprobate depicted in this cartoon is so bad that he doesn't live by any morals or standards.

   ⓐ religious person   ⓑ educated person

   ⓒ illiterate person   ⓓ immoral person

30. Luis: Where's the football game going to be?

   Ben: In the ___ downtown.

   ⓐ stadium   ⓑ gymnasium   ⓒ office   ⓓ spot

31. Following animal _______ is a kind of skill practiced by many hunters.

   ⓐ trays   ⓑ tracks   ⓒ means   ⓓ tribute

32. Tom got lost in the ___ for seven days and had to be rescued by helicopter.

   ⓐ wilderness   ⓑ mall   ⓒ neighborhood   ⓓ cafe

33. What do you usually do for _____ on weekends?

   ⓐ exciting   ⓑ pleasant   ⓒ amusement   ⓓ delightful

34. You can find a small _____ in the front of the airplane, where you can hang up your coat or a garment bag.

   ⓐ tray   ⓑ compartment   ⓒ company   ⓓ lounge

35. While playing soccer a bone in my arm is broken. I have a(n) _____ .

   ⓐ fracture   ⓑ frame   ⓒ frank   ⓓ fraction

36. You can find a large sports _____ about five hundred meters from there.

   ⓐ faculty   ⓑ figure   ⓒ facility   ⓓ fitness

37. Checking the tires, engine and mission oil, water, and gasoline is a(n) _____ which should be taken before a long trip.

   ⓐ consumption   ⓑ attitude   ⓒ precaution   ⓓ reason

38. They're not going to Canada on business, they're going for _____ .

   ⓐ contest   ⓑ work   ⓒ luxury   ⓓ pleasure

39. The coming down of the colorful balloons was exciting to see. The crowd watched their _____ .

   ⓐ output   ⓑ descent   ⓒ gradual   ⓓ ascent

40. During the motor racing, the drivers encounter many hindrances blocking the road.

   ⓐ obstacles   ⓑ terrains   ⓒ log   ⓓ bridges

41. Ann wants to visit Europe. She intends to go there someday.

ⓐ by the day
ⓑ for a long time
ⓒ if she has the time
ⓓ at some future time

42. People from different countries have lived in different culture and different surroundings.

ⓐ resources
ⓑ environments
ⓒ relatives
ⓓ neighborhood

43. The upward movement of the balloon held the spectators' attention. They watched the balloon's _____ .

ⓐ delay   ⓑ ascent   ⓒ descent   ⓓ input

44. The ad agency recently sliced the baby-boom generation into three sections: the optimistic "satisfied selves," the "conservative homebody traditionalists," who never go anywhere, and the insecure "worried traditionalists."

ⓐ one who never leaves the house

ⓑ one whose life is centered around the house

ⓒ one who body builds at home

ⓓ one who promote anarchy

45. The copywriter designed and developed the cereal commercial with craft. It's the best work I've seen.

ⓐ lack of talent
ⓑ special skill or art
ⓒ aircraft
ⓓ sculpture

정답 / 해석

1. ⓐ 그들은 비행기로 아프리카를 여행하였다.

2. ⓑ 우리는 국경에서 경비원에게 두 번 여권 검사를 받았다.

3. ⓐ "생각하는 사람"은 유명한 황동 동상이다.

4. ⓓ 이것은 고전음악이고, 저것은 현대 음악이다. 그래서 그것들은 같은 범주에 속하지 않는다.

5. ⓐ 축구팀은 재 시합에 대한 패자들의 도전을 받아들였다.

6. ⓐ 등산가들은 낭떠러지의 꼭대기에 올라가기 위해 로프를 사용하였다.

7. ⓑ 나는 지난 밤 TV에서 재미있는 광고를 보았다.

8. ⓒ 당신은 비행기 좌석 밑에 들어갈 수 있는 조그만 가방이 필요할 겁니다.

9. ⓑ 나침판은 여러분이 가야 할 방향을 말해준다.

10. ⓐ 우리는 피곤하고 허기진 채로 목적지에 도착했다.

11. ⓓ 만국기 게양은 보기 좋았다.

12. ⓓ 웨스트 이병: 샌 안토니오에서 오스틴까지 거리가 얼마입니까?

　　킹 이병: 80마일 가량 됩니다.

13. ⓐ 그가 좋아하는 스포츠는 다이빙이다. 그는 겨울에도 물 속에 가는 것을 좋아한다.

14. ⓐ 우리는 시합을 할 때 정당한 경기와 즐거움에 중점을 두되, 게임의 승패에 중점을 두어서는 안된다.

15. ⓒ 관중은 그 멋진 연예인에게 매우 열광하였다.

16. ⓐ 뉴욕까지 왕복 비행기 값은 얼마죠?

17. ⓑ 그 대학교 인근에 경기장이 있지. 거기서 축구 할 수 있어.

18. ⓓ 헨크가 그 수영 대회의 마지막 선수였다.

19. ⓐ 니콜라스와 올리비아는 결혼하고 유럽으로 신혼여행 갔다.

20. ⓑ 낯선 길에서 길을 찾는 데 도움이 되는 가장 좋은 이정표는 무엇입니까?

21. ⓒ 여가 시간에 주로 무엇을 즐깁니까?

22. ⓐ 그 군인은 은퇴했기 때문에 여가시간에 여행할 수 있다.

23. ⓒ 비행기가 만원이었다. 250명이 탑승하였다.

24. ⓒ 등산할 때 나뭇가지에 매달린 붉은 천을 보면 당신은 길을 제대로 가고 있는 것이다.

25. ⓑ 데이비드는 새 카메라를 사자, 사진 촬영을 취미로 하게 되었다.

26. ⓑ 나는 그 공연장에서 가장 멋진 좌석 가운데 하나에 앉았다. 공연자의 동작과 목소리를 아주 자세히 보고 들을 수 있었다.

27. ⓐ 당신 팀은 작년에 3대1로 우리를 눌렀다.

28. ⓐ 그 시골을 차타고 가보기로 하자. 날씨도 정말 좋네.

29. ⓓ 이 만화에 묘사된 부도덕한 사람은 너무 약해서 어떤 도덕이나 기준에 따라 생활하지 않는다.

30. ⓐ 루이스: 어디서 축구경기를 하지?

벤: 시내 경기장입니다.

31. ⓑ 동물 발자취를 따라가는 것은 많은 사냥꾼의 숙련된 기술이다.

32. ⓐ 탐은 황야에서 7일 동안 길을 잃었다. 헬기로 구조할 수밖에 없었다.

33. ⓒ 주말에 재미로 대개 무엇을 합니까?

34. ⓑ 비행기 앞부분에 작은 칸이 있습니다. 거기에 코트나 옷가방을 걸어 둘 수 있습니다.

35. ⓐ 축구하면서 내 팔뼈가 부러졌다. 골절상을 당했다.

36. ⓒ 거기에서 약 500미터 떨어진 지점에 큰 스포츠 시설이 있을 것이다.

37. ⓒ 타이어, 엔진과 미션오일, 물, 휘발유를 점검하는 것은 장거리 여행 전에 취해야 할 예방책이다.

38. ⓓ 그들이 캐나다로 가는 것은 사업 때문이 아니다. 놀러 가는 것이다.

39. ⓑ 형형색색의 풍선들이 내려오는 것을 보면 흥미롭다. 군중들은 내려오는 풍선들을 쳐다보았다.

40. ⓐ 자동차 경주 동안 운전자들은 도로를 막는 많은 장애물을 마주친다.

41. ⓓ 앤은 유럽을 방문하고 싶다. 그녀는 언젠가 거기에 갈 예정이다.

42. ⓑ 다른 나라 사람들은 문화도 다르고, 환경도 다르다.

43. ⓑ 위로 날아가는 풍선이 관중들의 시선을 이끌었다. 그들은 풍선이 날아가는 것을 보았다.

44. ⓑ 그 광고회사는 베이비붐 세대를 세부분으로 나누었다: 만족한 사람들, 나다니지 않는 보수적인 가정중심의 전통주의자, 불안한 걱정하는 전통주의자.

45. ⓑ 그 광고작성자는 곡물식품광고를 솜씨좋게 개선, 발전시켰다. 내가 본 작품 가운데 가장 훌륭하다.

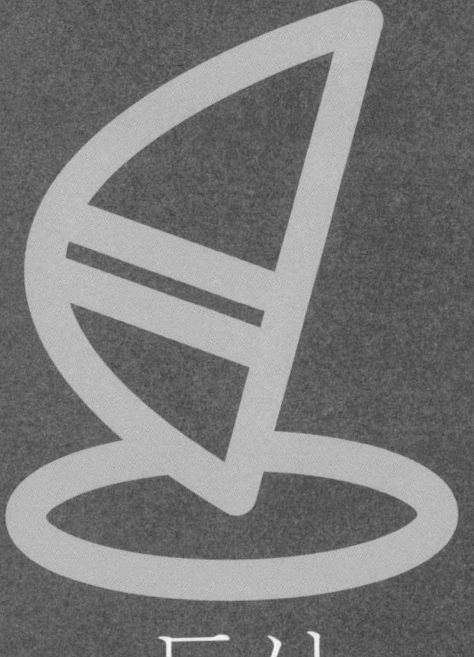

New American Language Course

1. 기본어휘   동사

attach / 붙이다, 달다 (to fasten or affix, connect)

We should attach a photograph to our applications with a staple.

(우리는 철침으로 지원서에 사진을 첨부해야 한다.)

bathe / 목욕하다, 씻다 (to take a bath, to apply a liquid for healing)

The nurse bathed the wound with iodine.

(간호원은 요오드로 상처를 씻었다.)

beat / 치다, ~에 이기다 (to defeat someone in a game, competition, election, or battle)

In 2000, George W. Bush narrowly beat Al Gore in the election.

(2000년도 선거에서 부시는 앨 고어에게 근소한 차이로 승리했다.)

board / 타다, 탑승시키다 (to get onto a ship, aircraft, train, or bus)

We're boarding through gate 15.

(우리는 15번 출구를 통해서 비행기에 탑승한다.)

bounce / 되튀다, 펄쩍 뛰다 (to move or walk in a lively manner)

The ball bounced down the stairs.

(공이 계단 아래로 굴러갔다.)

calculate / 계산하다, 산정하다 (to figure or estimate)

How much do you calculate the new golf club will cost?

(그 새 골프채가 얼마인지 계산할 수 있느냐?)

challenge / 도전하다, 요구하다 (to invite somebody to enter a competition or fight)

Their objections challenged me to think of better arguments for my ideas.

(그들의 반대로 나는 내 의견에 대한 더 좋은 논점을 생각해야 했다.)

confirm / 확실히 하다, 승인하다 (to render valid by formal assent, to strengthen)

He refused to deny or confirm.

(그는 부정도 긍정도 하지 않았다.)

crash / 무너지다, 부서지다 (to break or fall to pieces, to collapse or fail suddenly)

The stock market crashed.

(주식시장이 붕괴하였다.)

draw / 끌다, 당기다, 그리다(to make pictures, attract)

The concert drew a large audience.

(연주회는 많은 관중을 끌어들였다.)

drain / 배수하다, 빠지다 (to become empty or dry)

His anger is slowly draining away.

(그의 분노가 서서히 사그라들고 있다.)

drift / 표류하다, 표류시키다 (to be carried along by a current, to move easily or gradually)

Ash clouds can drift thousands of miles from an erupting volcano.

(분출하는 화산으로부터 화산재가 수천 마일 떠내려갈 수 있다.)

glorify / 찬미하다, 찬송하다 (to praise or worship)

It's very easy to glorify the past.

(과거를 미화하는 것은 매우 쉽다.)

injure / 상처를 입히다, 손해를 주다 (to hurt someone and cause damage to their body)

Nine people died and 55 were injured in the accident.

(그 사고로 9명이 사망하고 55명이 부상당했다.)

proceed / 나아가다, 전진하다 (to move or go forward or onward)

Our behaviour proceeds from hidden motives.

(우리의 행위는 감추어진 동기에서 진행된다.)

preserve / 보전하다, 유지하다 (to take care of a place in order to prevent it from being harmed)

The society works to preserve the district's historic buildings.

(그 모임은 그 지역의 역사적인 건물들을 보존하기 위해 일하고 있다.)

rise / 일어나다, 오르다 (to get up, to extend directly)

The tower rises to a height of 60 meters.

(탑은 60미터 높이까지 솟아있다.)

steer / 조종하다, 나아가다 (to guide or direct the course of)

The captain steered the warship into the port.

(함장은 군함을 항구에 운항하였다.)

trace / 그리다, 추적하다 (to copy an image by following the lines with your pencil)

He lifted his hand to trace the line of her cheekbone.

(그는 그녀의 광대뼈 선을 그리기 위해 그의 손을 올렸다.)

urge / 재촉하다, 몰아대다 (force or impel)

The senator urged against the confirmation of the appointment.

(그 상원위원은 그 임명의 비준에 반대하도록 촉구하였다.)

2. 연습문제

1. The best route to the lodge is marked on the _______ map.

   ⓐ attaching   ⓑ attached   ⓒ to attach   ⓓ attach

2. We lost the tennis ball because it _______ into the crowd.

   ⓐ bounded   ⓑ bounced   ⓒ bent   ⓓ moved

3. Can you _______ what our hotel bill is?

   ⓐ calculate   ⓑ approve   ⓒ count on   ⓓ accord

4. Did you _______ your room reservation at the hotel ?

   ⓐ affirm   ⓑ confirm   ⓒ confine   ⓓ define

5. All of the crew and passengers were afraid the airplane was going to _______ into the mountain.

   ⓐ faint   ⓑ deposited   ⓒ crash   ⓓ passout

6. Bob has _______ cartoons ever since he was about six years old.

   ⓐ drew   ⓑ drawn   ⓒ drown   ⓓ drone

7. After playing soccer, basketball, and swimming, the kids were _______ of energy, so they had to take a nap.

   ⓐ drained   ⓑ spread   ⓒ concluded   ⓓ spent

8. The Civil War was _______ in that movie.

   ⓐ glorified   ⓑ glory   ⓒ glorify   ⓓ glossy

9. Matthew broke his leg while he was playing soccer. He _______ himself.

   ⓐ depicted   ⓑ operated   ⓒ injured   ⓓ killed

10. The Millers planned to leave on their vacation early so they _______ at 5:00 am.

   ⓐ set forth   ⓑ set out   ⓒ set apart   ⓓ set about

11. It's hard to _______ a car in thick fog because you can't see where you're going.

   ⓐ steer   ⓑ step   ⓒ steel   ⓓ clutch

12. The travel agent is _______ us to buy our tickets right away. He's afraid we won't get seats on that flight if we don't hurry.

   ⓐ urging   ⓑ informing   ⓒ commanding   ⓓ making

13. Gregory copied the drawing by laying a thin sheet of paper over it and _______ it with a pencil.

   ⓐ drying   ⓑ rolling   ⓒ tracing   ⓓ dipping

14. Jane: Did John's team win last night?

   Linda: No, they _______ John's team 6 to 2.

   ⓐ run   ⓑ lose   ⓒ beat   ⓓ read

15. The boy _______ his friends to swim across the lake in 10 minutes.

   ⓐ challenged on   ⓑ challenged

   ⓒ challenged with   ⓓ challenged against

16. The excursion boat ______ slowly down the river with the slow current.

    ⓐ drafted   ⓑ dreaded   ⓒ drifted   ⓓ dodged

17. Always ______ a horse from the animal's right side.

    ⓐ put away   ⓑ pile   ⓒ mount   ⓓ leave out

18. The homes of famous people are often ______ as historical places.

    ⓐ raised   ⓑ resided   ⓒ rejected   ⓓ preserved

19. This photograph isn't clear. I can't ______ the people in the group.

    ⓐ implement   ⓑ defy   ⓒ distinguish   ⓓ simplify

20. Cartoon shows and reruns were doused heavily with ads for sugary breakfast foods, candy, and toys.

    ⓐ liquefied   ⓑ extinguished   ⓒ blamed   ⓓ loaded

21. It's time to board the plane.

    ⓐ leave   ⓑ live   ⓒ get off   ⓓ get on

22. The Statue of Liberty's outstretched arm beckons the humble, the poor and the disenfranchised of the world to come here to this land of opportunity.

    ⓐ allows   ⓑ calls   ⓑ oppresses   ⓒ stops

23. To enable its clients to tailor messages more specifically, the ad agency recently sliced the baby-boom generation into three sections.

    ⓐ design   ⓑ explain   ⓒ cut out   ⓓ announce

24. **Triggering** the "right" emotional response in a large group of people is not easy.
   - ⓐ Pulling the trigger
   - ⓑ Concealing
   - ⓒ Initiating
   - ⓓ shooting off

25. When you sell a kid on your product, if he can't **get it**, he'll throw himself on the floor and cry.
   - ⓐ convince him
   - ⓑ make a sale
   - ⓒ state a price
   - ⓓ give for nothing

26. Daniel couldn't decide whether to go by plane or by car. He kept **vacillating** between the two.
   - ⓐ showing great bravery
   - ⓑ calculating how much money the trip would take
   - ⓒ changing from one opinion to another
   - ⓓ introducing vaccine in to the body

정답 / 해석

1. ⓑ 오두막집으로 가는 가장 좋은 길은 첨부된 지도에 표시되어 있다.

2. ⓑ 테니스공이 군중 속으로 튀어 들어가서 공을 잃어버렸다.

3. ⓐ 호텔 요금이 얼마인지 계산할 수 있습니까?

4. ⓑ 호텔에 객실 예약을 확인했느냐?

5. ⓒ 모든 승무원들은 비행기가 산 속에 충돌할까 두려워하였다.

6. ⓑ 봅은 6살 때부터 만화를 그렸다.

7. ⓐ 축구, 농구 그리고 수영을 한 뒤에 아이들은 힘이 빠져서, 낮잠을 자야했다.

8. ⓐ 내란이 그 영화에서는 미화되었다.

9. ⓒ 매튜는 축구하다가 다리가 부러졌다. 그는 상처를 입었다.

10. ⓑ 밀러 부부는 일찍 휴가갈 계획을 하여서, 오전 5시에 출발하였다.

11. ⓐ 어디로 가는지 알 수 없기 때문에 짙은 안개 속에서 차를 운전하기는 어렵다.

12. ⓐ 여행사 직원은 우리가 즉시 표를 사도록 재촉하고 있다. 그는 우리가 서두르지 않으면 비행기 좌석이 없을
   까 두려워한다.

13. ⓒ 그레고리는 그림 위에 얇은 종이를 펼쳐 놓고 그 그림을 베끼고, 연필로 그렸다.

14. ⓒ 제인: 어제 밤 경기에서 존이 속한 팀이 이겼니?

   린다: 아니, 상대편이 존이 속한 팀을 6:2로 이겼어요.

15. ⓑ 그 소년은 10분내 그 호수를 헤엄쳐 건너기로 하고 친구들에게 도전하였다.

16. ⓒ 그 유람선은 느린 조류를 따라 강 아래로 천천히 떠내려갔다.

17. ⓒ 말을 탈 때에는 항상 말의 오른쪽에서 타도록 해야 한다.

18. ⓓ 유명한 사람의 집들은 종종 사적지로 보존되고 있다.

19. ⓒ 이 사진은 선명하지 않다. 나는 그 그룹에서 누가 누군지를 구분할 수 없다.

20. ⓓ 만화쇼와 재방영이 설탕이 많은 아침식사 대용 음식과, 캔디, 장난감 광고와 뒤덮였다.

21. ⓓ 비행기에 오를 시간이다.

22. ⓑ 자유의 여신상은 비천하고, 가난하고, 박탈당한 세상 사람들에게 여기 이 자유의 땅 으로 오라고 손짓하고
   있다.

23. ⓐ 의뢰인들이 메시지를 보다 세부적으로 만들 수 있게하기 위해서, 광고회사는 최근 베이비붐 세대를 세 부

분으로 분할하였다.

24. ⓒ 다수의 사람들에게서 올바른 정서적인 반응을 유발하기는 어렵다.

25. ⓐ 어린이를 설득하여 제품을 팔 때, 그 애가 그것을 사지 못하면, 그는 마루바닥에 몸을 던져 울게 된다.

26. ⓒ 다니엘은 비행기로 갈지 차로 갈지 결정할 수가 없었다. 그는 그 둘 사이에서 갈등하고 있다.

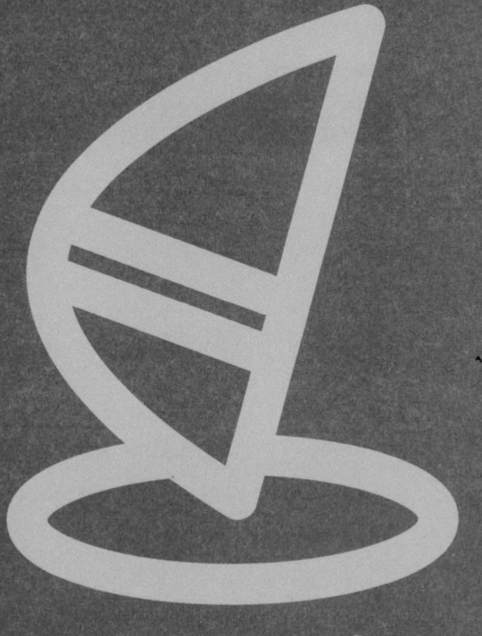

형용사

기본어휘 / 연습 문제

C

New American Language Course

either / 어느 한 쪽 (one or the other of two people of things)

Check or credit card - you can use either.

(현금이나 신용카드 중 어떤 것을 사용하실 겁니까? 어떤 것이라도 괜찮습니다.)

indefinite / 불명확한, 무기한의 (continuing in the future with no fixed end)

He is on indefinite sick leave.

(그는 무기한 병가 중이다.)

intimate / 친밀한, 잘 아는 (very familiar, closely acquainted)

Americans usually do not stand close to one another unless they are intimate.

(미국인들은 친하지 않으면 서로 가까이 서지 않는다.)

overseas / 해외(로 부터)의 (happening across the ocean from your country)

The number of overseas visitors is increasing every year.

(외국 관광객의 수가 매년 늘어나고 있다.)

professional / 직업의, 직업상, 전문적인 (earing one's living from an activity)

The doctor has been charged with professional misconduct.

(의사는 직업상의 비행으로 고발당했다.)

similarly / 유사하게, 비슷하게 (in the same way)

The Japanese people are similarly dressed when traveling in other countries.

(일본사람들은 다른 나라에 여행할 때 비슷한 옷차림을 한다.)

smooth / 매끄러운, 순조로운 (causing no difficulty, problems, or delays)

We are changing systems, but we expect a smooth transition.

(우리는 시스템을 바꾸고 있다. 하지만 부드러운 변화를 기대한다.)

tremendous / 무서운, 커다란 (very large, enormous)

His departure will be a tremendous loss for our school.

(그가 떠나는 것은 우리 학교에 매우 큰 손실이다.)

typical / 전형적인, 표준이 되는 (normal, representative)

He has the mannerism typical of his class.

(그는 자기 부류의 사람에게 전형적인 메너리즘을 가지고 있다.)

worth / 가치가 있는 (worthy of, meriting)

The leathers is worth 1 million won.

(그 가죽옷은 백만 원이다.)

2. 연습문제

1. You don't _______ want to go to the movies this evening, do you?
   ⓐ overall　　　ⓑ actually　　　ⓒ comparatively　　　ⓓ rarely

2. All the tickets to the game have been sold None are _______ .
   ⓐ sold　　　ⓑ available　　　ⓒ passing　　　ⓒ included

3. We can't go swimming because we don't have a _______ suit.
   ⓐ bathing　　　ⓑ bath　　　ⓒ bathed　　　ⓓ bathe

4. Mike: Which movie do you want to see?
   Mane: _______ one is okay with me.
   ⓐ Either　　　ⓑ None　　　ⓒ Furthermore　　　ⓓ Likewise

5. We're traveling to Europe and Asia this fall. We're going _______ .
   ⓐ foreign　　　ⓑ domestic　　　ⓒ country　　　ⓓ abroad

6. Yoon's travel plans are _______ . He doesn't know yet when he'll get his vacation time.
   ⓐ point out　　　ⓑ without doubt　　　ⓒ indefinite　　　ⓓ definite

7. Adam performs in musical comedies. Henry _______ acts in humorous plays.
   ⓐ rather than　　　　　　ⓑ neither
   ⓒ likewise　　　　　　ⓓ because of

8. Brian took a trip to Africa this past summer. He went ______ .

   ⓐ city   ⓑ alive   ⓒ overseas   ⓓ ocean

9. Maria: Is this a ______ edition of this magazine?

   Richard: Yes, I just received it last week.

   ⓐ dense   ⓑ recent   ⓒ rapid   ⓓ late

10. Donna and her brother play tennis ______ . Both of them stroke the ball very hard.

   ⓐ similarly   ⓑ moreover   ⓒ optional   ⓓ differently

11. The flight was very ______ . There were no problems.

   ⓐ occasional   ⓑ problematic   ⓒ smooth   ⓓ accidental

12. The Statue of Liberty in New York is ______ in size.

   ⓐ tremendous   ⓑ genuine   ⓒ numerous   ⓓ tiny

13. The actress is wearing a ______ dress of that time in the ceremony.

   ⓐ typical   ⓑ tropical   ⓒ tyrannous   ⓓ typology

14. The crew and passengers haven't gone aboard ______ .

   ⓐ already   ⓑ yet   ⓒ deck   ⓓ ship

15. The film was terrible! It certainly isn't ______ the price of the ticket.

   ⓐ amount   ⓑ worthless   ⓒ worth   ⓓ worthy

16. The name of Ellis Island soon became synonymous with all the loftiest hopes and dreams of a future in America.

   ⓐ brightest   ⓑ highest   ⓒ lowliest   ⓓ modest

17. The Statue of Liberty beckoned the disenfranchised of the world to a nation founded on the principles of freedom, individual dignity, and equality.
    - ⓐ without a business
    - ⓑ without organization
    - ⓒ without rights or privileges
    - ⓓ without hope or peace

18. The travel agent made such an alluring offer on a Caribbean cruise that we could not resist taking it.
    - ⓐ existing
    - ⓑ tempting; fascinating
    - ⓒ reasonable
    - ⓓ highly competitive

19. Some commercials have an ephemeral quality in that they don't last very long.
    - ⓐ lengthy
    - ⓑ permanent
    - ⓒ boring
    - ⓓ short-lived

20. The zany language was so cleverly used in the pizza commercial that it made us laugh.
    - ⓐ not understandable
    - ⓑ funny in a silly way
    - ⓒ childlike
    - ⓒ not practical

21. Advertisers don't tolerate eccentric copywriters, especially when they don't conform to the advertisers' standards.
    - ⓐ pleasant
    - ⓑ uninterested
    - ⓒ brilliant
    - ⓓ odd

정답 / 해석

1. ⓑ 너는 오늘 저녁 사실상 극장에 가기를 원하지 않지?

2. ⓑ 그 경기의 표는 모두 팔렸다. 한 장도 구할 수 없다.

3. ⓐ 우리는 수영복이 없어서 수영을 할 수가 없다.

4. ⓐ 마이크: 어떤 영화를 보러 갈래?

   메인: 어떤 영화도 좋아.

5. ⓐ 우리는 이번 가을에 유럽과 아시아를 여행할 것이다. 우리는 외국으로 간다.

6. ⓒ 윤씨의 여행계획은 불명확하다. 아직도 언제 휴가를 받게 될지 모르고 있다.

7. ⓒ 아담은 뮤지컬 코미디에서 활약하고 있다. 헨리도 또한 유머극에서 공연하고 있다.

8. ⓒ 브라이언은 작년 여름 아프리카로 여행하였다. 그는 해외에 갔다.

9. ⓑ 마리아: 이것이 이 잡지의 최신 판이니?

   리차드: 그래. 나도 바로 지난 주에 받았다.

10. ⓐ 도나와 그의 동생은 테니스를 유사하게 친다. 둘 다 볼을 매우 강하게 친다.

11. ⓒ 그 비행은 아주 순조로웠다. 아무런 문제도 없었다.

12. ⓐ 뉴욕에 있는 자유의 여신상은 엄청나게 크다.

13. ⓐ 여배우는 그 예식에서 그 시대의 전형적인 복장을 하고 있다.

14. ⓑ 승무원과 승객들은 아직 탑승하지 않았다.

15. ⓒ 그 영화는 아주 나쁘다! 그 것은 표값의 가치가 없다.

16. ⓑ 엘리스 섬이라는 이름은 미국에서는 미래의 가장 고상한 희망과 꿈이라는 말과 동의어가 되었다.

17. ⓒ 자유의 여신상은 세상의 박탈당한 사람들에게 자유와 개인의 존엄성과 평등의 원칙하에 건설된 나라로 오 라고 손짓하였다.

18. ⓑ 여행사직원이 카리브해 순항에 대한 아주 매력적인 제안을 해서, 우리는 거부할 수가 없었다.

19. ⓓ 어떤 상업광고는 일시적인 성격을 지녀서 오래 지속하지 않는다.

20. ⓑ 우스꽝스런 언어는 피자광고에서 아주 교묘하게 사용되어 우리를 웃긴다.

21. ⓓ 광고주들은 별난 광고작성자들을 싫어한다. 특히 그들이 광고주의 기준에 맞지 않으면.

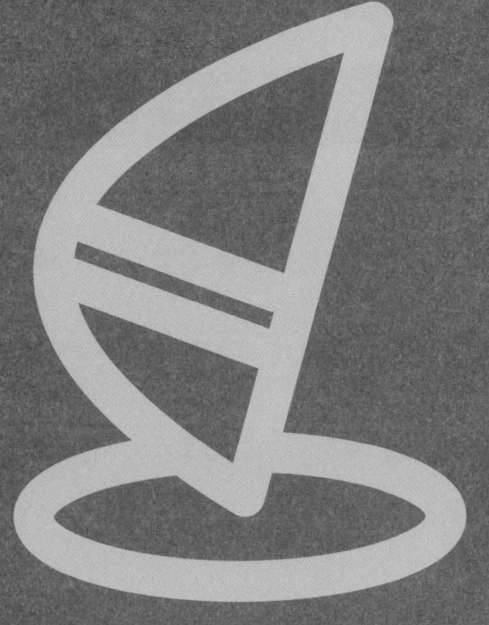

어휘, 관용구, 문형 종합

기본어휘 / 연습 문제

D

New American Language Course

1. 기본어휘 — 어휘, 관용구, 문형 종합

anyway / 어쨌든, 여하튼 (in any manner or way, at least, carelessly)

He wasn't qualified to apply for the job really but he got it anyway.

(그는 실제 그 직업에 지원할 자격이 없었지만, 여하튼 그 직업을 얻었다.

be about to / 막...하려고 하다 (to be going to do something soon)

The ship is about to leave port.

(배가 막 항구를 떠나려고 한다.)

fall apart / 산산조각이 나다, 깨어지다 (to break into pieces, disintegrate)

He tried everything to stop his marriage falling apart.

(결혼의 파탄을 막기 위해서 그는 모든 노력을 하였다.)

look forward to / 기대하다 (expect)

He had worked hard and was looking forward to working with you.

(그는 열심히 일했으며, 당신과 같이 일하기를 기대하였다.)

no matter how / 어떤 방식이라도 (however)

No matter how you smoke or chew tobacco can cause heart attacks.

(피우건 씹건, 담배는 심장마비를 유발 할 수 있다.)

set out / 출발하다, 떠나다 (to leave, to begin (a journey))

The ship is setting out for the island.

(그 배는 섬을 향하여 출발하고 있다.)

try out / 테스트해보다, 시험해보다 (to test something to see whether they are appropriate or effective)

John hopes to try out his new running shoes this weekend.

(존은 이번 주말에 그의 새 조깅화를 신어 보고 싶어 한다.)

turn (up) / 발굴하다, 발견되다 (to be found after being lost or not known about)

The police haven't turned up anything new, have they?

(경찰은 새로운 사실을 발견하지 못했죠?)

use up / 다 써버리다, 소모하다 (spend or consume completely)

We are using up the world's resources quickly.

(우리는 지구의 자원을 빠르게 소모하고 있다.)

watch / 살펴보다, 주시하다 (to look at someone or something for a period of time)

Have you been watching the presidential campaign?

(대통령 선거전을 살펴보았습니까?)

1. The movie that is being shown now was made 30 years ago. The movie _______ was made 30 years ago.

    ⓐ being shown that   ⓑ is shown now

    ⓒ now that it's shown   ⓓ being shown now

2. Their plans to go hiking for the weekend _______ when the typhoon hit.

    ⓐ got together   ⓑ fell apart   ⓒ withstood   ⓓ fell off

3. Always check your oil before you leave. _______ , you might want to check the tires.

    ⓐ Especially   ⓑ Eventually   ⓒ First of all   ⓓ In addition

4. You'd better hurry up. The commuter bus _______ leave.

    ⓐ were about to   ⓑ was about to

    ⓒ is about to   ⓓ be about to

5. John is excited about his trip. He's _______ it.

    ⓐ looking forward to   ⓑ giving for

    ⓒ believing in   ⓓ received on

6. I feel sorry that she could _______ sing _______ dance at all.

    ⓐ not/but   ⓑ both/and   ⓒ neither/nor   ⓓ not only/but also

7. Alli: Where's the museum?

   Sue: It's one block _____ the school.

   ⓐ far   ⓑ past   ⓒ next to   ⓓ on

8. Jennifer: How do you know the baseball game has been put off?

   David: I can't remember who told me, but _____ did.

   ⓐ anybody   ⓑ somebody   ⓒ something   ⓓ anything

9. Steve bought some weight lifting equipment. After class, we're going to his house to

   _____ .

   ⓐ take part in   ⓑ take it up   ⓒ try it out   ⓓ decide them

10. Wasn't that movie too scary _____ ?

    ⓐ watch   ⓑ to watch   ⓒ watching   ⓓ had watched

11. Henry: Did you find the map you lost?

    Burt: Not right away. It _____ two days later in my desk.

    ⓐ decides upon   ⓑ looked forward to
    ⓒ blew out   ⓓ turned up

12. There will be a baseball game this afternoon, except if it rains.

    ⓐ unless   ⓑ no matter what   ⓒ obstruct   ⓓ although

13. Is the woman who has the camera a professional photographer? Is the woman _____ a

    professional photographer?

    ⓐ with the camera   ⓑ whose camera has
    ⓒ has the camera   ⓓ that she has the camera

14. The Smiths would like to stay in Europe for a month, but they had ______ all of their money after only ten days.

    ⓐ gotten through   ⓑ used up

    ⓒ drop in   ⓓ kept away from

15. The grown-ups can see any movie they like.

    ⓐ whenever   ⓑ whichever   ⓒ however   ⓓ wherever

16. Most Air Lines ______ dinner on the plane.

    ⓐ serving   ⓑ are going

    ⓒ will serve   ⓓ going to serve

17. Lauren: What kind of car would you like to have?

    James: I ____ a sports car.

    ⓐ have wished   ⓑ I'd wished   ⓒ I wish that   ⓓ wish I had

18. You can travel anyway you want to.

    ⓐ however   ⓑ whenever   ⓒ whoever

19. Children's shows have become commercials for toys. The Federal Communications Commission (FCC) cracked down on this practice in 1969.

    ⓐ broke into pieces   ⓑ allowed legally

    ⓒ enforced stricter rules   ⓓ eliminated it completely

20. Creativity goes out the window when selling a toy takes priority over producing a good show.

    ⓐ is seen from the window   ⓑ is forgotten

    ⓒ is thrown out the window   ⓓ is developed rapidly

21. After the traffic light, keep going east on Highway 10.

    ⓐ process   ⓑ propose   ⓒ proceed   ⓓ persist

22. A group of housewives formed a group called Action for Children's Television (ACT) to change the development of commercials on children's TV. The group touched a nerve among the nation's parents.

    ⓐ aroused emotions   ⓑ started a disturbance

    ⓒ demanded satisfaction   ⓒ caused nervous breakdowns

23. Federal scrutiny of stations at license renewal time helped to keep the stations in line.

    ⓐ stay on one side of the street

    ⓑ keep them on the telephone line

    ⓒ make a complaint against them

    ⓓ make sure they adhere to regulations

24. Toymakers are juicing up their ads with fancy animation that was frowned on before.

    ⓐ making advertisements more appealing

    ⓑ drinking more juice

    ⓒ showing more juice advertisements

    ⓓ testing the fit or appearance of

25. James: Do you remember the name of that gorgeous island we went to in Greece?

Diana: It's on the tip of my tongue.

    ⓐ I know it, but I can't recall it right now.

    ⓑ Of course. I'll always remember it.

    ⓒ I remember it, but I can't pronounce it right.

    ⓓ I remember every place that we went to

26. Harry: Did we get authorization for this trip?

  Sally: No, it wasn't approved, but they said if we just go anyway, they'll look the other way.

  ⓐ reconsider approving it.   ⓑ pretend they don't know about the trip.

  ⓒ turn our request down again.   ⓓ reject their request

27. Adam prefers going to the rock concert rather than the symphony because classical music is not his bag.

  ⓐ Greg doesn't have the money to go to the symphony.

  ⓑ Classical music isn't one of his interests.

  ⓒ Greg left the ticket to the symphony in his suitcase.

  ⓓ Greg didn't afford to learn classic music.

28. A host of cheering fans crowded around the winning soccer team.

  ⓐ A small number of   ⓑ A large number of

  ⓒ Chief members of   ⓓ A small group of

29. Adam has diverse interests such as reading, playing the piano, and weight lifting.

  ⓐ uninteresting   ⓑ causing problems

  ⓒ noble and unique   ⓓ different and various

30. Because the two soccer teams have been bitter rivals for years, it was inevitable that they'd get into a fight on the field.

  ⓐ there was no fight on the field   ⓑ the fight was certain to happen.

  ⓒ the team are trying to avoid a fight   ⓓ the two teams decided not to play.

31. William plays tennis for a South Conference school and has been selected all-conference player. The South Conference is an association of school athletic teams in the southern part of the U.S.

ⓐ a player who has been chosen as outstanding in his conference

ⓑ a player who plays three sports in his conference

ⓒ a player who never plays outside his conference

ⓓ a player who scored most goals in his conference

32. Although Jack played football quite well, his coach used him as a second string player and allowed him to only during the second quarter.

   ⓐ superior   ⓑ substitute   ⓒ skilled   ⓓ useless

33. Having to pick the winner is not an enviable task. I'm glad I don't have to do it.

   ⓐ a challenging job   ⓑ a job desired by others

   ⓒ a time consuming job   ⓓ an unavoidable job

34. Lt Brown was planning to ride to Houston with us, but he backed out at the last minute.

   ⓐ left   ⓑ cancelled   ⓒ drove   ⓓ joined

정답 / 해석

1. ⓓ 지금 상영되는 영화는 30년 전에 제작되었다.

2. ⓑ 주말에 등산 가려던 그들의 계획은 태풍으로 인해 취소되었다.

3. ⓓ 출발하기 전에는 항상 연료를 확인하세요. 또한 타이어도 확인해야 합니다.

4. ⓒ 서두르는 것이 좋다. 통근버스가 떠나려고 한다.

5. ⓐ 존은 여행갈 생각에 흥분되었다. 그는 여행 가기를 손꼽아 기다린다.

6. ⓒ 그녀가 노래도 못하고 춤도 못추는 것이 유감이다.

7. ⓒ 알리: 박물관이 어디에요?

　　수 : 학교에서 한 블록 떨어져 있어요.

8. ⓑ 제니퍼: 야구시합이 연기된 것을 어떻게 알았니?

　　데이비드: 누가 말했는지 몰라. 그러나 누군가 말했어.

9. ⓒ 스티브는 들어올리는 운동기구를 샀다. 수업이 끝나면 우리는 그 운동기구를 시험하러 그의 집에 갈 것이다.

10. ⓑ 그 영화를 볼 때 무섭지는 않았나요?

11. ⓓ 헨리: 잃어버린 지도를 찾았니?

　　버트: 바로 찾지 못했어요. 2주 후에 내 책상에서 발견되었어요.

12. ⓐ 비가 오지 않으면, 오후에 야구경기를 한다.

13. ⓐ 카메라를 가진 여자는 전문 사진사인가?

14. ⓑ 스미스씨 가족은 한 달 동안 유럽에 머물고 싶었지만, 단 10일 만에 돈을 전부 써 버렸다.

15. ⓑ 성인은 좋아하는 영화는 어떤 것이든 볼 수 있다.

16. ⓒ 대부분의 항공사는 기내 식사를 제공할 것이다.

17. ⓓ 로렌 : 어떤 종류의 차를 갖고 싶으세요?

　　제임스 : 스포츠카를 갖고 싶습니다.

18. ⓐ 당신이 원하는 어떤 방식으로든 여행할 수 있다.

19. ⓒ 어린이 쇼가 장난감 광고가 되었다. 연방통신위원회는 1969년 이러한 관행을 엄격히 단속하였다.

20. ⓑ 훌륭한 공연을 제작하는 것보다 장난감을 파는 것이 우선되면 창조력은 사라진다.

21. ⓒ 신호등을 지나서, 고속도로 10번을 따라 동쪽으로 계속 가세요.

22. ⓐ 가정주부들이 어린이 TV에 상업광고가 확장되는 것을 변화시키기 위해 어린이 TV를 위한 행동이라 불리는

그룹을 결성했다. 그 그룹은 그 나라의 부모들의 심기를 건드렸다.)

23. ⓓ 면허갱신에 대한 연방정부의 엄격한 검사는 방송국들이 규정을 준수하도록 하는데 일조하였다.

24. ⓐ 장난감 제조업자들은 과거에는 눈살을 찌푸리게 하던 환상적인 만화영화로 그들의 광고가 재미있게 보이게 한다.

25. ⓐ 제임스: 그리스에서 우리가 갔던 그 멋진 섬의 이름이 기억나니?

다이아나: 내 혀끝에 맴돌아.

26. ⓑ 해리: 이 여행에 대해 허락 받았니?

셀리: 아니, 허락 받지 못했어. 그러나 우리가 여하튼 가면 그들은 눈감아 주겠다 고 말했다.

27. ⓑ 아담은 교향악 보다는 록 콘서트에 가기를 좋아한다. 클래식 음악은 그가 좋아하는 것이 아니기 때문이다.

28. ⓑ 환호하는 팬들이 그 승리 한 축구팀에 몰려들었다.

29. ⓓ 아담은 독서, 피아노, 역도와 같은 다양한 취미를 가지고 있다.

30. ⓑ 그 두 축구팀은 수년 동안 한 맺힌 적수 였기 때문에 그들이 필드에서 싸우게 될 것은 불가피하다.

31. ⓐ 윌리엄은 남부경기 연맹 소속 학교 테니스 선수로서, 연맹 최고선수로 선발되었다. 남부연맹은 미국 남부에 있는 학교 체육팀 연맹이다.

32. ⓑ 잭은 미식축구를 아주 잘했지만, 코치는 그를 교체 선수로 사용하여, 단지 2쿼터 동안만 활동하도록 허락했다.

33. ⓑ 승자를 선발해야 하는 일은 부러운 일이 아니다. 나는 그럴 필요가 없어서 기쁘다.

34. ⓑ 브라운 대위는 우리와 함께 휴스턴으로 갈 계획이었지만, 마지막 순간에 이를 철회했다.

New American Language Course

환경과 건강: 기후, 요리, 질병

5

A. 명사   B. 동사   C. 형용사   D. 어휘, 관용구, 문형 종합

ECL시험 대비 NEW ALC 필수어휘 완성

명사

기본어휘 / 연습 문제

A

New American
Language Course

advances / 진보, 진행 (progress)

Modern people can live longer because of advances in the medical field.
(현대인은 의학의 진보로 더 오래 살 수 있다.)

anesthetic / 마취제 (a drug that gets a man not to feel or respond to pain)

They gave the patient general anesthetic. (그들은 환자에게 전신 마취를 하였다.)

bandage / 붕대, 안대 (a strip or fabric for tying around a part of the wounded body, to wrap a bandage)

Don't bandage the wound too tightly. (상처를 너무 단단히 감지 마라.)

beam / 대들보, 광선 (a line of light or electric waves)

The approaching car's headlight were on full beam, so I couldn't see anything.
(다가오는 차의 헤드라이트가 매우 밝아서, 나는 아무 것도 볼 수가 없었다.)

blurry / 흐릿한, 더러워진 (difficult to see clearly, or causing difficulty in seeing something clearly)

For the time being, everything was blurry.
(잠깐 동안 모든 것이 희미하였다)

blood pressure / 혈압 (the pressure at which blood flows from your heart around your body)

Check your blood pressure every day! (매일 혈압을 확인하세요!)

chart / 도표, 해도 (a fact or an information given in the form of a graph or diagram)

The sales chart shows a distinct decline in the past few months.

(판매 수치가 지난 몇 달간 뚜렷한 하락을 보이고 있다.)

crop / 농작물, 곡물 (a plant grown for food, usually on a farm)

Tobacco is the state's largest cash crop.

(담배는 그 주의 가장 큰 현금원이다.)

destruction / 파괴 (damage that is so severe that something never returns to its normal state)

The building must be saved from destruction.

(그 빌딩은 파괴되지 않아야 한다.)

digestion / 소화, 동화흡수 (the act or process of digesting food)

Liquids interferes with the digestion of meals.

(수분은 음식의 소화를 방해한다.)

dirt / (진)흙, 오물 (soil or mud)

Groups of children were playing in the dirt.

(아이들이 진흙에서 놀고 있었다.)

disease / 질병 (morbid symptom, malady)

The first symptom of the flu is a very high temperature.

(유행성 독감의 첫 번째 징후는 고열이다.)

double / 이중의, 두배로 (consisting of two things or parts of the same type)

He went through the double doors. (그는 이중 문을 빠져 나갔다.)

emission / 방사, 발산 (discharge of fluid)
Exhaust emission systems are crucial for reducing air pollution.
(배기가스 방출 장치는 공기오염을 줄이기 위해 필수적이다.)

epidemiology / 병역학 (the branch of medicine that deals with the study of the causes, distribution, and control of disease in populations)
Medical studies include epidemiology, biostatistics, and health care research.
(의학에는 전염병학, 생물통계학, 건강연구가 포함된다.)

equator / 적도 (an imaginary circle around the earth equally distant from the North and South Poles)
The equator runs through parts of South Africa and Asia.
(적도는 남아프리카와 아시아의 일부를 관통한다.)

filling / 충전재, 충전물 (a thing used to fill something, material to fill a hole in a tooth)
I have two gold fillings in my teeth. (나는 두개의 금니가 있다.)

geography / 지리, 지형 (the descriptive science dealing with the surface of the earth)
The geography of the lodge is impossible to understand without a map.
(오두막집의 위치는 지도 없이 이해할 수 없다.)

handicap / 불리한 조건, 신체장애 (disadvantage, difficulty)
In case of severe mental handicap, he will not be promoted.
(여러 가지 정신적인 결함이 있을 경우에는 승진하지 못할 것이다.)

hardship / 고난, 곤란 (lack of comfort, suffering, difficulty)
These days many Koreans are suffering economic hardship.
(요즈음 한국은 경제적인 어려움을 겪고 있다.)

indications / 지시, 표시 (a sign that something will happen, is true, or exists)

The indications are that the economy has become more efficient and successful.

(그 신호는 경제가 더욱 효율적으로 그리고 성공적으로 흘러가고 있음을 말한다.)

interval / 간격, 거리 (gap, a space between two things)

There is an interval of 50 yards between street lamps.

(가로등 사이에는 50 야드의 간격이 있다.)

lung / 폐, 허파 (either of the two respiratory organs in the animals)

Lungs serve to remove caron dioxide and provide oxygen to the blood.

(폐는 이산화탄소를 제거하고, 혈액에 산소를 제공하는 역할을 한다.)

mass / 덩어리, 모임 (a body of indefinite shape and size)

The winter sky is often full of masses of snow.

(겨울 하늘은 종종 눈덩이로 가득 찬다.)

moisture / 습기 (small drops of water)

Moistures are misting up the windshield.

(습기가 앞 유리를 흐리게 한다.)

meteor / 유성, 운석 (any of the small solid extraterrestrial bodies that hits the earths's atmosphere)

We often see a meteor streak across the night sky.

(우리는 종종 밤하늘에 운석의 광선을 본다.)

measure / 재다, 측량하다 (to find the exact size, amount, speed, etc. of something)

We measured from the back of the house to the fence.

(우리들은 집 뒤쪽에서부터 울타리까지의 거리를 재었다.)

5. 환경과 건강: 기후, 요리, 질병

273

moisture / 습기, 수분 (very small drops of water)

The skin's natural moisture prevents sunburn.
(피부의 자연적인 습기는 볕에 타는 것을 막아준다.)

nerve / 신경, 용기 (the long thin thread in your body)

I need something to calm my nerves.
(나는 신경을 가라앉히기 위한 것이 필요하다.)

outskirt / 변두리, 교외 (outer area, areas away from the central area)

Because of the possibility of heavy pollution, the citizens of the city forced the company to build its factory on the outskirts of the city.
(심한 공해를 야기할 가능성 때문에, 그 도시민들은 그 회사가 도시 외곽에 공장을 짓도록 강요하였다.)

pharmacist / 조제사, 약사 (a person licensed to prepare and dispense drugs and medicines)

In Korea drugs and medicines are sold by a pharmacist.
(한국에서는 약품과 내복약을 약사가 판다.)

pharmacy / 약국, 약학 (a store where medicines are prepared and sold

Is there any pharmacy near your house? (당신 집 부근에 약국이 있습니까?)

precipitation / 강수량, 강우량 (rain or snow that falls)

Annual precipitation is increasing for several years. (매년 강수량이 수년 동안 증가하고 있다.)

ranch / 목장, 농장 (a very large farm where cows, horses, or sheep are kept)

The ranch over there produces a particular animal.
(저 너머 목장에서는 특수한 동물을 기른다.)

respite / 중간 휴식, 유예 (rest, break)

After studying for three hours, the young boy took a short respite before continuing.
(3시간동안 공부한 뒤에 그 어린 소년은 계속하기에 앞서 짧은 휴식을 취했다.)

scenery / 풍경, 경치 (features of a landscape)

The tourists are enjoying the beautiful scenery.
(관광객들은 아름다운 경치를 즐기고 있다.)

skeleton / 골격, 해골 (the set of bones that supports a human or animal body)

He dug up some bones from a human skeleton.
(그는 사람의 골격으로부터 뼈를 파내고 있었다.)

soil / 흙, 토양 (the top layer of the earth)

The area is covered with sandy and chalky soil.
(그 지역은 모래가 많은 백악질의 흙으로 덮여 있다.)

strength / 힘, 기력 (the physical energy that someone has to lift or move things

I didn't have the strength to get out of bed)
(나는 침대에서 일어날 만큼의 기력이 없다.)

sweat / 땀 (liquid that forms on your skin when your are hot)

She wiped the sweat off her forehead with a towel.
(그녀는 타월로 이마의 땀을 닦았다.)

tension / 긴장, 긴장 상태 (mental or nervous strain)

Tension can easily build up when one is involved in a high-pressure career.
(긴장감이 높은 직업에 종사하면 쉽게 긴장이 쌓인다.)

thermostat / 온도조절장치 (a device that measures and controls the temperature)

A thermostat maintains a constant temperature. (온도조절기는 일정한 온도를 유지한다.)

torch / 횃불 (a piece of wood with a flame at one end)

Our country must carry the torch of freedom and toleration.
(우리나라는 자유와 관용의 횃불을 들고 가야 합니다.)

trash / 쓰레기 (rubbish, refuse)

The trash stinks badly, why don't you take it out right now?
(그 쓰레기는 악취가 난다. 지금 즉시 그것을 바깥으로 가져가라.)

vein / 정맥, 맥처럼 뻗히다 (branching vessels or tubes conveying blood, to extend over or through)

Broad new highways vein the countryside. (넓고 새로운 고속도로가 시골길에 뻗는다.)

vision / 시력, 통찰 (the ability to perceive something, the act or power of anticipating)

We need strategic vision for our future life. (미래에 대한 전략적인 전망이 필요하다.)

view / 전망, 조망 (sight or vision)

We have a clear view of the gulf from our farm. (우리 농장에서는 해안이 잘 보인다.)

wells / 우물, 광천 (a deep hole in the ground)

The cameras are used to detect leaks in oil wells and pipelines.
(그 카메라는 유정과 정유관의 누수를 파악하기 위해서 사용된다.)

zone / 지대, 지역 (an area or region), 구획하다

The country is in an earthquake zone. (그 나라는 지진대에 있다.)
The property could now be zoned commercial. (그 땅은 이제 상업지구로 될 수 있다.)

2. 연습문제

1. Many doctors are making great ______ in curing cancers.

　ⓐ advances　　　ⓑ invent　　　ⓒ compulsory　　　ⓓ achieve

2. ______ are used so patients don't have to feel pain.

　ⓐ Antibiotics　　　ⓑ Anesthetics　　　ⓒ Allergy　　　ⓓ Amphibious

3. He looked thin after a few days in the hospital. His ______ wasn't so good.

　ⓐ appearing　　　　　　　　　ⓑ appeared

　ⓒ appearance　　　　　　　　ⓓ disappearance

4. You should cover the wound with a ______ .

　ⓐ procedure　　　ⓑ profile　　　ⓒ band　　　ⓓ bandage

5. Before Alexis saw the doctor, the nurse took her ______ .

　ⓐ blood pressure　　　　　　ⓑ leg

　ⓒ arm　　　　　　　　　　　ⓓ injury

6. We call it a ______ plant because it blooms only once every 100 years.

　ⓐ decade　　　ⓑ central　　　ⓒ century　　　ⓓ millenium

7. The doctor asked the nurse to bring the patient's record. He checks his ______ regularly.

　ⓐ dismiss　　　ⓑ attitude　　　ⓒ chart　　　ⓓ feature

8. A slice of _____ tastes good on a sandwich.
   ⓐ cheese   ⓒ sauce   ⓓ mayonnaise   ⓑ chocolate

9. We get milk from _____ .
   ⓐ cows   ⓑ pig   ⓒ horses   ⓓ plants

10. They will harvest the corn _____ later this month.
    ⓐ location   ⓑ crop   ⓒ crash   ⓓ forest

11. The heavy rains caused a lot of _____ in the valley.
    ⓐ cattle   ⓑ reflection   ⓒ fish   ⓓ destruction

12. Some people don't eat meat. Their _____ is made up of fruits and vegetables.
    ⓐ scale   ⓑ diet   ⓒ height   ⓒ weight

13. The process of _____ begins in the mouth where food is chewed and moistened.
    ⓐ organ   ⓑ concession   ⓑ distraction   ⓒ digestion

14. You were playing in the _____ . Don't forget to wash your hands.
    ⓐ fence   ⓑ dirt   ⓒ crop   ⓓ class

15. _____ includes all kind of illnesses and injuries that can lower the health of every
    individual.
    ⓐ Incidence   ⓑ Disease   ⓒ Epidemics   ⓓ Accident

16. I'm not hungry now. I just had a _____ dip of ice cream.
    ⓐ limited   ⓑ bounded   ⓒ double   ⓓ compact

17. Penicillin and sulfa are ______ .

    ⓐ drugs   ⓑ refreshments   ⓒ muscles   ⓓ bones

18. My son raises cows and sheep. He's a ______ .

    ⓐ farmer   ⓑ worker   ⓒ rancher   ⓓ hiker

19. My tooth is hurting again. I suppose my old ______ needs to be replaced.

    ⓐ filling   ⓑ feeing   ⓒ peeling   ⓓ pilling

20. The study of the earth's surface, shape, climate, and residents is ______ .

    ⓐ geology   ⓑ biology   ⓒ geography   ⓓ meteorology

21. His hearing loss has not been a ______ to this fine painter.

    ⓐ merit   ⓑ handicap   ⓒ characteristic   ⓓ talent

22. It won't be any ______ for me to be stationed in Korea because I have many friends there.

    ⓐ advantage   ⓑ hardship   ⓒ amusement   ⓓ suppression

23. The red sun sank quickly below the ______ .

    ⓐ beacon   ⓑ horizon   ⓒ holding   ⓓ bearing

24. James is the person who welcomes the guests at the Red Barn restaurant. He's the

    ______ .

    ⓐ flavor   ⓑ booth   ⓒ host   ⓓ taste

25. The lake's calm surface reflected the boat's ______ .

    ⓐ cycle   ⓑ scope   ⓒ level   ⓓ image

5. 환경과 건강: 기후, 요리, 질병

26. His cough and runny nose were _______ of a cold.

   ⓐ officials   ⓑ indications

   ⓒ departments   ⓓ positions

27. The storm warning on TV has been repeated at 20-minute _______ .

   ⓐ impacts   ⓑ intercourse   ⓒ internals   ⓓ intervals

28. The patients were impressed with the way the doctor treats them. He has a really good _______ .

   ⓐ unconscious   ⓑ conscious   ⓒ consideration   ⓓ manner

29. The doctor must wears _______ when he operates at the clinic.

   ⓐ mask   ⓑ flap   ⓒ goggles   ⓓ helmet

30. A continent is a large land _______ .

   ⓐ axis   ⓑ mass   ⓒ zones   ⓓ district

31. It feels humid today; there's a lots of _______ in the air.

   ⓐ atmosphere   ⓑ energy   ⓒ moisture   ⓓ moderation

32. The doctor injected the anesthetic into the _______ to relieve his pain.

   ⓐ nerve   ⓑ cavity   ⓒ nervous   ⓓ cave

33. A system of _______ connects the brain with the rest of the body.

   ⓐ nerves   ⓑ anesthetics   ⓒ needles   ⓓ limb

34. _______ must be able to read the prescriptions that doctors write for their patients.

   ⓐ Pedestrians   ⓑ Plumbers   ⓒ Physiologists   ⓓ Pharmacists

35. William went to the _____ to get some medicine.

ⓐ pharmacy ⓑ grocery ⓒ record ⓓ ground

36. The farmer _____ wheat and corn.

ⓐ planted ⓑ flies ⓒ grazed ⓓ destroyed

37. The fine light snow feels like _____ .

ⓐ a firearm ⓑ powder ⓒ a cartridge ⓓ shells

38. They raise horses on a _____ .

ⓐ boat ⓑ ship ⓒ jet ⓓ ranch

39. We should preserve all of our natural _____ such as oil, iron, and forests.

ⓐ prophecy ⓑ confusion ⓒ resources ⓓ discourses

40. Jejudo is famous for its beautiful _____ .

ⓐ scenery ⓑ density ⓒ industry ⓓ irrigation

41. The nurse told the young girl to go to the waiting room and take a _____ .

ⓐ home ⓑ pulse ⓒ view ⓓ seat

42. Tyler has never seen anything. He lost his _____ at birth.

ⓐ site ⓑ sight ⓒ seat ⓓ cite

43. The _____ supports the human body.

ⓐ core ⓑ brain ⓒ skeleton ⓓ kidney

44. There's some _____ stuck to the bottom of my boots.
ⓐ soil ⓑ muddy ⓒ floor ⓓ sting

45. Jane has been sick for a long time. I don't think she has enough _____ to get up.
ⓐ age ⓑ length ⓒ line ⓓ strength

46. The officer is feeling his blood pressure going up because he's under so much _____ at work these days.
ⓐ obstacles ⓑ stress ⓒ problem ⓓ questions

47. Only a heart _____ can perform that kind of operation.
ⓐ physician ⓑ oculist ⓑ surgery ⓓ surgeon

48. The imaginary circle around the center of the earth is _____ .
ⓐ the latitude ⓑ the equator
ⓒ the geography ⓓ the geology

49. Jeremy got his hand too close to the flame of the _____ .
ⓐ rivet ⓑ tubing ⓒ torch ⓓ dining

50. A _____ is between mountains.
ⓐ valley ⓑ ocean ⓒ dirt ⓓ reflection

51. Did you find the best rocks in the _____ or the mountains?
ⓐ crop ⓑ valley
ⓒ temple ⓓ destruction

52. The ______ of the valley from the top of the mountain is fantastic.

   ⓐ obstacle   ⓑ view   ⓒ review   ⓓ floor

53. Christopher has trouble seeing at night these days. His night ______ seems to become poor.

   ⓐ expectation   ⓑ skill   ⓒ vision   ⓓ version

54. Before I got sick, my ______ was 125 pounds.

   ⓐ width   ⓑ measure   ⓒ weight   ⓓ height

55. The medical assistant took her to a dark room for an ______ .

   ⓐ Xerox   ⓑ x-ray   ⓒ eyesight   ⓓ exchange

56. There is an hour between these two time ______ .

   ⓐ masses   ⓑ zones   ⓒ axis   ⓓ volume

57. The roe deer looked frozen in the ______ of the flashlight; it couldn't move.

   ⓐ beam   ⓑ laser   ⓒ bean   ⓑ razor

58. A ______ is a part of the body used for breathing.

   ⓐ barometer   ⓑ heart   ⓒ lung   ⓓ layer

59. We need to get some ______ in a few days or the water level of this reservoir will be quite low.

   ⓐ prediction   ⓑ perseverance

   ⓒ precipitation   ⓓ preparation

5. 환경과 건강: 기후, 요리, 질병

60 When a person gets too hot, _____ helps the body cool down.

   ⓐ refreshment   ⓑ sweat   ⓒ polish   ⓓ break

61. The _____ of the new nuclear energy plant is situated five kms east of the city of Pohang.

   ⓐ side   ⓑ site   ⓒ sight   ⓓ cite

62. The _____ in our building doesn't work. The temperature is set at 72 degrees, but it's 60 degrees in here.

   ⓐ temper   ⓑ thermostat   ⓑ thermometer   ⓒ heat

63. Heating and air conditioning bills cost a lot here. Our _____ bills are always a little high.

   ⓐ lease   ⓑ utility   ⓒ rent   ⓓ laundry

64. It is well known that there are oil _____ in many parts of Texas.

   ⓐ ditches   ⓑ wells   ⓒ streams   ⓓ springs

65. There is no _____ on the moon.

   ⓐ air   ⓑ dust   ⓒ rock   ⓓ volcano

66. Without my glasses everything I see is _____ .

   ⓐ vision   ⓑ focused   ⓒ blurry   ⓓ audio

67. To clean up the air, all sorts of vehicle are required to have _____ controls.

   ⓐ emission   ⓑ breath   ⓒ epidemic   ⓓ emergent

68. A thermometer _____ temperature

   ⓐ measures   ⓑ gains   ⓒ scales   ⓓ catches

69. Where's the ______ ? I want to find out how many pounds I have lost.

    ⓐ scale   ⓑ height   ⓒ weight   ⓓ measure

70. A(n) ______ is a tiny tube that carries blood from the body back to the heart.

    ⓐ artery   ⓑ stream   ⓒ vein   ⓓ vessel

71. Craters were formed when ______ hit the moon.

    ⓐ satellites   ⓑ meteors   ⓒ dirt   ⓓ volcanoes

72. The moon is the earth's only ______ satellite.

    ⓐ surrounding   ⓑ weather   ⓒ natural   ⓓ artificial

73. The predicted storm is likely to hit today. Rain and high winds are imminent, so make whatever preparations you can while you still have the chance.

    ⓐ precise   ⓑ recent   ⓒ immediate   ⓓ strong

74. Don't throw trash on the floor. Put it in that basket.

    ⓐ bush   ⓑ resources   ⓒ waste   ⓓ tray

75. Since this terrain is so rough and bumpy, no road goes through it.

    ⓐ shield   ⓑ obstacle   ⓒ land   ⓓ cliff

정답 / 해석

1. ⓐ 많은 의사들이 암치료에 커다란 진전을 이루고 있다.

2. ⓑ 마취제는 환자가 고통을 느끼지 않게 하기 위해서 사용된다.

3. ⓒ 그는 입원해서 며칠 지나자 야위어 보였다. 그의 외모가 별로 좋지 않다.

4. ⓓ 상처를 붕대로 감아야 한다.

5. ⓐ 알렉시스가 의사에게 가기 전에 그 간호사는 그녀의 혈압을 측정했다.

6. ⓒ 그것은 100년에 단 한번 피기 때문에 100년 식물이라고 부른다.

7. ⓒ 의사는 간호원에게 환자의 진료기록을 가져올 것을 요구하였다. 그는 그의 수치기록을 규칙적으로 확인한다.

8. ⓐ 치즈 한 조각이 샌드위치를 맛있게 만든다.

9. ⓐ 우리는 암소로부터 우유를 얻는다.

10. ⓑ 그들은 이번 달 늦게 옥수수 수확을 하게 될 것이다.

11. ⓓ 그 많은 비가 그 계곡의 많은 부분을 파괴해 버렸다.

12. ⓑ 몇몇 사람들은 고기를 먹지 않는다. 그들의 음식은 과일과 야채로 이루어진다.

13. ⓒ 소화과정은 음식이 씹혀지고 적셔지는 입에서 시작한다.

14. ⓑ 너희들은 진흙 속에서 놀았다. 손 씻는 일을 잊지 마라.

15. ⓑ 질병에는 개인의 건강을 약화시키는 모든 종류의 질병과 부상이 포함된다.

16. ⓒ 나는 지금 배고프지 않습니다. 방금 아이스크림을 두 번 떠 먹었습니다.

17. ⓐ 페니실린과 술파제는 약이다.

18. ⓐ 내 아들은 소와 양을 기른다. 그는 농부다.

19. ⓐ 이빨이 다시 아프다. 과거의 금니를 교체해야 할 필요가 있다.

20. ⓒ 지구의 표면, 형태, 기후, 주민에 대한 연구가 지리학이다.

21. ⓑ 청각상실이 이 훌륭한 화가에게는 결점이 아니었다.

22. ⓑ 나는 한국에 친구가 많기 때문에 거기에 정착하는 데에는 어려움이 없을 것이다.

23. ⓑ 그 붉은 해는 갑자기 수평선 아래로 사라졌다.

24. ⓒ 제임스는 레드 반 식당에서 손님을 환영한다. 그는 남자 주인이다.

25. ⓓ 그 호수의 잔잔한 표면은 그 보트의 형상을 반사한다.

26. ⓑ 기침과 흐르는 콧물은 그가 감기 걸렸음을 알려주고 있었다.

27. ⓓ TV에서 폭풍경보가 20분 간격으로 되풀이 되었다.

28. ⓓ 환자는 의사가 치료하는 방법에 감동하였다. 그는 매우 태도가 좋다.

29. ⓐ 의사는 병원에서 수술할 때 마스크를 껴야 한다.

30. ⓑ 대륙은 거대한 땅덩어리이다.

31. ⓒ 오늘은 습도가 높다. 대기 중에 많은 습기가 있다.

32. ⓐ 의사는 그의 고통을 완화하기 위해서 마취제를 신경 속에 투여했다.

33. ⓐ 신경체계는 두뇌를 신체의 나머지 부분과 연결한다.

34. ⓓ 약사는 의사가 환자에게 쓴 처방전을 읽을 수 있어야 한다.

35. ⓐ 윌리엄은 약간의 약을 사러 약국으로 갔다.

36. ⓐ 그 농부는 보리와 옥수수를 심었다.

37. ⓑ 미세한 가벼운 눈은 분말처럼 느껴진다.

38. ⓓ 그들은 목장에서 말을 기른다.

39. ⓒ 기름, 철, 숲과 같은 모든 천연자원을 보존해야 한다.

40. ⓐ 제주도는 아름다운 경치로 유명하다.

41. ⓓ 그 간호사는 젊은 여자에게 대기실로 가서 자리에 앉으라고 말했다.

42. ⓑ 타일러는 아무 것도 보지 못했다. 그는 날 때부터 시력을 잃었다.

43. ⓒ 그 골격이 인간의 몸을 지탱하고 있다.

44. ⓐ 신발 밑바닥에 흙이 들러붙어 있다.

45. ⓓ 제인은 오랫동안 아팠다. 회복하기에는 아직 충분하지 않다고 생각한다.

46. ⓑ 그 장교는 요즈음 직장에서 스트레스를 많이 받기 때문에 혈압이 오르는 것을 느끼고 있다.

47. ⓓ 단지 심장 외과의사만이 그런 종류의 수술을 할 수 있다.

48. ⓑ 지구 중심을 두르는 가상의 선이 적도다.

49. ⓒ 제레미는 그의 손을 횃불 불꽃에 아주 가까이 하여 데었다.

50. ⓐ 계곡은 산과 산 사이에 있다.

51. ⓑ 그 계곡 혹은 산맥에서 최고의 돌을 찾았니?

52. ⓑ 산 꼭데기에서 본 계곡의 모습은 환상적이다.

53. ⓒ 크리스토퍼는 요즈음 밤에 사물을 잘 볼 수 없다. 그의 밤눈이 약화되는 것 같다.

54. ⓒ 아프기 전에 내 몸무게는 125파운드였다.

55. ⓑ 그 의료보조원은 액스레이를 찍기 위해 그녀를 암실로 데려갔다.

56. ⓑ 두개의 시간대에는 한 시간의 차이가 있다.

57. ⓐ 노루가 불빛이 비치자 얼어붙은 듯이 보였다. 노루는 움직일 수가 없었다.

58. ⓒ 폐는 호흡하기 위해 사용되는 신체의 일부이다.

59. ⓒ 며칠 안에 비가 오지 않으면 이 저수지의 저수량이 매우 낮아질 것이다.

60. ⓑ 아주 더울 때, 땀은 우리 몸을 식히는데 도움을 준다.

61. ⓑ 새로운 핵에너지 발전소의 부지는 포항시로부터 동쪽 5키로미터에 위치해 있다.

62. ⓑ 건물의 온도조절기가 작동하지 않는다. 온도가 72도에 고정되어 있지만 여기는 60도다.

63. ⓑ 여기는 냉난방비가 비싸다. 우리들이 내는 시설 사용료는 항상 비싸다.

64. ⓑ 텍사스의 여러 지역에는 유정이 있다는 것은 잘 알려져 있다.

65. ⓐ 달에는 공기가 없다.

66. ⓒ 나는 안경이 없으면 모든 것이 희미하게 보인다.

67. ⓐ 공기를 정화하기 위해서, 모든 차량은 배기 조절장치를 부착하도록 되어 있다.

68. ⓐ 체온계는 체온을 잰다.

69. ⓐ 체중계가 어디 있지요? 몸이 얼마나 빠졌는지 확인해보려고 합니다.

70. ⓒ 혈관은 신체에서 심장으로 피를 운반하는 작은 관이다.

71. ⓑ 분화구는 운석이 달에 부딪힐 때 형성된다.

72. ⓒ 달은 지구의 유일한 천연 위성이다.

73. ⓒ 오늘 예상되는 폭풍이 강타할 것 같다. 비와 강풍이 임박하니, 기회가 있는 동안 할 수 있는 모든 준비를 하라.

74. ⓒ 쓰레기를 바닥에 버리지 마라. 쓰레기통에 버려라.

75. ⓒ 이 땅은 너무 거칠고 험해서, 여기에 도로를 낼 수 없다.

동사

기본어휘 / 연습 문제

B

New American Language Course

1. 기본어휘   동사

adapt / 적응시키다, 순응하다 (to adjust to new or changed circumstances)

We will have to adapt to the change of the climate in future.

(우리는 미래의 기후변화에 적응해야 할 것입니다.)

affect / 영향을 주다, 침범하다 (influence)

Although meningitis can affect people of any age, young children are most susceptible.

(뇌수막염은 모든 연령의 사람들에게 영향을 주지만, 특히 어린애들이 걸리기 쉽다.)

apply / 적용하다, 지원하다 (request a job etc.)

We advertised three jobs, and over 60 people applied.

(우리는 일자리 3개를 광고하였다. 그리자 60명 이상의 사람들이 응시하였다.)

assure / 보증하다, 안심시키다 (convince, guarantee)

The mechanic assured me that my car would be ready tomorrow.

(그 기술자는 내 차가 내일이면 준비될 것이라고 확신하였다.)

boil / 끓다, 화나게하다 (to change from a liquid to a gaseous state, to be unable to repress anger.)

Any mention of the incident makes me boil over. (그 사건만 언급하면 나는 화가 끓는다.)

complain / 불평하다 (to say that you are not satisfied with something)

"It's far too hot," she complained.

("너무 더워요." 하고 그녀가 불평하였다.)

confine / 제한하다, 감금하다 (to restrict, to be kept in a small space)

The seamen concerned were confined to barracks.

(관련된 수병은 막사에 갇혀있었다.)

dismiss / 해산시키다, 해고하다 (to send away, to allow to leave)

At 11:50 the class will be dismissed. (11시 50분에는 수업이 끝날 것이다.)

dissolve / 녹이다, 녹다 (melt)

You can dissolve the sugar in a boiled water. (끓는 물에 설탕을 녹일 수 있다.)

elevate / 올리다, 향상시키다 (to lift up, raise)

They don't try to elevate the status of teachers.

(그들은 선생님의 지위를 올리려고 노력하지 않는다.)

encircle / 둘러싸다, 일주하다 (to completely surround something)

A high fence encircles the property. (높은 울타리가 그 땅을 둘러싸고 있다.)

endure / 견디다, 지탱하다 (experience, continue to exist)

The company endured heavy financial losses this year.

(그 회사는 올 해 심한 재정적 손실을 겪었다.)

fluctuate / 오르내리다, 변동하다 (to move back and forth or up and down)

Vegetable prices fluctuates every season in here.

(이 지역에서는 야채가격이 계절마다 오르내린다.)

gain / 얻다, 도달하다 (to get or achieve something)

In her final exam she gained a B grade.

(그녀는 기말고사에서 B 등급을 받았다.)

5. 환경과 건강: 기후, 요리, 질병

gripe / 불평하다, 괴롭히다 (to complain or grumble, to annoy or irritate)

His tone of voice often gripes me.

(그의 어조는 종종 나를 화나게 한다.)

import / 수입하다 (to bring in from a foreign country)

Korea spends lots of money importing food abroad.

(한국은 외국 식품을 수입하는 데 많은 돈을 쓴다.)

infect / 감염시키다, 영향을 미치다 (to affect or contaminate with gems, to affect so as to influence feelings or action)

His courage infected the others.

(그의 용기는 다른 사람들에게 영향을 주었다.)

inhale / 빨아들이다, 흡입하다 (to breathe in, draw in by breathing)

We inhale the polluted air when we smoke.

(담배를 피울 때는 오염된 공기를 들이 쉰다.)

irritate / 화나게 하다, 자극하다 (to annoy, to make sore or painful)

Some drugs irritate my stomach.

(어떤 약은 위를 자극한다.)

isolate / 고립시키다, 격리하다 (to set apart, to place alone)

The police tried to isolate the demonstrators in a side street from pedestrians.

(경찰은 샛길에 있는 시위대들을 보행자와 격리하려고 노력하였다.)

monitor / 감시하다, 추적하다 (to regularly check something or watch someone)

He will monitor and review company policy.

(그는 회사 정책을 확인하고 점검할 것이다.)

restrict / 제한하다, 한정하다 (to limit the size, amount, or range of something)

In Korea speed is restricted to 100 kms per hour in the highway.

(한국 고속도로에서 속도는 시간당 100킬로로 제한된다.)

relieve / 경감하다, 완화하다 (to free from pain or discomfort, to lighten)

Drugs relieve much of our pain. (약은 고통을 많이 완화시킨다.)

rub / 문지르다, 마찰하다 (move backward and forward)

My new shoes are rubbing against my toe, so I've got blisters.

(내 새 신발이 발가락에 마찰되어, 물집이 생겼다.)

saturate / 흠뻑적시다, 몰두시키다 (to make completely wet, to be thoroughly soaked, imbued, or penetrated)

Saturate the bandage with cool water before you put it on the burned area.

(화상입은 부위에 붙이기 전에 붕대를 차가운 물로 적셔라.)

skip / 가볍게 뛰다, 깡충깡충 뛰다 (to move forward by jumping)

The three girls were out in the courtyard skipping rope.

(그 세 여자 아이들은 안마당으로 나가서 줄넘기를 하였다.)

stress / 강조하다, 긴장시키다 (to emphasize, to give special importance to)

My father always stresses the importance of good health.

(나의 아버지는 항상 건강의 중요성을 강조한다.)

tap / 개발하다, 소모하다 (use up, deplete)

Nations need to be concerned about tapping their natural resources until they are exhausted.

(각 국가는 천연자원이 고갈되기 전에 그 사용에 관심을 가져야 한다.)

5. 환경과 건강: 기후, 요리, 질병

293

B 명사 / 환경과 건강: 기후, 요리, 질병

vanish / 사라지다, 자취를 감추다 (to go suddenly, disappear)
The cat vanished without trace. (고양이가 흔적없이 사라졌다.)

weigh / 무게가 나가다, 무게를 달다 (to have a particular weight)
The baby weighed 7 pounds when she was born.
(그 여자 아이가 태어날 당시 몸무게는 7파운드였다.)

wipe / 닦다, 지우다 (to clean or dry something by moving a cloth or something soft)
She wiped away her tears. (그녀는 눈물을 닦았다.)

wreck / 난파하대[시키다] (to severely damage a vehicle or building)
The town has been wrecked by the bombing.
(그 도시는 폭격으로 파괴되었다.)

2. 연습문제

1. As Mary is used to warm weather, it will take her a while to _____ living in a cold weather.

   ⓐ adjust to　　　ⓑ accomplish　　　ⓒ succeed　　　ⓓ object to

2. Sgt Martin: Did the weather _____ your winter vacation plans?

   Sgt Young: No, I didn't change them.

   ⓐ effect　　　ⓑ affect　　　ⓒ occur　　　ⓓ form

3. I left some soup _____ on the stove, so it got a mess.

   ⓐ boil　　　ⓑ boiled　　　ⓒ boiling

4. _____ a teaspoon of salt in a glass of warm water; then soak your sore finger in it.

   ⓐ Resolve　　　ⓑ Dissolve　　　ⓒ Involve　　　ⓓ Solve

5. Every person _____ going to visit their dentists.

   ⓐ threads　　　ⓑ treads　　　ⓒ dreads　　　ⓓ breathes

6. If a man is bleeding from a cut on his foot, you have to _____ his foot above his head.

   ⓐ elevate　　　ⓑ remove　　　ⓒ release　　　ⓓ rise

7. She _____ a lot of pain while in the hospital.

   ⓐ endured　　　ⓑ decayed　　　ⓒ enlarged　　　ⓓ resisted

8. James took aspirin after he _____ a headache.

    ⓐ got   ⓑ gets   ⓒ gotten   ⓓ has got

9. Our country must _____ coffee and bananas; it's too cold to grow these foods here.

    ⓐ import   ⓑ impart   ⓒ immigrate   ⓓ embroider

10. We _____ air when we breathe in.

    ⓐ melt   ⓑ exist   ⓒ inhale   ⓓ exhale

11. All the smoke in this room is _____ my eyes.

    ⓐ resisting   ⓑ irritating   ⓒ interfering   ⓓ irrespirable

12. The weatherman said it would be sunny today, but it's raining hard. You can't _____ his reports.

    ⓐ rely on   ⓑ deny   ⓒ prescribe   ⓓ describe

13. I need a lot of time to _____ from my knee injury.

    ⓐ recover   ⓑ discover   ⓒ uncover   ⓓ cover

14. Finally, her body became too weak to _____ another illness.

    ⓐ return   ⓑ resume   ⓒ result   ⓓ resist

15. He often _____ the sides of his head in order to get rid of a headache.

    ⓐ hugs   ⓑ rubs   ⓒ circulates   ⓓ filters

16. That mop is _____ with oil and grease ; you have to throw it away.

    ⓐ sunken   ⓑ scandalized   ⓒ saturated   ⓓ penetrated

17. Dylan cut his finger and _____ the blood with a clean cloth.

    ⓐ kept   ⓑ wiped   ⓒ digged   ⓓ treated

18. The heavy rain completely _____ our picnic last Saturday.

    ⓐ enjoyed   ⓑ called in   ⓒ wrecked   ⓓ rejected

19. The light _____ us to read at night.

    ⓐ enlist   ⓐ enables   ⓑ encounters   ⓒ endures

20. Was it easy to _____ eating English food when you were stationed in the U.K.?

    ⓐ adopt   ⓑ adept to   ⓒ adapt to   ⓓ apply to

21. Daniel and his brother are going to travel abroad. They _____ for passports.

    ⓐ cut   ⓑ postpone   ⓒ applied   ⓓ appointed

22. Mr. Garcia had been quite upset until the doctor _____ him that everything was okay.

    ⓐ discovered   ⓑ assured   ⓒ insured   ⓓ insisted

23. We can't _____ it when it's so hot! Please turn on the air conditioner.

    ⓐ overcome   ⓑ take   ⓒ bear   ⓓ beat

24. Michael has been staying in the hospital for two weeks. For the first week, he was _____ to his bed.

    ⓐ confined   ⓑ committed   ⓒ sticked   ⓓ defined

25. Joshua told us the soup was cold, the meat was salty, and the coffee was bitter. He _____ about the whole meal.

    ⓐ yelled   ⓑ complained   ⓒ scrubbed   ⓓ marched

5. 환경과 건강: 기후, 요리, 질병

26. The valley was _____ by snow-covered mountains.
   ⓐ amplified   ⓑ encircled   ⓒ overflowed   ⓓ actuated

27. The patient can't leave the hospital until next week. The doctor won't _____ him.
   ⓐ offer   ⓑ confine   ⓒ stick   ⓓ dismiss

28. The medicine cannot control this patient's temperature. It _____ from 38°C to 41°C.
   ⓐ plunges   ⓑ fluctuates   ⓒ undergoes   ⓓ flunks

29. He used to weigh 130 pounds, and now he weighs 150. He has _____ 20 pounds.
   ⓐ gained   ⓑ dieted   ⓒ diluted   ⓓ lost

30. The tourists were _____ because their hotel rooms were in a mess and the air
   conditioning didn't work in hot weather.
   ⓐ trimming   ⓑ griping   ⓒ protruding   ⓓ getting by

31. The wound got _____ because he didn't clean it properly.
   ⓐ installed   ⓑ infected   ⓒ invaded   ⓓ injected

32. The nurse _____ the baby's temperature during that night.
   ⓐ slammed   ⓑ breathed   ⓒ perspired   ⓓ monitored

33. If your arm is broken , you have to _____ its movement.
   ⓐ restrain   ⓑ restore   ⓒ replace   ⓓ restrict

34. I'm just going to faint. Please give me something to _____ the pain.
   ⓐ relieve   ⓑ endure   ⓒ receive   ⓓ resist

35. I do my exercises every day in the morning, but this morning, I ______ them because I got up late.

    ⓐ jogged   ⓑ skipped   ⓒ avoided   ⓓ examined

36. A: You didn't hear the physician ______ to the patient, did you?

    B: No, I just saw him read the chart of the patient.

    ⓐ be talked   ⓑ talk   ⓒ talked   ⓓ to talk

37. Jim likes to run. He's going to ______ a race on Saturday.

    ⓐ avoid   ⓑ skip   ⓒ take part in   ⓓ scan

38. His trouble seemed to ______ after he took the medicine.

    ⓐ induce   ⓑ vanish   ⓒ appear   ⓓ parish

39. All doctors are apt to ______ the need for exercise and a balanced diet.

    ⓐ stress   ⓑ emphasis

    ⓒ important   ⓓ strain

40. When I asked Steven to recommend a place to eat dinner, he ______ a Chinese restaurant in the suburbs.

    ⓐ informed   ⓑ contacted   ⓒ suggested   ⓓ regarded

41. When you don't know how to eat something properly at a dinner party, you should observe the other guests. You should ______ them.

    ⓐ show   ⓑ watch   ⓒ listen   ⓓ see

42. The man stole a loaf of bread from the store.

    ⓐ stalled   ⓑ hided   ⓒ brought   ⓓ took

43. We need to isolate those sick people.

    ⓐ separate   ⓑ train   ⓒ inject   ⓓ join

44. Jackson couldn't pass his flight physical because he wasn't able to discriminate between colors. Every time he saw the color red, he identified it as green.

    ⓐ to recognize all the colors clearly.

    ⓑ to treat all the colors fairly.

    ⓒ to recognize the difference between colors.

    ⓓ to see the distant object

정답/해석

1. ⓐ 메어리는 따뜻한 날씨에 익숙해 있으므로, 추운 날씨에 적응해 살려면 시간이 좀 걸릴 것이다.

2. ⓑ 마틴 부사관: 날씨가 당신의 겨울방학계획에 영항을 주었습니까?

   영 부사관: 아니, 나는 그 계획을 변경하지 않았습니다.

3. ⓒ 나는 수프를 난로 위에 끓도록 내버려 두었다. 그랬더니 덩어리가 되어버렸다.

4. ⓑ 소금 한 스푼을 따뜻한 물에 녹여라. 그런 다음 아픈 손을 거기에 적셔라.

5. ⓒ 모든 사람은 치과의사에게 가기를 두려워한다.

6. ⓐ 발에 상처가 나서 피가 나면, 머리 위로 발을 올려야 한다.

7. ⓐ 병원에 있는 동안 그는 많은 고통을 겪었다.

8. ⓐ 제임스는 두통이 난 뒤에 아스피린을 복용했다.

9. ⓐ 우리나라는 커피와 바나나를 수입해야 한다. 이곳에서 그러한 과일을 기르기에는 너무 온도가 낮다.

10. ⓒ 우리는 호흡할 때 공기를 들이쉰다.

11. ⓑ 이 방의 모든 담배연기는 내 눈을 자극한다.

12. ⓐ 기상관은 오늘 날씨가 좋을 것이라고 했다. 그러나 비가 많이 내린다. 그의 예보를 믿을 수가 없다.

13. ⓐ 나는 무릎 상처를 회복할 충분한 시간이 필요하다.

14. ⓓ 마침내 그녀의 신체가 너무 허약하여 다른 병에 저항할 수 없게 되었다.

15. ⓑ 그는 두통을 처치하기 위해서 종종 옆머리를 문지른다.

16. ⓒ 그 자루걸레는 기름과 유지로 젖어있다. 그것을 버려야 한다.

17. ⓑ 딜란은 손가락을 베고 깨끗한 천으로 피를 닦았다.

18. ⓒ 폭우는 지난 일요일 우리 소풍을 완전히 망쳤다.

19. ⓐ 불빛은 우리가 밤에 책을 읽을 수 있게 해준다.

20. ⓒ 영국에 있을 때 영국음식에 적응하기가 쉬웠습니까?

21. ⓒ 다니엘과 그의 동생은 외국 여행을 가려고 한다. 그들은 여권을 신청하였다.

22. ⓑ 가르사씨는 의사가 모든 것이 정상이라고 확인해 줄때까지 아주 우울해했다.

23. ⓒ 너무 더우면 참을 수 없다. 에어컨을 켜세요.

24. ⓐ 마이클은 2주 동안 병원에 머물고 있다. 첫주 동안 그는 병원에 갇혀있었다.

25. ⓑ 죠수아는 국은 식고, 고기는 짜고, 커피는 쓴 맛이었다고 말했다. 그는 식사 전체에 대해 불평하였다.

26. ⓑ 그 계곡은 눈으로 뒤덮힌 산들이 에워싸고 있다.

27. ⓓ 그 환자는 다음 주까지 병원을 벗어날 수 없다. 의사는 그를 보내지 않는다.

28. ⓑ 그 약은 이 환자의 체온을 조절 할 수 없다. 38도에서 41도로 오르내린다.

29. ⓐ 그의 몸무게는 130파운드였다. 지금은 150파운드다. 20파운드가 더 늘었다.

30. ⓑ 호텔방이 지저분하고, 더운 날씨에 에어컨이 작동되지 않았기 때문에 여행객들이 불평하고 있었다.

31. ⓑ 그 상처는 적절히 닦아내지 않았기 때문에 감염되었다.

32. ⓓ 그 간호사는 야간에 아이들의 체온을 주시하였다.

33. ⓓ 팔이 부러지면 움직임을 제한해야 한다.

34. ⓐ 기절할 것 같다. 고통을 완화 시켜 주세요.

35. ⓑ 나는 매일 아침에 운동하지는 않는다. 하지만 오늘 아침에 나는 늦게 일어나서 운동을 걸렀다.

36. ⓐ A: 너는 내과 의사가 그 환자에게 말하는 것을 들었느냐?

   B: 아니, 나는 그가 환자의 차트를 읽는 것만 보았다.

37. ⓒ 짐은 달리기를 좋아한다. 그는 토요일의 경주에 참가할 것이다.

38. ⓑ 약을 복용한 후 그의 고통이 사라진 것 같았다.

39. ⓐ 모든 의사들은 운동과 균형잡힌 식사를 강조하는 경향이 있다.

40. ⓒ 내가 스티븐에게 저녁식사 장소를 추천하라고 했을 때, 그는 교외에 있는 중국식당을 권하였다.

41. ⓑ 저녁 파티에서 어떻게 먹어야 할지 모를 경우에는 다른 손님들을 관찰해야 한다. 다른 사람들을 유심히 보아야만 한다.

42. ⓓ 그 남자는 가게에서 빵을 훔쳤다.

43. ⓐ 이 환자들을 격리할 필요가 있다.

44. ⓒ 잭슨은 색을 구별할 수 없었기 때문에 그는 비행신체검사를 통과할 수 없었다. 그는 붉은 색을 볼 때마다, 그것을 녹색으로 식별한다.

형용사, 어휘, 관용구, 문형 종합

기본어휘 / 연습 문제

C

New American Language Course

adjust to / 맞추다, 조정하다 (to change or adapt to)

Many students have trouble adjusting to the food in the U. K.
(많은 학생들은 영국 음식에 맞추기가 힘들다.)

allergic / 알레르기에 걸린, 신경과민의 (affected by an allergy)

She's allergic to milk. (그녀는 우유 알레르기가 있다.)

clear away / 제거하다, 치우다 (to remove, to take away)

She cleared away the food and made coffee for the guests.
(그녀는 음식을 치우고 손님을 위해 커피를 만들었다.)

conclusive / 결정적인, 최종적인 (final, decisive)

Because the test results were not conclusive, Carter's doctor will have to do exploratory
surgery. (시험결과가 확정적이지 않았기 때문에 카트의 의사는 조사를 위한 수술을 해야 할 것 이다.)

dispose of / 처분하다, 버리다 (to get rid of, throw away)

It is a little difficult to dispose of nuclear waste. (핵폐기물을 처리하기는 다소 어렵다.)

frazzled / 녹초가 된, 너덜너덜한 (tired or worn out)

Richard is an elementary school teacher with thirty small children who run around all day.
When he leaves work to go home, he feels frazzled.
(리차드은 온 종일 뛰어다니는 30명의 어린이를 데리고 있는 초등학교 선생님이다. 그가 직장을 귀가
할 때는 그는 녹초가 된다.)

give in / 굴복하다 (to stop competing or arguing), 제출하다

The champion refused to give in and went on to win the set.
(그 챔피언은 포기하지 않고 계속하여, 그 개임을 이겼다.)

get down to / 내리다, 착수하다 (descend, concentrate)

We should get down to the matter at hand.
(우리는 임박한 문제를 처리해야 한다.)

guard against / 경계하다, 대비하다 (take precautions against, prevent)

We should always guard against accidents. (우리는 항상 사고를 예방해야한다.)

go on / 계속하다, 지속하다 (to continue happening or doing something)

The meeting went on a lot longer than I expected.
(그 회의는 생각했던 것보다 더 오래 지속 되었다.)

harried / 피곤에 지친, 근심어린 (worried or tired)

Because of too much work and too little time, John always has a harried look on his face.
(일이 말고 시간이 없어서, 존은 항상 얼굴에 피곤한 모습을 하고 있다.)

poisonous / 유독한, 유해한 (harmful, destructive)

Dangerously high levels of poisonous chemicals were found in the lake.
(위험할 정도로 높은 수준의 유독성 화학물질이 호수에서 발견되었습니다.)

regardless of / 개의치 않고, 관계없이 (in spite of, without regard to)

We should endure regardless of all the obstacles. (우리는 모든 장애에도 불구하고 참아야한다.)

stick out / 튀어나오다, 돌출하다 (to project, to be noticeable or easily seen)

The limb stuck out from the trunk of the pine tree. (가지가 소나무 줄기에서 튀어 나왔다.)

5. 환경과 건강: 기후, 요리, 질병

swollen / 부푸어 오른, 부은 (increased in size as a result of an injury or illness)

Their eyes were red and swollen from the smoke.

(연기로 인해 그들의 눈은 빨갛게 부풀어 올랐다.)

take after / 닮다, 흉내내다 (to be or look alike)

I take after my mother in looks, but I've got my father's character.

(나는 외모는 어머니를 닮았으나, 성격은 아버지를 닮았다.)

turn up / 소리를 높이다, 밝게 하다 (to increase the amount of sound, heat, or light) h

Don't turn the TV up – I'm trying to read.

(TV 소리를 크게 하지 마세요. 책을 읽으려고 하니까요.)

up to / 감당할 수 있는, 종사하는 (capable of, fit for)

We chose him to be captain because he was up to the job.

(그가 그 일을 할 수 있기 때문에 우리는 그를 우두머리로 선택했다.)

2. 연습문제

1. David can't eat strawberries. He's _______ to them.

   ⓐ good   ⓑ allergic   ⓒ twisted   ⓓ perfect

2. _______ clouds are moving slowly towards the local area.

   ⓐ Rainy gray heavy   ⓑ Gray rain heavy
   ⓒ Rain heavy gray   ⓓ Heavy gray rain

3. When you finish your picnic be sure to _______ all your trash.

   ⓐ bring up   ⓑ get along   ⓒ dispose of   ⓓ get down

4. We went on a picnic _______ the heavy rain and cold weather.

   ⓐ despite   ⓑ without   ⓒ as far as   ⓓ in regard of

5. David didn't want to, but he finally _______ and went to the medical doctor.

   ⓐ gave in   ⓑ pass over   ⓒ fought off   ⓓ took on

6. Jeff couldn't _______ his weight , so he had to get out of the military.

   ⓐ lose track of his weight   ⓑ in charge of his weight
   ⓒ get his weight down   ⓓ throw his weight around

7. We should _______ sickness by eating well.

   ⓐ concentrate on   ⓑ cancel   ⓒ argue against   ⓓ guard against

8. If you want to lose weight, you have to _____ or exercise.

    ⓐ eat a diet   ⓑ go on a diet

    ⓒ have side dishes   ⓓ scale

9. When Tyler gets a cold, he treats it himself. He doesn't _____ .

    ⓐ take care of himself   ⓑ eat anything

    ⓒ take any medicine   ⓓ go to the doctor

10. The doctor examined Lauren's ankle.

    ⓐ He fixed it immediately.   ⓑ He cut it down

    ⓒ He gave her a prescription.   ⓓ He looked at it carefully.

11. Epidemiology is, in part, the study of _____ .

    ⓐ serious contagious diseases

    ⓑ communicable diseases when can be contagious

    ⓒ how and why a disease spreads

    ⓓ knowledge to solve the problems in the future

12. I like sweet potato; _____ , I don't eat it every day.

    ⓐ but   ⓑ however   ⓒ despite   ⓓ instead

13. Floyd was sure that he had the flu; nevertheless, he went to work this morning.

    ⓐ thus   ⓑ however   ⓒ therefore   ⓓ on the contrary

14. Kayla is a very good cook; _____ , she's often too tired to cook after she gets home from work.

    ⓐ therefore   ⓑ nevertheless   ⓒ such as   ⓓ however

15. It is a nice day though _____ pretty cold.

   ⓐ even if   ⓑ it is   ⓒ in spite of   ⓓ however

16. Air pollution is a problem ___ for advanced countries _____ for developing ones.

   ⓐ both/and   ⓑ neither/nor

   ⓒ either/or   ⓓ not/but

17. She couldn't help having the dental work done, _______ the cost and pain.

   ⓐ regardless of   ⓑ with regard to

   ⓒ even so   ⓓ in regard of

18. The dentist prescribed a special toothpaste for Daniel.

   ⓐ She made a new toothpaste to Daniel.

   ⓑ She described a new kind of toothpaste to Daniel.

   ⓒ She asked him if he used a this toothpaste.

   ⓓ She told Daniel to use a certain kind of toothpaste.

19. Sarah is ill.

   ⓐ She doesn't feel that way   ⓑ She's never felt better

   ⓒ She doesn't feel well   ⓓ She's went to work.

20. The European's nose _______ quite far from his face.

   ⓐ caught on   ⓑ stuck out   ⓒ put out   ⓓ stood still

21. Laura _____ her father. She has his hair, his nose, and his eyes.

   ⓐ keeps up with   ⓑ takes after

   ⓒ calls off   ⓓ take away

22. The "incidence rate" of a disease is __________ .

    ⓐ the number of sick persons in one country.

    ⓑ the number of times a person gets sick in his life

    ⓒ the number of people having the disease per 1,000

    ⓓ the number of people who get sick every year.

23. I didn't realize ______ .

    ⓐ was that insect poison   ⓑ was that a poisonous insect

    ⓒ that insect was poisonous   ⓓ that a poisonous insect

24. Smoking is a ______ our health.

    ⓐ threat to   ⓑ battle with   ⓒ defense against   ⓓ fighting with

25. In the winter, Martin ___ the heat when the room temperature is below 60 ° F.

    ⓐ continues   ⓑ stops   ⓒ turns up   ⓓ turns down

26. This is your first day home from the hospital. Are you sure that you are ______ going out?

    ⓐ up for   ⓑ up to   ⓒ up on   ⓓ up with

27. You'll feel better once you've seen the doctor.

    ⓐ when   ⓑ at once   ⓒ because   ⓓ once over

28. Because Mr. Wright is a cigarette smoker, he took issue with the company policy of no smoking in the building.

    ⓐ He disagreed with the policy.

    ⓑ He bought a magazine dealing with the subject.

    ⓒ He took some cigarettes without paying for them.

    ⓓ He was obliged to stop smoking.

29. Since no one volunteered to go and pick up the pizza, we decided to draw straws to see who would have to do it.

    ⓐ to determine by a matter of chance   ⓑ to decide whether to go or stay

    ⓒ to select several straws   ⓓ to put off the decision

30. Jacob's finger is swollen.

    ⓐ His finger is dizzy.   ⓑ He can't take off his ring.

    ⓒ His finger is long enough   ⓓ His ring keeps slipping off.

정답 / 해석

1. ⓑ 데이비드는 딸기를 먹지 못한다. 그는 딸기 알레르기가 있다.

2. ⓓ 짙은 회색구름이 천천히 그 지방으로 움직이고 있다.

3. ⓒ 소풍을 끝냈을 때에는 반드시 쓰레기를 처리하세요.

4. ⓐ 심한 비와 차가운 날씨에도 불구하고 우리는 소풍을 갔다.

5. ⓐ 데이비드는 원하지 않았지만, 결국 포기하고 의사에게 갔다.

6. ⓒ 제프는 몸무게를 줄일 수 없었다. 그래서 그는 재대해야 했다.

7. ⓓ 우리는 잘 먹어서 질병을 예방해야 한다.

8. ⓑ 몸무게를 빼고 싶거든 다이어트를 하거나 운동을 해야 한다.

9. ⓓ 타일러는 감기에 걸리면 자기 스스로 처리한다. 의사에게 가지 않는다.

10. ⓓ 그 의사는 로렌의 발목을 검사하였다.

11. ⓒ 전염병학은 부분적으로 어떻게 왜 질병이 퍼지는 가에 대한 연구이다.

12. ⓑ 나는 고구마를 좋아한다. 그러나 나는 그것을 매일 먹지는 않는다.

13. ⓑ 프로이드는 유행성 독감에 걸린 것을 확신했다. 그러나 그는 아침에 출근했다.

14. ⓓ 카일라는 훌륭한 요리사다. 그러나 그는 집으로 돌아가면 너무 피곤해서 요리를 할 수 없는 경우가 더러 있
    었다.

15. ⓑ 꽤 춥지만 화창한 날이다.

16. ⓐ 대기오염은 선진국뿐만 아니라 개도국에게도 문제다.

17. ⓐ 아무리 비용과 고통에도 불구하고 그녀는 이빨치료를 하지 않을 수 없다.

18. ⓓ 치과의사는 다니엘에게 특별한 치약을 처방하였다.

19. ⓒ 사라는 아프다.

20. ⓑ 유럽인의 코는 얼굴에서 아주 튀어 나왔다.

21. ⓑ 로라는 그녀의 아버지를 닮았다. 그녀는 머리, 코, 눈이 닮았다.

22. ⓒ 사고율은 천명 당 질병에 걸리는 사람들의 숫자이다.

23. ⓒ 나는 그 곤충이 독이 있는 것을 몰랐습니다.

24. ⓐ 흡연은 우리 건강에 위협이 된다.

25. ⓒ 겨울에 마틴은, 방의 온도가 화씨 60도 이하가 되면 히트를 높였다.

26. ⓑ 오늘이 너가 병원에서 집으로 온 첫날이다. 밖으로 나갈 수 있겠니?

27. ⓐ 의사를 만나면 나아질 것이다.

28. ⓐ 라이트씨는 흡연가였으므로 그는 건물 안에서 금연하는 회사 정책에 이의를 제기했다.

29. ⓐ 아무도 피자를 사러가기를 자원하지 않았기 때문에, 우리는 누가 해야 할 것인지를 위해 제비뽑기를 하기로 결정하였다.

30. ⓑ 제이콥의 손가락이 부풀어 올랐다.

New American
Language
Course

New American
Language Course

과학과 기술 6

A. 명사　B. 동사　C. 형용사　D. 어휘, 관용구, 문형 종합

ECL시험 대비 NEW ALC 必 필수어휘 완성

명사

기본어휘 / 연습 문제

A

New American Language Course

accomplishment / 성취, 수행 (successful completion)

Earning engineering degree was a big accomplishment for Daniel. (accomplish)
(공학사 학위를 받는 것은 다니엘에게는 큰 성취였다.)

alloy / 합금, 혼합물 (a mixture of two or more metals)

Steel is an alloy of iron, carbon, and other elements.
(강철은 철, 탄소와 다른 성분의 혼합물이다.)

altimeter / 고도계 (a device to measure how high it is from the ground)

An altimeter is used chiefly in aircraft for finding distance above sea level.
(고도계는 해발에서의 거리를 알기 위해 주로 비행기에서 사용된다.)

assembly / 집회, 모임 (the process of putting together)

The national assembly rejected the budget.
(국회는 예산안을 거부하였다.)

astronaut / 우주비행사 (a person engaged in or trained for space flight.)

Astronauts travel and work in a spacecraft.
(우주비행사는 우주선에서 항해하고 작업한다.)

attitude / 자세, 태도 (a position of the body, posture, aggressive behaviour)

I should abandon a pretty selfish attitude.
(나는 아주 이기적인 자세를 버려야 한다.)

axis / (지)축, 축선 (an imaginary line through the centre of an object)

Mars takes longer to revolve on its axis than the earth.

(화성은 지구보다 축으로 회전하는 데 오래 걸린다.)

blast / 돌풍, 폭발 (explosion, to run or destroy)

Indiscretion and arrogance can blast his good reputation.

(무분별과 오만이 그의 명성을 손상시킨다.)

board / 판자, 널판지 (a sheet of wood, cardboard, paper, etc)

When typhoons come people nail boards across the window.

(태풍이 오면 사람들은 창문을 가로질러 널빤지에 못을 친다.)

breakdown / 고장, 쇠약 (a failure to work or function properly)

get around : to go to a different place

The police must prevent the breakdown of law and order.

(경찰은 법과 질서의 붕괴를 막아야 한다.)

bubble / 기포, 거품 (a ball of air gas in a liquid)

Heat the milk until bubbles form around the edge of the pan.

(그 팬의 가장자리로부터 기포가 생길 때까지 우유를 끓이세요.)

capability / 역량, 가능성 (abilities or qualities to do something)

Our new computer system gives us the capability to branch out into new areas.

(우리의 새로운 컴퓨터체계는 새 영역으로 확장할 수 있는 능력을 준다.)

carbon / 탄소 (a nonmetallic chemical element found in many inorganic compounds)

Carbon compounds are the basis of all living things.

(탄소복합물은 모든 생물의 기초이다.)

contingencies / 우발적 사건, 부수적 사건 (a possible, unforseen happening that may cause a problem if it occurs.)

Effective leaders take into account future contingencies as part of their planning strategy. In doing so, they prepare themselves for whatever may happen.
(능률적인 지휘관은 자신들의 설계전략의 일부로 미래의 우발적 사건을 고려한다. 그렇게 함으로써 그들은 미래의 모든 상황에 대비하는 것이다.)

core / 핵심, 정수 (the most important or most basic part of something)

These 2,500 words form the core of the language.
(이 2천 5백 단어가 그 언어의 핵심을 이룬다.)

charge / 전하, 충전 (amount of electricity)

The proton has a positive electrical charge.
(프로톤은 양전기 전하를 가지고 있다.)

chopper / 헬리콥터 (a helicopter), 도끼

He wants to be a chopper pilot.
(그는 헬리콥터 조종사가 되기를 바란다.)

combustion chamber / 연소실 (a chamber, as in engine or boiler, where combustion occurs)

In combustion chamber, the gases from the fire become more thoroughly mixed and burnt.
(연소실에서는 불꽃에서 나온 가스가 보다 철저히 혼합되고 연소된다.)

composite / 합성[혼합]물 (compound)

The photograph is a composite of dozens of pictures put together.
(그 사진은 합성한 12개의 사진의 복합체이다.)

composition / 구성성분, 조직 (a mixture of several part or ingredients, a short piece of writing)

What is the composition of the lipstick? (립스틱의 구성물질은 무엇이냐?)

compound / 합성[혼합]물 (the mixture or combination of two or more parts or elements)

Soap is a compound substance. (비누는 혼합물질이다.)

cylinder / 원통, 원기둥 (barrel, a hollow figure with round ends and long straight sides)

Candles are shaped like a cylinder. (초는 원통모양이다.)

drawback / 결점, 약점 (disadvantage, shortcoming)

pitfalls / 함정, 예기치 않는 위험 (unexpected dangers)

The greatest drawback to insect robots is that, like their biological cousins, they often do dumb things. They're not smart enough to avoid many pitfalls.

(곤충로봇의 가장 큰 결점은 자신들의 생물학적 사촌과 마찬가지로, 종종 바보같은 짓을 한다는 것이다. 그들은 많은 예기치 않은 위험을 피할 정도로 영리하지 않다.)

echo / 메아리, 반향 (a noise that is repeated because the sound returns)

His argument contains clear echoes of 1980s free-market philosophy.

(그의 주장은 1980년대 자유시장에 철학을 명확히 반향하고 있다.)

electricity / 전기 (a form of energy that can produce light, heat, and power, etc.)

The machines run on electricity. (그 기계는 전기로 가동된다.)

emission / 방사(물) (gas that is sent out into the air)

Every firm must clean up industrial emissions.

(모든 회사는 산업 폐기물을 깨끗이 처리해야 한다.)

fuse / 신관, 도화선 (a piece of string or paper, a strip of easily melted material)

My hair drier stopped working. I suppose the fuse has gone.
(헤어드라이기가 작동하지 않는다. 도화선이 나간 것 같다.)

fuselage / 동체, 기체 (the main body of an aircraft)

A close investigation revealed minute cracks in the aircraft's fuselage.
(면밀히 조사한 결과 미행기의 동체에 미세한 균열이 있었다.)

friction / 마찰, 불화 (rubbing of one object against to another)

The U.S. experiences friction over North Korea policy.
(미국은 북한의 정책과 마찰을 겪고 있다.)

glue / 아교, 접착제 (to fix or attach firmly with adhesives)

We glued a model ship together.
(우리는 모형배를 접착제로 붙였다.)

gravity / 중력, 근엄 (the force that attracts the object)

Gravity acts between stars and planets.
(행성과 위성 사이에는 중력이 작용한다.)

grid / 격자, 모눈 (a pattern of straight lines that cross each other to form squares)

Each spreadsheet page is made up of a grid of columns and rows.
(각 매트리트 정산표 페이지는 가로 세로의 격자로 구성되어 있다.)

junk / 쓰레기, 폐물 (old or broken things)

You should get rid of all that junk in your garage.
(당신은 당신 차고에 있는 폐물들을 없애버려야 한다.)

kit / 연장통, 용구 (a small tub, equipment for some activity, a set of tools or implements)

I keep a repair kit in the trunk of my car. (나는 내 차의 트렁크에 수리상자를 보관하고 있습니다.)

light bulb / 전구 (a round glass from which light shines)

A light bulb is simply called a bulb. (백열전구는 간단히 전구라고 부른다.)

limit / 제한, 한정 (the greatest number or amount allowed, to restrict)

The sale of alcoholic beverages is limited to those over 20.

(알콜음료의 판매는 20세 이상의 사람들에게 제한되어 있습니다.)

latitude / 위도, 허용범위 (the distance north or south from the equator, freedom of action)

We should allow our children a fair amount of latitude.

(우리는 자녀들에게 상당한 행동의 자유를 허락해야 한다.)

likeness / 비슷함, 닮음 (sameness in form)

Ever since Homer envisioned "handmaids of gold resembling living young damsels" in the Iliad, humans dreamed of building machines in their own likeness.

(호머가 살아있는 젊은 처녀를 닮은 금으로 된 하녀를 마음속에 상상한 이래로 인간들 은 자신을 닮은 기계를 만드는 것을 꿈꾸었다.)

longitude / 경도, 세로길이 (the distance of a place east or west of the Greenwich meridian)

Meridians of longitude and parallels of latitude together form a grid by which any position on the earth's surface can be specified.

(경도의 자오선과 위도의 평행선이 함께 격자를 형성하며, 그로 인해 지구표면의 모든 위치가 정해진다.)

lubricant / 윤활유 (a substance fro reducing friction)

A lubricant is a substance to reduce the friction between two moving surfaces.

(윤활유는 두개의 움직이는 표면의 마찰력을 줄이는 물질이다.)

magnet / 자석, 자철 (a piece of iron that attracts objects, an object with a magnetic surface)

The magnet has attraction for iron.
(자석은 철을 끌어당긴다.)

molecule / 분자 (the smallest particle of an element or compound)

A salt molecule have a wide range of jobs inside our bodies.
(소금 분자는 우리 몸 속에 다양한 일을 하고 있다.)

myriad / 무수함, 많음 (great number, variety)

Insect robots are able to perform a myriad of useful tasks: In nuclear power plants they could clean up spills too dangerous for humans to handle.
(곤충로봇은 수많은 유용한 일을 할 수 있다. 원자력 발전소에서는 그들은 인간이 다 루기에는 너무 위험한 유출물을 처리할 수 있다.)

niches / 분야, 활동범위 (positions or roles)

"Insects do a good job in the world," says Hans Moravec, a senior researcher at Carnegie-Mellon University. "We thought there ought to be some niches insects robots fill fairly well."
(카네기 멜론 대학의 고등연구원인 한스 모라벡은 "곤충은 세상에서 좋은 일을 한다. 우리는 곤충로봇이 아주 잘 메워 줄 수 있는 몇 가지 분야가 반드시 있다고 생각한다."고 말했다.)

panel / 판벽, 틀 (a piece of metal, a compartment or pane of a window)

There are dials and switches over the control panel.
(제어판에는 숫자판과 스위치가 있다.)

radiation / 방사 (에너지), 복사 (a form of energy produced during a nuclear reaction)

There is a clear link between exposure to radiation and some forms of cancer.
방사선 노출과 어떤 암들과는 확실한 연관이 있다.

punch / 천공(기), 구멍을 뚫다 (to make a hole in something with tool or machine)

She held out her ticket for the conductor to punch.

(그녀는 안내원이 구멍 내도록 표를 주었다.)

ore / 광석 (a natural minerals or substance)

Metal ores can be found mixed with rock or clay.

(광물은 바위와 진흙에 섞인 체로 발견된다.)

reverse / 역전, 불운 (the back or rear of something, change to the opposite, defeat, misfortune)

These days people are suffering a serious financial reverse.

(요즈음 사람들은 심한 재정적 역조로 고통을 겪고 있다.)

rod / 장대, 긴 막대 (a long straight piece of wood, metal or glass)

The fishing rod bowed like a question mark.

(낚싯대가 물음표와 같이 구부러졌다.)

rust / 녹 (a reddish-brown substances formed on iron or steel)

As water rusts iron, idleness rusts our mind.

(물이 쇠를 녹슬게 하듯이, 게으름은 마음을 녹슬게 한다.)

solids / 고형물 (a substance having a definite shape and volume)

The baby is not yet on solids.

(그 아이는 아직 딱딱한 것은 못 먹는다.)

state / 상태, 형편 (the condition of matter, status, rank)

He dresses in a manner befitting his state.

(그는 형편에 딱 맞게 옷을 입는다.)

technician / 기술자, 전문가 (someone with technical training whose job involves using special equipment or machine)

That company employes twenty technicians.
(그 회사는 20명의 기술자들을 고용하고 있다.)

tin / 주석 (a soft light silver metal)

Tin is a chemical element.
(주석은 일종의 화학 성분이다.)

turbine / 원동기 (a machine through which liquid or gas flows and turns a special wheel)

Turbine receives its power from a wheel that is turned by the pressure of water, air or gas.
(터빈은 물, 공기, 가스의 압력에 의해 돌아가는 바퀴로부터 힘을 받는다.)

vacuum / 진공, 공허 (a space entirely devoid of matter, a space not filled, emptiness)

The trouble left a vacuum in his heart.
(그 문제는 그의 마음 속에 공허함을 남겼다.)

vapor / 증기, 김 (a gas which results from the heating)

Warmer air can hold more water vapor than cold air.
(따뜻한 공기는 차운 공기 보다 더 많은 물의 증기를 담을 수 있다.)

velocity / 속력, 빠르기 (speed)

Tigers can move with an astounding velocity.
(호랑이는 놀라운 속도로 움직일 수 있다.)

viscosity / 점성(도) (the internal friction of a fluid, thickness)

The viscosity of engine oil generally decreases in six months.
(엔진오일의 점도는 일반적으로 6달 지나면 떨어진다.)

volt / 전압의 단위 (a unit for measuring the force of an electric current)

The blaze was caused by an electrical fault when a 220-volt multi-plug adaptor set fire to the end of a mattress.

(화재는 220볼트 누전으로 다중 어댑터가 담요 끝에 화재를 일으켜 누전으로 발생하였다.)

voltage / 전압량 (electrical force measured in volts)

A transformer changes a voltage to a higher or lower voltage.

(변전기는 전압을 높게 또는 낮게 변화시킨다.)

2. 연습문제

1. Steel and brass are examples of ______ .

   ⓐ valleys   ⓑ alumnus   ⓒ alloys   ⓓ allies

2. I need your help with the ______ of my new model warship.

   ⓐ assemble   ⓑ assembly   ⓒ assembler   ⓓ assemblage

3. The earth spins on its ______ .

   ⓐ axis   ⓑ equator   ⓒ longitude   ⓓ latitude

4. A nuclear bomb ______ emits light, heat and radioactive particles.

   ⓐ blast   ⓑ blush   ⓒ bluster   ⓓ blur

5. Jack bought several ______ to repair the wooden fence.

   ⓐ goggles   ⓑ scissors   ⓒ boards   ⓒ pliers

6. A ______ of communication occurred and no word of the emergency got around.

   ⓐ surge   ⓑ breakdown   ⓒ discrepancy   ⓓ mall

7. There were air ______ coming up from the bottom of the fish tank.

   ⓐ coats   ⓑ bubbles   ⓒ piles   ⓓ chow

8. The bridge was suspended from huge steel ______ .

   ⓐ desk   ⓑ cables   ⓒ beacons   ⓓ bearings

9. _____ is a gluey substance used to hold things together.

    ⓐ Cement   ⓑ Carbon   ⓒ Ceramics   ⓓ Cereal

10. Magnets, like electricity, have two different _____ .

    ⓐ switches   ⓑ charges   ⓒ cords   ⓓ powers

11. Sea water is supposed to be a _____ of more than 70 different substances.

    ⓐ commission   ⓑ corrosion   ⓒ fuse   ⓓ composition

12. An aluminum can is shaped like a _____ .

    ⓐ thermometer   ⓑ cylinder   ⓒ piston   ⓓ thermostat

13. A saw is a _____ used to cut wood or board.

    ⓐ borer   ⓑ device   ⓒ tip   ⓓ motion

14. A type of high explosive is _____ .

    ⓐ cosmetics   ⓑ fuse   ⓒ dynamite   ⓓ congestion

15. She shouted and then heard the _____ of her own voice.

    ⓐ image   ⓑ echo   ⓒ picture   ⓓ grid

16. A steam iron is an _____ appliance. Be careful!

    ⓐ electricity   ⓑ electrical   ⓒ electrify   ⓓ elective

17. A(n) _____ is part of an electrical circuit.

    ⓐ magnet   ⓑ pole

    ⓒ electrode   ⓓ electron

18. If you are planning on entering the branch of industry that produces radio, TV's, etc., you must study _____ in college.
    ⓐ electronics ⓑ elective ⓒ electrodes ⓓ equipment

19. The main function of oil is to reduce _____ .
    ⓐ pressure ⓑ weight ⓒ friction ⓓ speed

20. John used _____ to hold two pieces of wood together.
    ⓐ rust ⓑ scissors ⓒ glue ⓓ goggles

21. _____ keeps the atmosphere from floating off into space.
    ⓐ Flotage ⓑ Buoyance ⓒ Gravity ⓓ Resources

22. To locate points on a map, use the _____ .
    ⓐ blip ⓑ grid ⓒ cycle ⓓ booklet

23. His drill made the small _____ in the gate.
    ⓐ rust ⓑ hole ⓒ device ⓓ knob

24. That truck looks like a piece of _____ , but it runs well.
    ⓐ gorgeous ⓑ dent ⓒ junk ⓓ luxury

25. The repairperson always carries his tool _____ in his truck.
    ⓐ kite ⓑ kitten ⓒ kit ⓓ instrument

26. She doesn't have the right size of _____ for her lamp.
    ⓐ light bulb ⓑ course ⓒ bubble ⓓ hinge

27. This bridge has a weight _____ of 4 tons. You may not drive this container truck across it.

    ⓐ limit   ⓑ landmark   ⓒ mark   ⓓ permit

28. _____ are often used in the construction industry to lift large pieces of equipment.

    ⓐ Flashlights   ⓑ Magnets   ⓒ Beams   ⓓ Columns

29. The _____ is the thin, narrow indicator on instruments which is also used for sewing.

    ⓐ nickel   ⓑ nail   ⓒ needle   ⓓ noodle

30. You can find many gauges on the instrument _____ of the aircraft.

    ⓐ panel   ⓑ flap   ⓒ mask   ⓓ boarding

31. _____ was needed to run the automotive equipment.

    ⓐ Output   ⓑ Cool   ⓒ Storage   ⓓ Petroleum

32. This machine can _____ a hole through 50 pages at one time.

    ⓐ punch   ⓑ show   ⓒ reveal   ⓓ slam

33. Overexposure to X-rays can cause _____ sickness.

    ⓐ radiation   ⓑ frequency   ⓒ check   ⓓ amplifier

34. The blade of this _____ has been too dull to cut wood.

    ⓐ screw   ⓑ saw   ⓒ hammer   ⓓ bolt

35. The three forms of matter are gases, liquids, and _____ .

    ⓐ solids   ⓑ layers   ⓒ elements   ⓓ atoms

36. _____ is used extensively for bridges.
    ⓐ Brass   ⓑ Steel   ⓒ Ore   ⓓ Aluminum

37. We'll have to get a(n) _____ to fix that computer.
    ⓐ bearing   ⓑ image   ⓒ technician   ⓓ seaman

38. Modern _____ makes our lives easier.
    ⓐ site   ⓑ manufacture   ⓒ technology   ⓓ terminology

39. The roof of the building is made of _____ .
    ⓐ wine   ⓑ rivet   ⓒ tin   ⓓ alcohol

40. Sally: What _____ of chair is it?
    Henry: It's an antique of dark wood.
    ⓐ seat   ⓑ weight   ⓒ material   ⓓ type

41. Electricity has many _____ . Powering electrical motors is one.
    ⓐ appliance   ⓑ shocks   ⓒ uses   ⓓ shorts

42. A _____ is a space which is empty of air.
    ⓐ vacuum   ⓑ volume   ⓒ voice   ⓓ velocity

43. The airspeed indicator tells you the _____ of the aircraft.
    ⓐ altitude   ⓑ velocity   ⓒ windproof   ⓓ aviation

44. A _____ is a unit of electrical force.
    ⓐ intensity   ⓑ beam   ⓒ volt   ⓓ resistance

45. The _____ was regulated at the transformer.
   ⓐ voltage   ⓑ magnet   ⓒ flashlight

46. We can find how high the plane is flying by looking at the _____ .
   ⓐ altimeter   ⓑ compass   ⓒ attitude   ⓓ altitude

47. The _____ of an airplane is the position of the nose or wing.
   ⓐ attitude   ⓑ alternation   ⓒ aviation   ⓓ altitude

48. _____ is an element common in diamonds.
   ⓐ Carbon   ⓑ Steel   ⓒ Zinc   ⓓ Copper

49. This washing machine has three rinse _____ .
   ⓐ voice   ⓑ cycles   ⓒ images   ⓓ echoes

50. The _____ of the earth is made of hot, liquid rock.
   ⓐ curvature   ⓑ frame   ⓒ core   ⓓ surface

51. Air and fuel are mixed in an engine's combustion _____ .
   ⓐ shells   ⓑ division   ⓒ chamber   ⓓ cartridges

52. We breathe in oxygen and breathe out _____ .
   ⓐ lungs   ⓑ nitrogen   ⓒ carbon dioxide   ⓓ oxygen

53. This large atomic reactor is a _____ of many machines.
   ⓐ contact   ⓑ corrosion   ⓒ composite   ⓓ component

54. Some people don't buy gasoline because all their tractors have ______ engines.

    ⓐ petroleum   ⓑ diesel   ⓒ triangle   ⓓ remote

55. Don't run the engine with the windows closed. The ______ of the fumes from the exhaust can be hazardous.

    ⓐ emission   ⓑ advances   ⓒ admission   ⓓ omission

56. Nina has worked on computers for 10 years. She has a lot of ______ fixing them.

    ⓐ instruments   ⓑ violins   ⓒ experience   ⓓ ability

57. Smoke is one kind of ______ .

    ⓐ pollution   ⓑ malfunction   ⓒ combustion   ⓓ exhaust

58. We need a match to light this ______ .

    ⓐ fuse   ⓑ kit   ⓒ fuss   ⓓ fury

59. The cockpit and the tail of a plane are part of the ______ .

    ⓐ propeller   ⓑ flaps   ⓒ fuselage   ⓓ engine

60. Thomas used ______ to adhere the article to the page.

    ⓐ stick   ⓑ glue   ⓒ a nail   ⓓ a bolt

61. Lines of ______ run parallel to the equator and measure distance north and south.

    ⓐ latitude   ⓑ longitude   ⓒ axis   ⓓ altitude

62. Oil and grease are two kinds of ______ .

    ⓐ filters   ⓑ lubricants   ⓒ coolants   ⓓ gasoline

63. Lines that measure distance east and west and run perpendicular to the equator are lines of _______ .

    ⓐ latitude   ⓑ longitude   ⓒ height   ⓓ altitude

64. _______ is the stuff things are made of.

    ⓐ State   ⓑ Matter   ⓒ Form   ⓓ Shape

65. Liquids and gases consist of tiny, moving particles called _______ .

    ⓐ atoms   ⓑ electrons   ⓒ droplet   ⓓ molecules

66. _______ is mined from the ground.

    ⓐ Ore   ⓑ Concrete   ⓒ Cement   ⓓ Ceramics

67. Can you understand the _______ concerning the velocity of fluids relative to pressure?

    ⓐ principle   ⓑ principal   ⓒ privilege   ⓓ property

68. A _______ pole has a deficiency of electrons.

    ⓐ positive   ⓑ negative   ⓒ magnetic   ⓓ neutral

69. If you want to drive your car backwards put the gear in _______ .

    ⓐ rotor   ⓑ rotation   ⓒ recital   ⓓ reverse

70. A long narrow bar made of wood or metal is called a _______ .

    ⓐ cane   ⓑ rod   ⓒ lash   ⓓ column

71. Matter usually exists in three _______ , or forms.

    ⓐ states   ⓑ spaces   ⓒ atoms   ⓓ barometers

72. They have to build three _____ to support the electrical lines.
   ⓐ trenches   ⓑ tunnels   ⓒ towers   ⓓ prisons

73. A _____ is a type of engine.
   ⓐ fuselage   ⓑ propeller   ⓒ turbine   ⓓ wardrobe

74. Water _____ is a gas.
   ⓐ state   ⓑ vapor   ⓒ molecule   ⓓ drop

75. Is this the normal _____ for the engine oil used in this car?
   ⓐ viscosity   ⓑ moisture   ⓒ glue   ⓓ attraction

76. There is almost no air in a(n) _____ .
   ⓐ vacuum   ⓑ atmosphere   ⓒ volume   ⓓ lung

77. Because he was speaking before a group of laymen, the doctor had to explain a lot of the medical terminology.
   ⓐ people who are brick layers
   ⓑ people outside the medical profession
   ⓒ people who are well educated
   ⓓ people who had special training and a high level of education

78. The ballast of immigration ships, made up primarily of rocks and gravel, was later used as landfill to enlarge the island.
   ⓐ bow   ⓑ large wooden logs
   ⓒ heavy stabilizing materials
   ⓓ floating object that is used to show ships and boats

정답 / 해석

1. ⓒ 강철과 황동은 일종의 합금이다.

2. ⓑ 나는 새 모형 전함의 조립에 너의 도움을 필요로 한다.

3. ⓐ 지구는 축을 기준으로 회전한다.

4. ⓐ 핵폭탄의 폭발은 빛, 열, 그리고 방사능 낙진을 방출한다.

5. ⓒ 잭은 나무 울타리를 수리하기 위해서 여러 장의 널빤지를 샀다.

6. ⓑ 통신이 단절되어 긴급사태에 대한 어떤 말도 전달되지 않았다.

7. ⓑ 생선 탱크 바닥으로부터 기포가 올라왔다.

8. ⓑ 그 다리에는 커다란 강철 케이블이 매달려 있다.

9. ⓐ 시멘트는 물질을 붙이기 위해 사용되는 접착성 물질이다.

10. ⓑ 전기와 마찬가지로 자석에는 두 극이 있다.

11. ⓓ 소금물은 70종류의 다른 물질의 혼합물이다.

12. ⓐ 알루미늄 캔은 원통모양이다.

13. ⓑ 톱은 나무나 널빤지를 자르기 위해 사용되는 도구다.

14. ⓒ 고성능 폭발물의 한 유형이 다이나마이트이다.

15. ⓑ 그녀는 소리친 후 자신의 소리를 메아리로 들었다.

16. ⓑ 스팀다리미는 전기기구이다. 주의하여라!

17. ⓒ 전극은 전자회로의 일부이다.

18. ⓐ 라디오, TV 등을 생산하는 산업에 취업하려고 계획하고 있다면, 대학에서 전자를 공부해야 한다.

19. ⓒ 오일의 주 기능은 마찰을 줄이는 것이다.

20. ⓒ 존은 두개의 나무토막을 붙이기 위해서 접착제를 사용하였다.

21. ⓑ 중력은 물체가 대기 속으로 떠올라 가는 것을 막는다.

22. ⓑ 지도에서의 위치를 확인하려면 격자를 사용하세요.

23. ⓑ 그는 송곳으로 문에 작은 구멍을 내었다.

24. ⓒ 그 트럭은 고물처럼 보인다. 그러나 잘 달린다.

25. ⓒ 수리공은 자신의 트럭에 항상 공구연장통을 가지고 다닙니다.

26. ⓐ 그녀는 그녀의 램프에 맞는 크기는 전구를 갖고 있지 않다.

27. ⓐ 이 다리는 4톤의 무게제한이 있다. 이 컨테이너 트럭을 다리 위로 몰고 갈 수는 없습니다.

28. ⓑ 자석은 무거운 장비를 들어올리기 위해 종종 건설업에서 이용됩니다.

29. ⓒ 바늘은 계기에 있는 얇고 좁은 표시계로, 바느질에도 사용된다.

30. ⓐ 비행기의 계기판에는 많은 계기가 있다.

31. ⓓ 석유 원유는 자동 추진장치를 운행하는 데 필요하다

32. ⓐ 이 기계는 한 번에 50페이지를 구멍 낼 수 있다.

33. ⓐ X-선에 오래 동안 노출되면 방사선 병을 앓게 된다.

34. ⓑ 이 톱날은 너무 무뎌서 나무를 자를 수 없다.

35. ⓐ 물질의 세 가지 형태는 기체, 액체, 고체다.

36. ⓑ 강철은 교량에 널리 사용된다.

37. ⓒ 우리는 이 컴퓨터를 수리할 기술자를 구해야 한다.

38. ⓒ 현대기술은 우리 생활을 더 편안하게 한다.

39. ⓒ 그 건물의 지붕은 주석으로 만들어져 있다.

40. ⓓ 셸리: 의자는 어떤 타입입니까?

   헨리: 검은 색의 나무로 된 오래된 고전풍입니다.

41. ⓒ 전기는 여러 가지 용도에 사용된다. 전기 모타가 그 중 하나이다.

42. ⓐ 진공은 공기가 없는 공간이다.

43. ⓑ 항공기의 속도계는 비행기의 속도를 알려 준다.

44. ⓒ 볼트는 전력의 단위이다.

45. ⓐ 전압은 변전기에서 조절된다.

46. ⓐ 고도계를 보면 비행기가 얼마나 높이 나는지를 알 수 있다.

47. ⓐ 비행기의 비행자세는 기수나 날개의 위치이다.

48. ⓐ 탄소는 다이아몬드의 일반적인 성분이다.

49. ⓑ 이 식기 건조기는 세 차례 헹구도록 되어 있다.

50. ⓒ 지구의 중심은 뜨거운 액체 바위로 구성되어 있다.

51. ⓒ 공기와 연료는 연소실에서 혼합된다.

52. ⓒ 우리는 산소를 호흡하고, 이산화탄소를 내뱉는다.

53. ⓒ 이 큰 원자로는 많은 기계들의 복합체이다.

54. ⓑ 어떤 사람들은 휘발유를 사지 않는다. 왜냐하면 그들의 모든 트랙터는 디젤 엔진을 사용하기 때문이다.

55. ⓐ 창문을 닫고 엔진을 운전하지 마라. 배기가스에서 나온 방출된 매연은 위험할 수 있다.

56. ⓒ 니나는 10년 동안 컴퓨터 관련 일을 하였다. 그녀는 컴퓨터 수리한 경험이 많다.

57. ⓓ 연기는 일종의 배기가스이다.

58. ⓐ 이 심지에 불을 붙일 성냥이 필요하다.

59. ⓒ 조종석과 비행기의 꼬리는 기체의 일부이다.

60. ⓑ 토마스는 그 페이지에 기사를 붙이기 위해서 접착제를 사용하였다.

61. ⓐ 위도는 적도와 평행하며, 남북으로 거리를 측정한다.

62. ⓑ 오일과 그리스는 두 종류의 윤활유이다.

63. ⓑ 동서로 거리를 측정하고 적도에 수직인 선이 경도이다.

64. ⓑ 물질은 사물이 만들어지는 덩어리이다.

65. ⓓ 액체와 기체는 분자라는 작고 움직이는 입자로 구성되어 있다.

66. ⓐ 광물은 흙에서 채굴된다.

67. ⓐ 압력에 대한 액체의 속도에 대한 원리를 이해할 수 있습니까?

68. ⓐ 양극은 전자가 결여되어 있다.

69. ⓓ 차를 후진하려면, 기어를 후진으로 하라.

70. ⓑ 나무나 금속으로 된 길고 좁은 막대기를 장대라고 부른다.

71. ⓐ 물질은 세가지 상태 또는 상태로 존재한다.

72. ⓒ 그들은 그 전선을 지탱하기 위해 3개의 탑을 만들어야 한다.

73. ⓒ 터빈은 엔진의 일종이다.

74. ⓑ 물의 증기는 기체다.

75. ⓐ 이것은 이 차에 사용될 엔진 오일에 맞는 정상적인 점도입니까?

76. ⓐ 진공에는 공기가 없다.

77. ⓑ 그는 일반인에게 말해야 했기 때문에 그 의사는 많은 의학 용어를 설명해야 했다.

78. ⓒ 이민선의 벨러스트는 주로 바위와 자갈로 구성되었으며, 후에 섬을 확장하기 위한 매립용 쓰레기로 이용되었다.

동사

기본어휘 / 연습 문제

B

New American Language Course

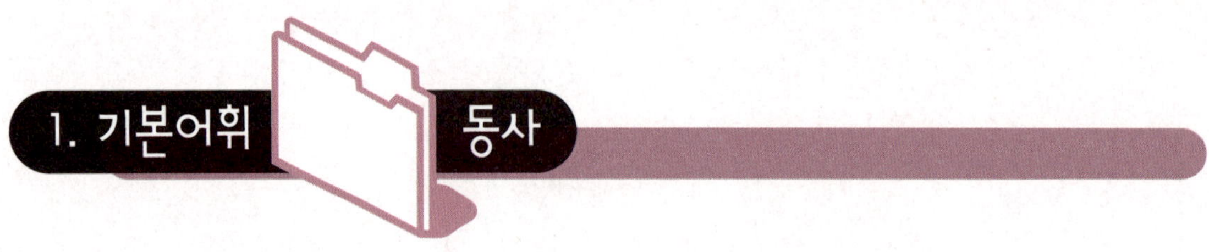

adjust / 맞추다, 조정하다 (to change in order to make it better or more accurate)

Stir in the lemon juice and adjust the seasoning.

(레몬 주스를 저으면서 조미료를 조절해 보세요.)

bother / 괴롭히다, 귀찮게 하다 (to worry, disturb, interrupt)

I don't want to bother you with my problems at the moment.

(나는 지금 내 문제로 당신을 괴롭히고 싶지 않다.)

cement / 시멘트(로 바르다) (a substance made of burned lime and clay, to join together using cement)

They cemented the front garden so that they could park the car.

(그들은 앞마당에 시멘트를 칠해서, 차를 주차할 수 있었다.)

circulate / 순환하다 (to move about, distribute)

In summer cooled air is circulated throughout the building.

(여름에는 서늘한 공기가 건물을 순환한다.)

coat / 덮다, 입히다 (to cover something with a layer of substance)

The wind had coated everything with a layer of sand. (바람이 모든 것을 모래로 덮었다.)

coil / 감은 것, 감다 (to wind into a series of circles)

He found a coil of rope on the beach.

(그는 해변에서 로프 묶음을 발견했다.)

compress / 압축하다, 다물다 (condense, press together)

She compressed her lips. (그녀는 입술을 깨물었다.)

compute / 계산[측정]하다 (to determine or calculate)

Compute the ratio of the column's heights and lengths.
(그 기둥의 높이와 길이의 비율을 계산하여라.)

contaminate / 더럽히다, 오염되게 하다 (to make impure, infected, and corrupt)

Much of our land are contaminated with toxic wastes and food.
(우리 대지의 많은 부분이 유독 폐기물과 음식으로 오염되었다.)

converge / 한 점에 모이다, 모아지다 (to meet in a point or line, come together)

The streets converge at a central square. (거리는 중심지에서 만난다.)

convert / 전환하다, 바꾸다 (transform)

They converted an automobile factory to the manufacture of tanks.
(그들은 자동차 공장을 탱크 제조업으로 바꾸었다.)

detonate / 폭발시키다, 폭음을 내다 (to explode violently and noisily)

In Baghdad there was a report of a bomb detonation in a crowded bus terminal.
(바그다드에서 번잡한 버스 정류장에서 폭탄이 폭발했다는 보고가 있었다.)

dissolve / 녹(이)다, 해체하다 (melt, be broken up)

The committees of our parliament have been dissolved. (우리 국회의 위원회가 해산되었다.)

distort / 찡그리다, 왜곡하다 (to change something so that it is no longer accurate)

The program presented a distorted picture of her life.
(그 프로그램은 일그러진 그녀의 생활의 한 단면을 보여주었다.)

corrode / 부식하다, 침식하다 (to destroy or be destroyed by chemical action, to eat by rusting)

Acid rain can corrode the metal pipes. (산성비는 금속 파이프를 부식할 수 있다.)

crush / 분쇄하다, 진압하다 (to press or squeeze with a force, to suppress or subdue)

They crushed the rebellion. (그들은 그 폭동을 격퇴했다.)

emit / 방출하다, 분출하다 (send out, give forth, discharge)

The crew didn't send out any distress signals.
(승무원들은 어떤 불편한 표시도 하지 않았다.)

evaporate / 증발하다, 증발시키다 (to change from a liquid or solid state into vapor, vanish)

His hope evaporated. (그의 희망이 사라졌다.)

exert / 발휘하다, 노력하다 (exercise as ability or influence)

You should exert every effort to pass the test.
(너는 시험에 통과하기 위해 모든 노력을 기울여야 한다.)

exhale / 내쉬다, 내뱉다 (to breathe out, emit)

The engine exhales steam. (그 엔진은 증기를 내뿜는다.)

exhaust / 다써 버리다, 소모하다 (discharge or release of used steam, gas, energy etc, use up)

Don't give up until you have exhausted all the possibilities.
(모든 가능성을 다 사용할 때까지는 포기하지 마라.)

exhibit / 전시하다, 진열하다 (to put something in a museum or other public place)

Where are you going to exhibit next?
(다음에는 무엇을 전시할 것입니까?)

expose / 노출시키다, 드러내다 (to leave without protection)

The soldiers were exposed to considerable danger.

(군인들은 상당한 위험에 노출되어 있었다.)

float / 뜨다, 표류하다 (to rest or remain on the surface of a liquid, to move lightly)

She floated down the stairs. (그녀는 계단 아래로 가볍게 내려갔다.)

gauge / 재다, 측정하다 (to calculate or measure, an instrument for measuring)

It's difficult to gauge how they will react.

(그들이 어떻게 반응할 지 예측하기가 어렵다.)

ground / 근거하다, 기초를 두다 (base, found)

Larson's research on sleep pattern is grounded upon the fact that younger people exert more energy that their older counterparts.

(라어손의 잠에 대한 이론은 젊은이는 나이든 사람보다 더 많은 에너지를 발산한다는 사실에 기초를 두고 있다.)

hoist / 올리다, 게양하다 (to raise, lift, pull up)

We must hoist the flag every morning.

(우리는 매일 아침 국기를 게양해야 한다.)

invent / 발명하다 (to come upon, to think out or produce)

The first safety razor was invented by K.C Gillette in 1903.

(최초의 안전면도기는 1903년 질렛에 의해 발명되었다.)

isolate / 고립시키다, 분리하다 (to set apart from others, to separate)

We can isolate a number of factors that contribute to a man's downfall.

(우리는 한 인간의 몰락에 영향을 주는 많은 요인들을 분리해 낼 수 있다.)

maneuver / 군사행동, 기동연습(을 하다) (manoeuvre (BE), to direct or guide with skill and dexterity, a planned and controlled movement)

In a well-rehearsed manoeuvre the navy swept into the port.
(잘 훈련된 기동작전으로, 해군은 항구에 급습하였다.)

melt / 녹(이)다 (to change from a solid to a liquid state)

Sunlight melts the snow. (햇볕은 눈을 녹인다.)

plot / 도모하다, 꾸미다 (to make a secret plan with other people)

He warned that they might be plotting a coup against the administration.
(그는 그들이 행정부에 대해 반란을 도모하고 있다고 경고하였다.)

pollute / 더럽히다, 오염시키다 (to make unclean or impure, contaminate)

Chemical fertilizers and pesticides can pollute the soil and the water supply.
(화학비료와 살충제는 흙과 상수원을 오염시킬 수 있다.)

propel / 추진하다, 몰아대다 (to drive or drive onward)

The tiny rocket is designed to propel the spacecraft towards Moon.
(우주선을 달로 발사하기 위해 작은 로켓이 설계되었다.)

remove / 옮기다, 제거하다 (to move away, to get rid of)

They are removing illegally parked cars in the street.
(그들은 거리에 불법 주차된 차를 견인하고 있다.)

repel / 격퇴하다, 저항하다 (to drive or force back, to resist)

We have troops along the border ready to repel any attack.
(국경을 따라 배치된 우리 군은 어떠한 공격도 격퇴할 준비가 되어 있다.)

revolve / 회전하다, 회전시키다 (to move in a circle around a central line)

The table is revolved by a small electric motor.

(탁자는 작은 전기로 회전한다.)

shape / 모양을 취하다, 적합하게 하다 (to fashion or form, to adjust)

He shaped everything to suit his taste.

(그는 모든 것을 그의 취향에 맞게 다듬었다.)

soak / 젖다, 스며들다 (to wet thoroughly, to become known)

His lesson didn't soak in.

(그의 수업은 잘 이해되지 않는다.)

stretch / 뻗(치)다, 늘이다 (to extend, spread)

She stretched herself out on the couch.

(그녀는 소파에 몸을 쭉 뻗었다.)

solidify / 응고시키다 [하다], 단결시키다 (to make or become firm or hard)

Our habits solidifies through carelessness and idleness.

(우리의 습관은 무관심과 나태함으로 인하여 굳어진다.)

suspend / 매달다, 보류하다 (to hang something, to officially delay)

The revision of the regulations has been suspended until next month.

(규정의 수정이 다음 달까지 보류되었다.)

vaporize / 증발하다[시키다] (to turn into gas)

Carburetors help vaporize the mixture for combustion.

(캬뷰레이터는 연소를 위해 혼합물을 증발시킨다.)

vibrate / 진동하다 (to quiver, to move rapidly back and forth)

When I start the engine in the morning, my old car vibrates.
(내가 아침에 시동을 걸면 낡은 차가 진동을 한다.)

vie / 경쟁하다, 다투다 (compete)

Computer makers vie to make their machines visually pleasing and fun to use.
(컴퓨터 제조업자들은 자신들의 기계를 시각적으로 보기 좋고 사용하기에 즐겁게 하려 고 경쟁한다.)

wage / 수행하다, 종사하다(engage in, carry on)

Some species, such as honeybees and army ants, when working in large colonies, can perform complex tasks – such as building hives and waging war.
(꿀벌과 병정개미 같은 몇몇 종들은 무리로 작업을 하여, 벌통을 짓거나 전쟁을 수행 하는 것과 같은 복잡한 일을 수행할 수 있다.)

weigh / 무게를 달다, 무게가 ...이다 (to have a particular weight, to consider carefully)

I weighed the benefit of the plan against the risks involved.
(나는 그 계획의 내제된 위험에 대비한 이익을 저울질 해보았다.)

2. 연습문제

1. The liquid can _______ if it's heated to a very high temperature.
   ⓐ vaporize   ⓑ condense   ⓒ evacuate   ⓓ evade

2. Air under pressure is _______ .
   ⓐ compressed   ⓑ solid   ⓒ melted   ⓓ tiny

3. We found tests that can be used to _______ the age of the bones under the ground.
   ⓐ compute   ⓑ compel   ⓒ comment   ⓓ command

4. Gasoline and oil leaked into the sea and _______ the water.
   ⓐ congested   ⓑ contemplated   ⓒ contaminated   ⓓ consumed

5. Parallel lines never _______ .
   ⓐ diversify   ⓑ transport   ⓒ converge   ⓓ diverge

6. Lots of elements can be easily _______ from one form into another form.
   ⓐ compressed   ⓑ floated   ⓒ converted   ⓓ contrived

7. The rock for the new highway is being _______ and spread by a machine.
   ⓐ crushed   ⓑ crowded   ⓒ clicked   ⓒ collapsed

8. Dr. Jones has _______ a simple way to treat backache.
   ⓐ guided   ⓑ developed   ⓒ annoyed   ⓓ disappoint

9. She _______ the nail into the wall with the hammer.

   ⓐ glued   ⓑ sawed   ⓒ drove   ⓓ sanded

10. That device sends out radio waves.

   ⓐ embroider   ⓑ emits   ⓒ expel   ⓓ embark

11. When water _______ from the rivers or seas, clouds are formed.

   ⓐ evaporates   ⓑ escapes   ⓒ evades   ⓓ escalates

12. We _______ carbon dioxide from our lungs.

   ⓐ expand   ⓑ exhale   ⓒ inhale   ⓓ expend

13. The atmosphere _______ pressure on all lives on the earth.

   ⓐ expands   ⓑ exhales   ⓒ exerts   ⓓ expends

14. Don't open your camera in the bright sunlight. You'll _______ the film.

   ⓐ expose   ⓑ exert   ⓒ crush   ⓓ extend

15. It takes at least seven people to _______ the heavy, metal drum.

   ⓐ hoist   ⓑ hog   ⓒ hoe   ⓓ huddle

16. In 1791, a father and his son _______ a machine for making nails.

   ⓐ expanded   ⓑ invented   ⓒ involved   ⓓ intervened

17. A solid turns into a liquid when it _______ .

   ⓐ exhales   ⓑ exists   ⓒ expands   ⓓ melts

18. The earth _____ around the sun.

   ⓐ recovers   ⓑ resolves   ⓒ revolves   ⓓ removes

19. When Armstrong and Aldrin left the moon, they _____ their direction of flight and came back to the earth.

   ⓐ conversed   ⓑ reversed   ⓒ diversified   ⓓ restore

20. Can you _____ the material into a ball?

   ⓐ manage   ⓑ affect   ⓒ safe   ⓓ shape

21. You should _____ the shirt in cold, soapy water to remove the blood.

   ⓐ drain   ⓑ stretch   ⓒ stay   ⓓ soak

22. Shoes are usually a little tight at first, but they will soon _____ as you wear them. Then they'll fit just right.

   ⓐ stretch   ⓑ scratch   ⓒ stitch   ⓓ squeeze

23. Water _____ when you boil it.

   ⓐ vapors   ⓑ vaporize   ⓒ vapor   ⓓ is vaporous

24. The blades of that fan _____ and make a loud noise because they're loose.

   ⓐ vibrate   ⓑ exchange   ⓒ faint   ⓓ confound

25. The engine worked just fine, after the mechanic _____ it.

   ⓐ copied   ⓑ figured   ⓒ adjusted   ⓓ keyed

26. Batteries left in a flashlight too long may eventually _____ .

   ⓐ corrupt   ⓑ cohere   ⓒ corrode   ⓓ collide

27. The mechanic ______ the wire around the rod.

    ⓐ rocked   ⓑ coiled   ⓒ roared   ⓓ curbed

28. If we ______ salt in hot water, we can get salty water right now.

    ⓐ dissolve   ⓑ solve   ⓒ distract   ⓓ soothe

29. Studies by scientists ______ that the surface of the moon is rocky and dusty.

    ⓐ indicate   ⓑ suggest   ⓒ contend   ⓓ know

30. He planned to ______ the explosive with a short fuse.

    ⓐ denote   ⓑ denounce   ⓒ detonate   ⓓ depose

31. The first U.S. space rockets are ______ in Houston, Texas.

    ⓐ exhibited   ⓑ defeated   ⓒ resided   ⓓ defied

32. Some nuclear wastes ______ radioactive particles.

    ⓐ absorb   ⓑ emit   ⓒ partake   ⓓ derive

33. If you burn your hand, you should ______ it in cold water.

    ⓐ course   ⓑ roll   ⓒ dip   ⓓ slide

34. I left my tape in the car and the heat ______ it.

    ⓐ distorted   ⓑ amplified   ⓒ started   ⓓ terminated

35. If you put ice in water it will ______ .

    ⓐ float   ⓑ exert   ⓒ expand   ⓓ sink

36. Those parts are _____ with oil so they won't rust.
   ⓐ traced ⓑ switched ⓒ alternated ⓓ coated

37. You need to have the car's front wheels _____ so it will drive properly.
   ⓐ discount ⓑ dismounted ⓒ lined up ⓓ piled

38. The driver quickly _____ the car to avoid an accident.
   ⓐ manufactured ⓑ manifested ⓒ maneuvered ⓓ master

39. Thompson built a car that is _____ by burning cooking oil.
   ⓐ burnt ⓑ propelled ⓒ maneuvered ⓓ operating

40. The navigator _____ the aircraft's course.
   ⓐ started ⓑ plotted ⓒ amplified ⓓ actuated

41. Like poles of a magnet _____ while unlike poles attract.
   ⓐ repel ⓑ surge ⓒ represent ⓓ reveal

42. The expert designed an experiment that would _____ that his theory was correct.
   ⓐ kick ⓑ come out ⓒ prove ⓓ announce

43. On an icy road a car may _____ when the brakes are applied.
   ⓐ slide ⓑ dismount ⓒ account ⓓ pull apart

44. Cement _____ when it dries.
   ⓐ solidity ⓑ solid ⓒ solicits ⓓ solidifies

B 동사 / 과학과 기술

45. Plastic can be used to _____ real wood.

   ⓐ simulate   ⓑ copy   ⓒ appreciate   ⓓ formulate

46. The wood feels like silk. How many times did you _____ it?

   ⓐ sew   ⓑ drive   ⓒ sand   ⓓ smash

47. Before we can build our new house, we must cut down many trees.

   ⓐ chop   ⓑ hoist   ⓒ fall   ⓓ divide

48. We often notice the shining objects moving across the sky at night, but they suddenly disappear.

   ⓐ vanish   ⓑ banish   ⓒ verify   ⓓ disappoint

49. Don't go into that area. It's been exposed to atomic rays.

   ⓐ radical   ⓑ interactive   ⓒ radioactive   ⓓ racial

50. After they knocked down the apartment, they brought dozers and trucks to remove the pieces of bricks.

   ⓐ clear away   ⓑ set out   ⓒ put off   ⓓ put down

정답/해석

1. ⓐ 매우 높은 온도로 열이 가해지면, 액체는 증발한다.

2. ⓐ 압력을 받는 공기는 압축된다.

3. ⓐ 우리는 땅속에 있는 뼈의 연대를 계산하기 위해 사용될 수 있는 시험방법을 발견했다.

4. ⓒ 휘발유와 기름이 바다로 누출되어 물을 오염시켰다.

5. ⓒ 평행선은 결코 만나지 않는다.

6. ⓒ 많은 성분들은 쉽게 형태가 변경된다.

7. ⓐ 새 고속도로를 만들기 위해 기계로 바위를 깨고 뿌렸다.

8. ⓑ 존스 박사는 요통을 치료하기 위한 간단한 방법을 개발했다.

9. ⓒ 그녀는 망치로 벽에 못을 박았다.

10. ⓑ 그 장치는 무선파를 내 보냅니다.

11. ⓐ 물이 강이나 바다에서 증발하면, 구름이 형성된다.

12. ⓑ 우리는 폐에서 이산화탄소를 내뿜는다.

13. ⓒ 대기는 지상의 모든 생물에 압력을 가한다.

14. ⓐ 밝은 햇볕에 카메라를 열지 마라. 필름이 노출된다.

15. ⓐ 그 무거운 금속 드럼을 들어 올리려면 적어도 7명이 필요하다.

16. ⓑ 1791년에 한 부자가 못을 만드는 기계를 발명했다.

17. ⓓ 고체는 녹으면 액체로 변한다.

18. ⓒ 지구는 태양 둘레를 회전한다.

19. ⓑ 암스토롱과 앨드린이 달을 떠날 때, 그들은 비행방향을 돌려서 지구로 돌아왔다.

20. ⓓ 그 물체를 공 모양으로 만들 수 있느냐?

21. ⓓ 피를 제거하려면 찬 비눗물에 셔츠를 담궈야 한다.

22. ⓐ 신발은 대개 처음에는 약간 조인다. 그러나 신으면 곧 늘어나며, 그 후에는 딱 맞다.

23. ⓐ 물은 끓으면 증발합니다.

24. ⓐ 그 팬의 날개가 너무 헐거워서 진동하고 큰소리가 난다.

25. ⓒ 정비사가 엔진을 정비한 이후로 엔진은 원활하게 작동한다.

26. ⓒ 휴대용 전등에 너무 오래 넣어 둔 밧데리는 결국 부식한다.

27. ⓑ 기술자가 막대 둘레에 철사를 감았다.

28. ⓐ 소금을 뜨거운 물에 녹이면, 즉시 소금물을 얻을 수 있다.

29. ⓐ 과학자들의 연구는 달의 표면이 바위가 많고 흙으로 덮인 것을 지적하고 있다.

30. ⓒ 그는 짧은 퓨즈로 그 폭발물을 터뜨리려고 계획하였다.

31. ⓐ 첫 번째 미국 우주선은 텍사스 주 휴스턴에 전시되어있다.

32. ⓑ 몇 몇 핵 폐기물은 방사능 입자를 방출한다.

33. ⓒ 만약 손이 데이면 찬물에 그 손을 넣어야 한다.

34. ⓐ 나는 테이프를 차에 두고 내렸는데 열이 테이프를 망쳐버렸다.

35. ⓐ 얼음을 물 속에 두면 뜬다.

36. ⓓ 그 부분들은 오일 코팅이 되어 있기 때문에 녹슬지 않습니다.

37. ⓒ 자동차가 제대로 나아가도록 하기 위해서는 앞바퀴를 정렬시켜야 한다.

38. ⓒ 운전사는 사고를 피하려고 차를 재빨리 조종하였다.

39. ⓑ 톰슨은 요리용 오일을 연소하여 추진되는 차를 만들었다.

40. ⓑ 그 조종 장치는 항공기 진로를 도면에 표시하였다.

41. ⓐ 자석의 같은 전극은 밀어내고, 다른 전극은 끌어당긴다.

42. ⓒ 그 전문가는 그의 이론이 옳다는 것을 증명하는 실험을 준비했다.

43. ⓐ 얼음 길 위에서 브레이크를 잡으면 자동차는 미끄러질 것이다.

44. ⓓ 시멘트는 마르면 굳어진다.

45. ⓐ 플라스틱은 실제 나무와 유사한 것처럼 흉내 낼 수 있다.

46. ⓒ 나무가 비단 같다. 몇 번이나 샌드페이프로 닦았니?

47. ⓐ 새 집을 짓기 전에 많은 나무를 잘라야 한다.

48. ⓐ 우리는 반짝이는 물체가 밤하늘을 가로지르는 것을 종종 목격하지만, 그들은 곧 바로 사라진다.

49. ⓒ 그 지역에 가지 마세요. 그것은 방사선에 노출되었습니다.

50. ⓐ 그들은 아파트를 무너뜨린 다음에, 불도저와 트럭을 가져와서 벽돌 조각을 제거하였다.

형용사

기본어휘 / 연습 문제

C

New American
Language Course

1. 기본어휘   형용사

abrupt / 갑작스러운, 느닷없는 (unexpected, sudden)

Many people catch a cold because of an abrupt change in the winter weather.

(겨울날씨가 갑자기 변하여 많은 사람들이 감기에 걸린다.)

acid / 신 맛의 (sour, sharp and biting), 산 (a sour substance)

Vinegar is an acid. (식초는 산이다.)

coarse / 조잡한, 거친 (not fine or delicate)

The stiff, coarse fabric irritated her skin.

(뻣뻣하고 거친 직물이 그녀의 피부를 자극하였다.)

commercial / 상업의, 무역상의 (connected with commerce or trade)

These cassette are not for commercial use, but for private use only. (commerce)

(이 카세트는 상업용이 아니며, 단지 개인용일 뿐이다.)

compatible / 양립하는, 조화하는 (working well together)

Two computers are said to be compatible if programs can be run on them without alteration, or if they can communicate with each other.

(프로그램이 전환하지 않고 운용되고, 서로 통할 수 있으며, 두개의 컴퓨터가 호환한다고 말한다.)

compress / 압축하다, 요약하다 (to force into less space, to condense or shorten)

The series were compressed by 100 pages.

(그 시리즈는 100페이지로 압축되었다.)

dual / 둘의, 이중의 (composed or consisted of two people or items)

This room has a dual purpose serving as both a study and a living room.

(이 방은 서제와 거실의 이중 목적을 가지고 있다.)

essential / 필수적인 (indispensable, absolutely necessary)

Discipline is essential in the army.

(훈련은 군대에서 필수적이다.)

fixed / 고정된, 일정한 (staying the same, not changing, to keep in sight)

His eyes were fixed on the beautiful girl.

(그의 눈은 예쁜 소녀에게 고정되어 있었다.)

mechanical / 기계(상)의 (having skill in the use of machinery or tools, automatic)

Air safety investigators are focusing on mechanical failure rather than human error.

(항공 안전 조사관들은 인간의 실수보다 기계적인 실수에 초점을 두고 있다.)

negative / 부정의, 음의 (of negative electricity, opposite to something positive)

The negative pole of a battery is the part which releases electrons.

(밧데리의 음극은 전자를 방출하는 부분이다.)

primitive / 원시의, 원시적인, 소박한 (crude, simple, uncivilized)

Human laws was considered unchangeable in primitive times.

(인간의 법칙은 원시시대에는 변하지 않는 것으로 간주되었다.)

principal / 주요한, 중요한 (most important, main)

The guiding principle of the new legislation is that the wellbeing of the poor comes first.

(새 법률제정의 지침이 되는 원칙은 가난한 자의 행복이 우선이라는 것이다.)

radioactive / 방사성의, 방사능의 (sending out harmful radiation)

The government stored radioactive waste at a remote island.
(정부는 외딴 섬에 방사능 폐기물질을 보관했다.)

reliable / 의지가 되는, 믿음직한 (a reliable person is someone you can trust to behave well, work hard, or do what you expect them to do well)

Alice can take care of the children. She is very reliable.
(엘리스는 그녀의 아이들을 돌볼 수 있다. 그녀는 믿을 만하다.)

rotary / 회전하는 (moving or turning on an axis), 로터리

Helicopters have rotary wings but airplanes have fixed ones.
(헬리콥터는 회전날개를 가지고 있으나, 비행기는 고정날개가 있다.)

rough / 거친, 울퉁불퉁한 (with a surface that is not smooth)

The walls were built of dark rough stone. (그 벽은 검고 거친 돌로 만들어졌다.)

rugged / 거칠거칠한, 울퉁불퉁한 (rough and uneven)

A robot called Attila will carry 150 sensors in its legs for position, force, surface hardness, surface color, and the proximity of objects. It will be able to crawl over objects and move around rugged landscapes freely.
(아틸라라는 로봇은 위치, 힘, 표면의 딱딱함, 표면의 색깔, 물체의 근접성에 대비한 150개의 감지기를 지니고 있다. 그것은 물체위로 기어갈 수 있고, 거칠은 표면 둘레로 자유롭게 움직일 수 있다.)

skeptical / 회의적인, 의심이 많은 (doubting)

A simple robot called Allen could perform some tasks better than far more expensive and complex conventional robots. A skeptical scientific community was impressed.
(알렌이라는 단순한 로봇이 훨씬 더 비싸고 복잡한 전통적인 로봇보다 어떤 임무는 더 잘 수행할 수 있었다. 회의적인 과학계도 감명을 받았다.)

soundproof / 방음의 (not penetrated by sound, to make soundproof)

Soundproof materials can be purchased online.
(방음물질은 온라인에서 구입할 수 있다.)

thorough 철저한, 완벽한 (very exact and accurate)

We should be very thorough in our preparation for the plot.
(우리는 계획을 짤 때 매우 철저해야 한다.)

valuable / 가치있는, 유용한 (having great value, of great merit or use)

Internet provides valuable information on current fashion.
(인터넷은 현대 유행에 대한 가치있는 정보를 제공한다.)

2. 연습문제

1. The solution changed color when the ______ was added.
   ⓐ acrid　　　　ⓑ acid　　　　ⓒ sweet　　　　ⓓ acorn

2. They were really ______ by the low-flying jets.
   ⓐ amazed　　　　ⓑ amazing　　　　ⓒ to amaze　　　　ⓓ amazement

3. The car came to an ______ stop because he slammed on the brakes.
   ⓐ slow　　　　ⓑ smooth　　　　ⓒ abrupt　　　　ⓓ ahhesive

4. A ______ can be used to transport cargo and passengers.
   ⓐ crop　　　　ⓑ chopper　　　　ⓒ motorist　　　　ⓓ rotor

5. When sandpaper is rough, it is ______ sandpaper.
   ⓐ course　　　　ⓑ fine　　　　ⓒ blunt　　　　ⓓ coarse

6. ______ air is air forced into a small container.
   ⓐ Compressed　　　　ⓑ Compressing　　　　ⓒ Compress　　　　ⓓ To compress

7. To support the heavy loads they carry, large containers usually have ______ rather than single tires.
   ⓐ dual　　　　ⓑ illegal　　　　ⓒ efficient　　　　ⓓ heavy

8. The gauge on my car is ______ . We cannot trust it.

    ⓐ erratic   ⓑ erect   ⓒ equivalent   ⓓ equator

9. Call Mr. Harris. He's a(n) ______ good plumber.

    ⓐ especially   ⓑ bluntly   ⓒ consciously   ⓓ special

10. This lens was made ______ for this bifocal glasses.

    ⓐ excessively   ⓑ primitive   ⓒ especially   ⓓ picturesque

11. These pieces of equipment are essential for this job.

    ⓐ original   ⓑ important   ⓒ inexpensive   ⓓ infective

12. The North Star has a(n) ______ position in the sky; it doesn't move.

    ⓐ sufficient   ⓑ fixed   ⓒ overall   ⓓ severe

13. He can do anything with machines; he's a ______ genius.

    ⓐ muscular   ⓑ mechanical   ⓒ orderly   ⓓ machinery

14. One end of the electrode has a ______ charge.

    ⓐ negative   ⓑ primitive   ⓒ neutral   ⓓ mutual

15. A car would weigh ______ on the moon as it does on earth.

    ⓐ one-sixth as much   ⓑ six times more

    ⓒ the same   ⓓ sixty times as much

17. We hope the mechanic can repair the car right now. ______ , we have to rent one.

    ⓐ In addition   ⓑ At least   ⓒ Otherwise   ⓓ In place of

18. They have a _____ method of farming in that underdeveloped country.

ⓐ mechanical ⓑ primitive ⓒ permanent ⓓ primary

19. The engine is the _____ part of a car.

ⓐ principal ⓑ principle ⓒ princely ⓓ principial

20. I'm sure the mechanic will repair the truck correctly. He's very _____ .

ⓐ reliable ⓑ dependable ⓒ lucky ⓓ character

21. The _____ movement of this blade is too slow to make the chopper fly. It should be turning much faster than this.

ⓐ rotary ⓑ static ⓒ stationary ⓓ roaring

22. The top of the table isn't smooth. In fact, it's _____ .

ⓐ idle ⓑ rough ⓒ lucky ⓓ neat

23. To make our tape recordings we need a studio protected from outside noise.

ⓐ soundproof ⓑ noisy ⓒ suspended ⓓ vacuum

24. Are you supposed to use _____ or thin oil in the winter?

ⓐ thick ⓑ cheap ⓒ wide ⓓ hot

25. The mechanic checked all of the items; he was very _____ .

ⓐ extreme ⓑ standard ⓒ thorough ⓓ adequate

26. Gold is a _____ metal.

ⓐ worthless ⓑ valuable ⓒ curious ⓓ vegetarian

27. Have NASA fired the rocket to the planet Mars _____ ?

    ⓐ long time ago   ⓑ still   ⓒ yet   ⓓ already

28. Because space exploration is a controversial subject, the students conducted a lengthy debate – each presenting a different view.

    ⓐ especially interesting   ⓑ marked by opposing views

    ⓒ very complex   ⓓ unanimous

29. Although the sisters are identical twins, they have very unique and discrete personalities.

    ⓐ similar   ⓑ distinctly different   ⓒ quite peculiar   ⓓ difficult

30. A prescriptive approach is needed in order to understand the details of how the specific features of a computer system can be applied to a particular need.

    ⓐ creative   ⓑ classifying the data

    ⓒ telling what should be done   ⓓ not judging but explaining

정답 / 해석

1. ⓑ 산이 첨가되면 용액은 색깔이 변한다.

2. ⓐ 그들은 낮게 비행하는 제트기에 깜짝 놀랐다.

3. ⓒ 그가 브레이크를 급하게 밟았기 때문에 차가 급작스럽게 정지하였다.

4. ⓑ 헬리콥터는 화물과 승객을 수송하기 위해서 사용될 수 있다.

5. ⓓ 사포가 까칠하면, 그것은 거친 사포이다.

6. ⓐ 압축공기는 작은 용기 속에 강제로 주입되는 공기이다.

7. ⓐ 운반하는 무거운 짐을 지지하기 위해서, 큰 컨테이너 화물차는 단일 바퀴가 아닌 이중 바퀴를 가지고 있다.

8. ⓐ 내 차의 계기가 불규칙하다. 우리는 그것을 믿을 수 없다.

9. ⓐ 헤리스씨에게 전화해라. 그는 아주 우수한 배관공이다.

10. ⓒ 이 렌즈는 이중 초점 안경을 위해 특별히 만들어졌다.

11. ⓑ 이 장비들은 이 일에 필수적이다.

12. ⓑ 북극성은 하늘에 위치가 고정되어 있다. 그것은 움직이지 않는다.

13. ⓑ 그는 기계로 무엇이든 할 수 있다. 그는 기계에 대한 천재다.

14. ⓐ 자석의 한 쪽 끝은 음극을 가진다.

15. ⓐ 차는 지구에 비해 달에서는 무게가 6분의 1이다.

17. ⓒ 그 기술자가 차를 즉시 수리하지 않으면, 우리는 차를 한 대 빌려야 한다.

18. ⓑ 미개발국가에서는 원시적인 농사법을 가지고 있다.

19. ⓐ 엔진은 차의 주요부품이다.

20. ⓐ 나는 그 수리공이 트럭을 확실하게 고칠 것이라고 믿는다. 그는 믿을 만 하다.

21. ⓐ 이 날개의 회전 운동이 너무 느려서 헬리콥터가 날게 만들 수 없다. 그것은 이보다 좀 더 빨리 돌아야 한다.

22. ⓑ 그 테이블 위는 부드럽지 않다. 사실은 꺼칠꺼칠하다.

23. ⓐ 테이프 녹음을 하기 위해서는 외부 소음에서 차단된 작업실이 필요하다.

24. ⓐ 겨울에는 걸쭉한 오일을 사용합니까 아니면 묽은 오일을 사용 합니까?

25. ⓒ 그 기술자는 모든 품목을 확인했다. 그는 매우 철저하다.

26. ⓑ 금은 가치있는 금속이다.

27. ⓒ 미항공우주국이 화성에 이미 로켓을 발사했느냐?

28. ⓑ 우주 탐험은 논쟁이 되는 주제였기 때문에, 학생들은 장황한 토론을 수행했다. 각자 다른 의견을 제시하였다.

29. ⓑ 그 자매들은 일란성 쌍둥이지만, 그들은 독특하고 전혀 다른 성질을 가지고 있다.

30. ⓒ 컴퓨터 체계의 특성이 특별한 필요에 어떻게 적용될지를 상세히 이해하기 위해서는 규범적인 접근이 필요하다.

어휘, 관용구, 문형 종합

기본어휘 / 연습 문제

D

New American Language Course

1. 기본어휘 — 어휘, 관용구, 문형 종합

come of age / 성년이 되다, 성숙하다 (become mature, respected, etc.)

The gene revolution finally came of age last year when the federal government launched the single most ambitious project in the history of biology: the $3 billion, 15-year Human Genome project to map and copy the 100,000 genes that make up a human being.
(연방정부가 생물학 연구에서 단일과제로는 가장 야심적인 과제를 시작한 지난 해 유전자 혁명은 성년에 도달했다: 인간을 구성하는 십 만개의 유전자 지도를 그려내고 복사하기 위해 투자하는 30억 달러를 15년에 걸친 인간 유전자 과제이다.)

despite / 불구하고 (notwithstanding, in spite of)

She is very generous despite her background and education.
(그녀는 배경과 교육에도 불구하고 매우 관대하다.)

drive away / 몰아내다, 격퇴하다 (to push or press onward forcibly, to repulse)

They drove the enemy's attacks away.
(그들은 적의 공격을 격퇴하였다.)

fall apart / 깨어지다, 붕괴하다 (to break off, to break into pieces, to fall away)

Every person must try to stop their marriage falling apart.
(모든 사람은 결혼이 깨어지지 않도록 노력해야 한다.)

fall down / 쓰러지다, ~에 있다 (to topple or sink, to come by right)

The accent falls down on the first syllable.
(강세는 첫음절에 있다.)

line up / 세우다, 정렬하다 (to form a row or to put people or things in a row)

The books are lined up on a shelf above the desk.

(그 책들은 책상 위 서가에 가지런히 정리되어 있다.)

look into / 들여다보다, 조사하다 (to examine carefully, investigate)

A working party has been set up to look into the terrible scandal.

(그 나쁜 추문을 조사하기 위해서 특별조사 위원회가 설치되었습니다.)

put to rest / 잠재우다, 누그러뜨리다 (calm one's fears)

As it has matured over the past decade, genetic engineering has put some fears to rest by showing it can work within regulatory limits and without unpleasant surprises.

(지난 10년간 성숙했기 때문에 유전공학은 그것이 통제 범위내에서 불쾌한 놀라운 사건 없이 작동할 수 있다는 것을 보여 줌으로써 몇 가지 두려움을 잠재울 수 있었다.)

take apart / 분해하다, 분석하다 (to separate an object into pieces)

My watch stopped, so I take it apart.

(내 시계가 멈춰 버렸다. 그래서 시계를 분해하고 있다.)

wind up / 감다, 끝내다 (to tighten, to arrange or settle)

He wound up the toy car and let it run across the living room.

(그는 장난감 차를 감아서 거실을 가로질러 달리게 하였다.)

work on / 종사하다, 영향을 미치다 (to do mental or physical effort as a part of a job)

I've been working on my assignment all day long.

(나는 온 종일 숙제를 하고 있었다.)

2. 연습문제

1. The fluorescent lights in the living room ______ from the ceiling.
   ⓐ suspends   ⓑ are suspended   ⓒ is suspended   ⓓ suspense

2. ______ recording songs from the radio, we can play music with our cassette tape recorder.
   ⓐ Also   ⓑ Luckily   ⓒ Poorly   ⓓ Besides

3. Because his helicopter's radio wouldn't work, Lt. Smith had to use hand signals to ______ the other pilots.
   ⓐ count on   ⓑ adjust to
   ⓒ communicate with   ⓓ account for

4. A water molecule ______ two hydrogen atoms and one oxygen atom.
   ⓐ compose of   ⓑ consists of   ⓒ exerts   ⓓ converts to

5. Rust on the car's body resulted from its exposure to the sea air.
   ⓐ Corrosion   ⓑ Contact   ⓒ Commission   ⓓ Condition

6. We could still hear outside noises ______ the fact that this studio is supposed to be soundproof.
   ⓐ in respect of   ⓑ on condition that   ⓒ despite   ⓓ although

7. The surface of this car decayed so much that I think it's going to ______ if I drive it.
   ⓐ get together   ⓑ feign   ⓒ fall apart   ⓓ leave out

8. Astronauts are people who travel ______ .

    ⓐ by boat   ⓑ into the forests   ⓒ in space   ⓓ under the sea

9. There seems to be a problem with this hydraulic system. Could you ______ it?

    ⓐ look after   ⓑ look into   ⓒ look down on   ⓓ look forward to

10. That earring is alloy ______ gold and copper.

    ⓐ for   ⓑ of   ⓒ on   ⓓ from

11. The smoke from the manufacturing factories can make the air dirty.

    ⓐ clear the air   ⓑ pollutes the air   ⓒ consume the air   ⓓ clean the air.

12. We must ______ the machine ______ before we can find its problem.

    ⓐ take apart   ⓑ cut down   ⓒ lend a hand   ⓓ take advantage of

13. The scientist was able ______ the germ causing the cancer.

    ⓐ to reprimand   ⓑ to isolate   ⓒ to challenge   ⓓ to despair

14. Can you ______ this wire on that spot?

    ⓐ turn over   ⓑ wind up   ⓒ blow up   ⓓ turn over

15. John: Can you repair this machine?

    Daniel: No, but I ______ .

    ⓐ wish I could   ⓑ wish I couldn't   ⓒ if I wished to   ⓓ don't wish

16. The mechanic was ______ my car when his friend called him.

    ⓐ working for   ⓑ working with   ⓒ working against   ⓓ working on

6. 과학과 기술

17. The company had to shut the nuclear power plant down for two days because one of the systems malfunctioned.

ⓐ reopen　　　ⓑ computerize　　　ⓒ repair　　　ⓓ close

18. Because I didn't know anything about computers, and there was no one available to teach me, it was a matter of "sink or swim" in learning to use our computer.

ⓐ Since I didn't know how to use the computer, I decided to go to the beach.

ⓑ I had to try very hard to learn by myself or I would fail.

ⓒ The computer was too heavy to carry.

ⓓ I couldn't learn computer for myself.

정답 / 해석

1. ⓑ 거실에 있는 형광등은 천장에 매달려 있다.

2. ⓐ 카세트는 라디오에서 나오는 노래의 녹음 뿐만 아니라, 음악을 틀 수도 있다.

3. ⓒ 그의 헬리콥터 무선이 작동하지 않기 때문에, 스미스 대위는 다른 비행사와 의사소통하기 위해서 수신호를 사용해야 했다.

4. ⓑ 물 분자는 두개의 수소원자와 한 개의 산소 원자로 구성된다.

5. ⓐ 차체의 녹은 바닷물에 노출된 결과이다.

6. ⓒ 이 작업실이 방음이 되어 있지만 그래도 우리는 외부의 소음을 들을 수 있다.

7. ⓒ 이 차의 표면이 너무 부식되어서, 운전하면 떨어져 나갈 것 같다.

8. ⓒ 우주비행사는 우주에서 항해하는 사람들이다.

9. ⓑ 이 유압계에 이상이 있습니다. 살펴 봐 주겠습니까?

10. ⓑ 그 귀고리는 금과 구리의 합금이다.

11. ⓑ 제조공장의 매연은 대기를 오염시킨다.

12. ⓐ 우리는 기계의 문제를 발견하기 전에 기계를 뜯어보아야 한다.

13. ⓑ 과학자는 암을 유발하는 세균을 분리할 수 있었다.

14. ⓑ 이 철사를 저 지점에 감아라.

15. ⓐ 존 : 이 기계를 수리할 수 있어요?

   다니엘 : 아니오. 수리할 수 있으면 좋겠지만.

16. ⓓ 친구가 전화했을 때, 기술자가 내 차에 작업을 하고 있었다.

17. ⓓ 그 회사는 그 원자력 발전소를 2일 동안 닫아야 했다. 왜냐하면 시스템의 하나가 작동하지 않았기 때문이다.

18. ⓑ 나는 컴퓨터를 몰랐고 나를 가르칠 수 있는 사람이 없었기 때문에 컴퓨터를 사용하는 것을 배우기 위해서
    는 필사적으로 할 수 밖에 없었다.

New American
Language
Course

New American
Language Còurse

군사 및 무기 7

A. 명사　　B. 동사　　C. 형용사　　D. 어휘, 관용구, 문형 종합

ECL시험 대비 NEW ALC 必 필수어휘 완성

명사

기본어휘 / 연습 문제

A

New American Language Course

1. 기본어휘 — 명사

ally / 동맹국, 연합국 (a group joined with another for a common purpose)

North Korea is one of China's staunchest allies.
(북한은 중국의 가장 충실한 동맹국의 하나이다.)

appearance / 모습, 생김새 (the way that someone or something looks)

His thinning hair gave him the appearance of much older man.
(그의 가느다란 머리카락은 자신의 나이보다 더 늙은 사람으로 보이게 한다.)

armed forces / 군대, 전군 (a country's army, navy, and air force)

Without the armed forces, we cannot survive in this world.
(군대가 없다면, 우리는 이 세계에서 살아남지 못한다.)

ammunition / 탄약 (projectiles such as bullets and shot)

These two guns use the same type of ammunition. (이 두개의 총은 같은 탄약을 사용한다.)

armor / 갑옷, 방호복 (any defensive or protective covering)

Police put on body armor before confronting the demonstrators.
(경찰은 시위대와 맞서기 전에 방호복을 입는다.)

artillery / 대포 (large heavy guns which are often moved on wheels)

Naval gunfire and ground-based artillery are generally less accurate than many aircraft-borne weapons.
(해군의 포격과 지상군의 포는 일반적으로 많은 항공무기보다 정확하지 않다.)

behavior / 행동, 행위 (the way that someone behaves)

Anna was sick of her brother's annoying behavior.

(애나는 남동생의 성가신 행동에 지쳐있다.)

benefit / 이익, 이득 (extra money or other advantage that you get)

The benefits include medical insurance and a company car.

(그 혜택 가운데에는 의료보험과 회사차량 제공이 포함된다.)

blunders / 실책, 실수 (foolish or careless mistake)

A supervisor should make unscheduled, informal visits in the subordinate's work areas to show interest in their work and to make it possible for the superior to catch blunders before they become too serious.

(감독관은 하급자의 작업지역에 비계획적으로 비공식적인 방문을 하여 그들의 작업에 대한 관심을 보여주고, 상급자는 너무 심각해지기 전에 실책을 포착할 가능성을 가져야 한다.)

captain / 함장 (the person in charge of a ship or aircraft), (해군) 대령, (육,공군) 대위

We were invited to dine with the captain of the ship.

(우리는 그 함정의 함장과 함께하는 저녁 초대를 받았다.)

club / 클럽 (an organization for people who have a common interest in a particular activity or subject

Have you thought about becoming a member of our model airplane club?

(우리 모델 항공기 클럽 멤버가 되실 생각이 있었습니까?)

crux / 핵심, 욧점 (the central part of a problem)

The crux of successful delegation is knowing the amount of responsibility and authority that should be delegated.

(성공적인 위임의 핵심은 위임되는 책임과 권한의 양을 아는 것이다.)

dichotomy / 이분법, 분열 (division into two parts or direction)

The soldiers were confused by the dichotomy in philosophy exhibited by their two leaders.
(그 군인들은 그들의 두 지도자가 보여준 철학이 달라서 혼란스러웠다.)

discipline / 훈련, 규율 (the practice of making people obey rules of behavior and punishing them if they do not)

He believes in strict discipline.
(그는 엄격한 규율을 신봉한다.)

ensign / 소위 (an officer of low rank in the US navy or coast guard)

Ensign Kim will be promoted to the Lieutenant Junior Grade next month.
(김소위는 다음 달에 중위로 진급하게 될 것이다.)

etiquette / 예절, 행동규범 (rules of proper behaviour)

While at formal social functions, military personnel need to observe proper military etiquette
(공식적인 사회활동에서 군인은 적절한 군대 예절을 지킬 필요가 있다.)

explosion / 폭발, 격정 (detonation, noisy outburst, violent expression of emotion)

The fire was brought about by a gas explosion.
(화재는 가스 폭발로 발생되었다.)

facility / 편의 시설, 설비 (a building, a special room, services)

The company provides the researchers with every facility for accomplishing a task.
(그 회사는 연구원들에게 임무를 수행하기 위한 모든 시설을 제공한다.)

flap / 퍼득거리다, 아래위로 움직이다 (move quickly up and down)

The gulls flapped their wings and flew away.
(갈매기는 날개를 파닥거리다 날라가 버렸다.)

flag / 기, 깃발 (a piece of cloth decorated with the pattern and colors that represent a country or organization)

The American flag is called the stars and stripes.

(미국 국기는 성조기라고 한다.)

general / 장군 (an officer of high rank in the army, air force, or marines)

Instead of general, admiral is always used in the navy.

(해군에서는 장성이라는 용어 대신에 항상 제독이라고 한다.)

hardship / 고난, 곤경 (difficulty, hard circumstances)

The 2000's is a time of high unemployment and economic hardship all over the world.

(2000년대 전 세계는 높은 실업과 경제적인 역경의 시대이다.)

hearsay / 소문, 풍문 (unverified or unofficial information gained from another person)

Reporting systems should include not only statistical and official reports but also hearsay reports given by a variety of personal contacts.

(보고체계는 통계적 공식적 보고 뿐만 아니라, 다양한 개인적 접촉에 의한 소문에 대한 보고도 포함되어야 한다.)

hierarchy / 계급조직, 계층조직 (the arrangement of objects, elements or values in a graduated series)

Notice how one's responsibilities changes as one gets higher and higher up in the hierarchy.

(계층조직에서 승진하면 할 수록 자신의 책임이 어떻게 변하는 지를 주목하라.)

infantry / 보병(대) (foot soldiers collectively)

I joined an infantry regiment.

(나는 보병연대에 소속되었다.)

insignia / 기장, 표지 (a mark or sign that shows someone's rank or status, or what organization they belong to)

Each rank or rate has its own insignia.

(각 계급이나 등급에는 그에 상응하는 계급장이 있다.)

installation / (군사)시설, 설비 (a building or structure, especially one that is important for an army, industry, or government)

It's on the list of military installations that are scheduled to be closed.

(그것은 곧 폐쇄 예정인 군사 시설물들 가운데 들어있다.)

marksmanship / 사격술 (skill of a marksman)

Their marksmanship is remarkable. (그들의 사격술은 탁월하다.)

missile / 미사일, 탄도병기 (a weapon that is sent through the air)

Satellite photographs provide conclusive proof of the existence of the guided missiles.

(위성사진은 유도미사일의 존재에 대한 결정적인 증거를 제공한다.)

mission / 임무, 사명 (the special duty or function)

The squadron flew on a reconnaissance mission. (그 기병대대는 정찰임무에 뛰어들었다.)

morale / 사기, 의욕 (the amount of enthusiasm a person or group of people feel about their situation at a particular time)

The officers were struggling to boost morale.

(그 장교들은 사기를 드높이기 위하여 노력하였다.)

offense / 위반, 공격 (process of attacking)

The second offense was carried out on the Christmas Eve.

(그 두 번째 공격은 크리스마스 전날 밤에 감행되었다.)

privilege / 특권 (a special benefit that is available only to a particular person or group.)

Cheap air travel is one of the privileges of working for the airline.

(값싼 항공료는 항공사에 근무하는 사람들에게 제공되는 특권 중 하나다.)

resistance / 저항, 반항 (opposition to someone or something, especially a political or military opponents)

The government had taken elaborate precautions to crush any political resistance.

(정부는 정치적 반대세력을 쳐부수기 위하여 보다 정교한 조치를 택했다.)

rotary / 회전하는, 선회하는 (turn around a central point or axis)

A helicopter flies by the rotary movement of its blades.

(헬리콥터는 날개의 회전 운동에 의해 비행한다.)

subordinate / 부하, 하위 (someone who has less power or authority than someone else)

He never won the respect of his subordinates.

(그는 그의 부하들로부터 존경을 받지 못했다.)

trench / 참호, 도랑 (long narrow open hole dug in the ground)

They realize the importance of trenches.

(그들은 참호의 중요성을 인식하였다.)

scope / 범위, 영역 (the things that a particular activity, organization, subject, etc deals with)

These issues are beyond the scope of this book.

(이 문제들은 이 책의 범위를 벗어난다.)

trainee / 연습생, 훈련생 (someone who is being trained a particular profession or job)

The firm hired seven accountant trainees a year.

(그 회사는 매년 7명의 경리실습생을 고용한다.)

2. 연습문제

1. Kevin shot at the target until he ran out of ______ .
   ⓐ cases   ⓑ powder   ⓒ chambers   ⓓ ammunition

2. In the U.S., the ______ include the Army, the Navy, the Marine Corps, and the Air Force.
   ⓐ armed forces   ⓑ military ranks   ⓒ military duty   ⓓ assignment

3. Long time ago, Roman soldiers wore a protective metal ______ covering during warfare.
   ⓐ camouflage   ⓑ armor   ⓒ obstacle   ⓓ screen

4. The ______ destroyed all of the skyscrapers in the city. They collapsed under the heavy attack.
   ⓐ arrows   ⓑ rifles   ⓒ marksman   ⓓ artillery

5. The ______ have marched all morning and look a little tired.
   ⓐ drills   ⓑ ceremony   ⓒ BDUs   ⓓ trainees

6. The admiral was proud of the sailors' ______ during the emergency.
   ⓐ custom   ⓑ behavior   ⓒ privilege   ⓓ sleeping

7. Being in the military gives you a lot of ______ such as free medical care, travel, and BX commissary privileges.
   ⓐ employment   ⓑ points   ⓒ unemployment   ⓓ benefits

8. The soldiers ran out of the barracks when they heard the loud explosion.

   ⓐ exploitation   ⓑ explanation   ⓒ blast   ⓓ blade

9. Before Dora became a rear admiral (lower-half), she was a _____ .

   ⓐ captain   ⓑ colonel   ⓒ commander   ⓓ lieutenant

10. The air force base is well known for its medical and dental _____ .

   ⓐ nourishment   ⓑ vicinity   ⓒ facilities   ⓓ faculty

11. He's a foot soldier, but he doesn't handle large weapons. He's in the _____ .

   ⓐ targets   ⓑ infantry   ⓒ artillery   ⓓ air-force

12. They're afraid that the country has a secret _____ pointed at its enemies.

   ⓐ missile   ⓑ runway   ⓒ mystery   ⓓ mission

13. Sgt Kim's _____ is to locate a place where the Marines can cross the river.

   ⓐ routine   ⓑ confidence   ⓒ mission   ⓓ responsibility

14. After his promotion, Bernado's _____ was very high.

   ⓐ style   ⓑ morale   ⓒ character   ⓓ foundation

15. The troops practiced attacking, defending, and resisting. The exercise involved _____ ,
    defense, and resistance.

   ⓐ ascent   ⓑ output   ⓒ balance   ⓓ offense

16. The enemy put up a great deal of opposition to the forces.
    Their _____ was strong.

   ⓐ descent   ⓑ application   ⓒ petroleum   ⓓ resistance

17. A helicopter has a set of _______ blades on its top and tail.

   ⓐ horizontal   ⓑ rotary   ⓒ round   ⓓ vertical

18. He is able to hit the _______ with almost 100% accuracy.

   ⓐ purpose   ⓑ aim   ⓒ target   ⓓ presentation

19. The men are expert marksmen. They all hit the _______ .

   ⓐ event   ⓑ target   ⓒ phase   ⓓ bullit

20. The exercise tested the commander's ideas. They put his _______ into action.

   ⓐ emotion   ⓑ theories   ⓒ diesels   ⓓ codes

21. Those nations are allies.

   ⓐ They communicate with each other.

   ⓑ They're fighting against each other.

   ⓒ They help each other when necessary.

   ⓓ They are arguing with everything.

22. Military people must present a neat _______ . Their uniforms should be clean and pressed, their shoes shined, and their hair cut short.

   ⓐ appearance   ⓑ personality   ⓒ position   ⓓ character

23. The U. S. president can always _______ the reserves to strengthen the nation's armed forces.

   ⓐ call up   ⓑ call down   ⓑ take over   ⓒ take control of

24. Sgt Owen is going to meet Sgt Lowe and Sgt Wilson at the NCO _______ .

   ⓐ International   ⓑ Club   ⓒ Class A   ⓓ top notch

25. The practice and good _____ of the soldiers showed when they marched in the parade.

    ⓐ support   ⓑ display   ⓒ review   ⓓ discipline

26. Military personnel salute the _____ as it passes by.

    ⓐ parade   ⓑ hand   ⓒ flag   ⓓ review

27. A United States Army officer who wears four stars is _____ .

    ⓐ general   ⓑ an admiral   ⓒ captain   ⓓ lieutenant

28. This is Admiral Phillip's retirement party. He's the guest of _____ .

    ⓐ honor   ⓑ custom   ⓒ requirement   ⓓ courtesy

29. A senior officer always sits or walks on the right side of a junior officer.

    The right side is the place of _____ .

    ⓐ honor   ⓑ salute   ⓒ responsibility   ⓓ original

30. Notwithstanding lots of _____ while growing up, he turned out to be a wonderful officer in the Navy.

    ⓐ embarrassment   ⓑ hardships   ⓒ editorials   ⓓ hard line

31. An Army post is a military _____ .

    ⓐ salute   ⓑ privilege   ⓒ installation   ⓓ operation

32. A silver bar is the _____ for a first lieutenant in the Army.

    ⓐ opportunity   ⓑ ensign   ⓒ insignia   ⓓ medal

33. _____ is important for all military personnel.

    ⓐ Marksmanship   ⓑ Infantry   ⓒ Martyr   ⓓ Marksman

34. There'll be _______ for the celebration.

    ⓐ marched   ⓑ march   ⓒ marching   ⓓ to march

35. Bill is an ensign. He's in the _______ .

    ⓐ Army   ⓑ Navy   ⓒ Air Force   ⓓ Marine Corps

36. It was my _______ to serve under General Westfield.

    ⓐ right   ⓑ privilege   ⓒ control   ⓓ passenger

37. When Mr. Nickson says something in a meeting, everyone else says, "Yes, sir." They are his _______ .

    ⓐ authorities   ⓑ subordinates   ⓒ friends   ⓓ sons

38. The troops dug long deep ditches to use for cover from the enemy's weapons. They dug _______ .

    ⓐ towers   ⓑ quarters   ⓒ trenches   ⓓ theories

39. This radar _______ can show the position of 70 aircraft at one time.

    ⓐ note   ⓑ blip   ⓒ scope   ⓓ frequency

40. Located on the narrow edge of the wing, the _______ are lowered to slow down the plane while it is landing.

    ⓐ tails   ⓑ flaps   ⓒ propellers   ⓓ fuselage

41. The sergeant didn't say a word, but the frown on his face showed implicit disapproval.

    ⓐ His disapproval was not legal.

    ⓑ His disapproval was plainly suggested though not stated.

    ⓒ His disapproval was not practical.

ⓓ His disapproval was clearly shown with his attitude

42. The company commander is trying to establish cohesion within the unit by promoting unity, teamwork, and group loyalty.

ⓐ The company commander wants the members of the unit to feel a sense of attachment to each other.

ⓑ The company commander wants the soldiers to eat nutritious food.

ⓒ The company commander is trying to teach the soldiers about other religions.

ⓓ The company commander want all the members to follow his orders.

43. The men were billeted in the wooden cantonments until they were assigned to their permanent barracks.

ⓐ fox holes   ⓑ temporary quarters

ⓒ tents   ⓓ container

44. The colonel liked the research report. He gave it his stamp of approval.

ⓐ signature   ⓑ attention   ⓒ okay   ⓓ opinion

45. The area was designated as the place to keep the ammunition.

ⓐ storage   ⓑ kitchen   ⓒ prison   ⓓ tower

1. ⓓ 케빈은 탄약이 다 떨어질 때까지 표적을 쏘았다.

2. ⓐ 미국 군대는 육군, 해군, 해병대, 그리고 공군으로 이루어진다.

3. ⓑ 옛날에 로마군인들은 전쟁동안 보호용 금속 가리개를 착용했다.

4. ⓓ 대포가 도시의 모든 고층건물을 파괴하였다. 그것들은 심한 공격으로 붕괴되었다.

5. ⓓ 그 훈련생들은 아침 내내 행군했고, 약간 지쳐보였다.

6. ⓑ 그 제독은 비상시에 보여준 수병들의 행동을 자랑스럽게 여긴다.

7. ⓓ 군에서는 무료의료검진, 무료여행, 군내 매점사용권 등 많은 혜택이 주어진다.

8. ⓒ 강한 폭발소리를 듣자 군인들이 막사에서 뛰어 나왔다.

9. ⓐ 도라가 제독이 되기 전에 그녀는 대령이었다.

10. ⓒ 그 공군기지는 의료 및 치과 시설로 유명하다.

11. ⓑ 그는 보병이지만, 중화기는 다루지 않는다. 그는 보병에 속한다.

12. ⓐ 그들은 그 나라가 적을 향한 숨겨진 미사일을 가지고 있을 것을 두려워한다.

13. ⓒ 김하사의 임무는 해병들이 강을 건널 장소를 찾는 것이다.

14. ⓑ 베르나도는 진급한 후 사기충천 하였다.

15. ⓓ 그 부대원들은 공격, 방어, 저항 훈련을 실시하였다. 그 훈련은 공격, 수비 그리고 방어훈련을 포함한다.

16. ⓓ 적군은 엄청난 저항을 참아냈다. 그들의 저항은 대단했다.

17. ⓑ 헬리콥터는 앞부분과 꼬리에 한 쌍의 회전날개를 가지고 있다.

18. ⓒ 그는 거의 100% 정확하게 표적을 맞힐 수 있다.

19. ⓑ 그 사람들은 전문 저격수이다. 그들 모두는 표적을 맞혔다.

20. ⓑ 그 훈련은 지휘관의 생각을 시험하였다. 그들은 이론을 실전에 적용하였다.

21. ⓒ 그 국가들은 동맹군이다.

22. ⓐ 군인들은 깔끔한 외모를 보여주어야 한다. 군복은 깨끗하게 다려지고, 신발은 광이 나고, 머리는 짧게 유지해야 한다.

23. ⓐ 미국대통령은 군대를 강화하기 위해 항상 예비군을 소집할 수 있다.

24. ⓑ 오웬 상사는 NCO클럽에서 로웨 상사와 윌슨 상사를 만날 것이다.

25. ⓓ 병사들의 연습과 훈련 상태는 그들의 행진에서 드러났다.

26. ⓒ 군인들은 국기가 지날 때 경례한다.

27. ⓐ 4성의 미군 장교는 대장이라고 불린다.

28. ⓐ 이것은 필립 제독의 전역기념 파티이다. 그는 주빈이다.

29. ⓐ 고급 장교는 항상 초급장교의 오른쪽에 앉거나 걷는다. 오른쪽이 상석이다.

30. ⓑ 성장하는 동안 많은 역경에도 불구하고, 그는 해군에서 훌륭한 장교가 되었다.

31. ⓒ 육군 기지는 하나의 군사 시설이다.

32. ⓒ 은색 막대기는 육군 중위를 상징하는 계급장이다.

33. ⓐ 사격술은 모든 군인에게 중요하다.

34. ⓒ 축하를 위한 분열이 있을 것이다.

35. ⓑ 빌은 해군 소위다. 그는 해군에서 근무한다.

36. ⓑ 웨스트필드 장군 아래에서 일하는 것은 특별한 은혜다.

37. ⓑ 닉슨씨가 모임에서 어떤 말을 하면, 다른 모든 사람들은 "그렇습니다." 하고 말한다. 그들은 닉슨씨의 부하
들이다.

38. ⓒ 그 부대는 적군의 무기 공격을 막기 위하여 길고 깊은 굴을 팠다. 그들은 참호를 팠다.

39. ⓒ 이 레이더는 한 번에 70기의 항공기 위치를 보여줄 수 있다.

40. ⓑ 날개의 좁은 가장자리에 위치한 보조날개는 착륙시 비행기의 속도를 낮추기 위해 아래로 내려진다.

41. ⓑ 그 부사관은 한 마디 말도 안했다. 그러나 그의 얼굴의 찡그림 표정은 은연중에 불만을 보여주었다.

42. ⓐ 그 중대장은 단합, 협동, 집단의 충성심을 촉구함으로써 결속을 유지하려고 노력하고 있다.

43. ⓑ 그 군인들은 영구 막사를 할당받을 때까지는 나무로 된 임시 막사에 숙소를 할당받았다.

44. ⓒ 그 대령은 그 연구보고서를 좋아했다. 그는 거기에 인가하는 표시를 했다.

45. ⓐ 그 지역은 탄약을 보관할 장소로 지정되었다.

New American Language Course

adhere / 고수하다, 집착하다 (follow, to stay attached)

They adhered to their original plan.

(그들은 원래의 계획을 고수하였다.)

arrange / 배열하다, 조정하다 (to classify, to put in the proper order. to make ready)

The officers arrange matters so that one of them is always on duty.

(장교들이 상황을 정리하여, 그들 중 한 명이 항상 근무하도록 한다.)

clarify / 분명하게 하다, 명확히 하다 (to make or become clear)

Could you please clarify the second point?

(두 번째 사항을 상세히 말할 수 있습니까?)

conclude / 결론내리다, 끝내다 (end, finish)

She concluded her speech with a safe trip home.

(그녀는 집으로 안전하게 여행하라는 말로 연설을 마쳤다.)

discharge / 내리다, 해임하다, 귀가시키다 (to fire or shoot to release or send away)

The children were discharged early from school.

(학생들은 학교에서 일찍 귀가하게 되었다.)

disguise / 변장하다, 가장하다 (to hide or obscure, to change one's appearance)

The man disguised himself by putting on a false beard and a wig.

(그 사람은 가짜수염을 달고 가발을 써서 위장하였다.)

dismiss / 떠나게 하다, 해산시키다 (to send away or to allow to leave)

Don't dismiss the idea before you think about it.

(생각해 보지도 않고 아이디어를 버리지 마라.)

hide / 감추다, 보이지 않게 하다 (to conceal, to turn away)

I hide my private papers in a cabinet.

(나는 개인서류를 캐비넷에 감춘다.)

hover / 맴돌다, 공중에 떠있다 (to hang fluttering or suspended in the air)

The helicopter is hovering over a fortress.

(헬리콥터가 요새 위로 선회하고 있다.)

clear / 치우다, 소계하다 (to remove something that is not wanted)

Clear all of your books and notes off the desk.

(모든 책과 공책을 책상에서 치우세요.)

commit / 의무를 지우다, 위임하다 (to make someone agree or promise to do something)

The agreement commits them to a minimum number of performances per year.

(그 합의서는 1년에 최소한의 공연을 해야 하는 것으로 되어 있다.)

count on / 믿다, 의지하다 (rely on, trust)

The ship counts on the captain's making the right decision.

(함정은 함장의 올바른 결정에 좌우된다.)

delegate / 위임하다, 대리로 보내다 (to entrust authority to another person)

Since Col Kelly couldn't attend the meeting, he delegated Maj Owens to go in his place.

(캘리 대령은 그 모임에 참석할 수 없었기 때문에, 오웬 소령을 대리로 위임했다.)

7. 군사 및 무기

deviate / 벗어나다, 빗나가다 (to do something differently, to be different from)

The war on terror deviated much of the world's energy and attention away from other decisive problems.

(테러에 대한 전쟁으로 중요한 문제에 대한 세계의 에너지와 관심이 많이 분산되었다.)

disregard / 무시하다, 경시하다 (to pay little attention to, neglect)

The police and security forces must not disregard human rights.

(경찰과 안전요원들은 인권을 무시하지 않아야 한다.)

embark / 착수하다, 시작하다 (start or commence), 출항하다 (begin a journey)

The navy embarked on a new training program for admiral designees. Only time will tell whether or not the program is successful!

(해군은 제독지명자를 위한 새로운 훈련 계획을 시작했다. 시간이 지나면 그 계획이 성공적인지 알 수 있을 것이다.)

enlist / 입대하다, 모병하다 (join the military of country)

Charlie left shortly after he was enlisted in the Army.

(찰리는 육군에 잠시 입대한 후 떠났다.)

exhibit / 전시하다, 진열하다 (to put something interesting in a museum or other public place)

Where are you going to exhibit next?

(다음에는 어떤 것을 전시하려고 하십니까?)

extinguish / 끄다, 진화하다 (to put out)

The firefighters tried to extinguish the flames.

(소방요원들이 화재를 진압하려고 노력했다.)

formulate / 공식화하다, 명확하게 하다 (to develop a plan, system, or proposal carefully, thinking about all of its details)

The government is formulating a new strategy to combat crime.

(그 정부는 범죄와 전쟁하기 위한 새로운 전략을 짜고 있다.)

guard / 지키다, 보호하다 (protect someone/something from harm)

The male fish guards the eggs.

(수컷 고기들은 알을 보호한다.)

integrate / 통합하다, 결합시키다 (to bring parts together into a whole)

The mid-level leader needs to be concerned about how to integrate the activities of these multiple work groups into some sort of cohesive objective.

(중간 그룹의 지도자는 이 다양한 업무집단의 활동을 일종의 일관된 목적에 통합하는 방법에 관심을 기울여야 한다.)

issue / 내다, 발행하다 (to announce something or give it to people officially)

The bank issued a warning that charges are likely to rise sharply.

(그 은행은 부과금이 상당히 오를 것이라는 것을 경고하였다.)

minimize / 최소화하다, 경시하다 (to reduce something harmful or unpleasant to the smallest amount or degree)

I don't want to minimize their role in the campaign.

(나는 그 캠페인에서 그들의 역할을 최소화해야 한다고 생각하지 않는다.)

mobilize / 동원하다, 전시체제로 바꾸다 (to bring into readiness, to organize for active service)

The commander mobilized the troops for the upcoming mission.

(사령관은 다음 임무를 위해 군대를 동원하였다.)

ECL시험 대비 New ALC 필수어휘 완성

negate / 무효로 하다, 부인하다 (to take away effectiveness)

Supervisors must be careful to avoid giving their subordinates only the dull and boring jobs, for this will quickly discourage energetic subordinates and will negate the benefits of delegation.

(감독관은 부하에게 단지 지루하고 싫증난 일만 주지 않도록 해야 한다. 왜냐하면, 이는 활기 있는 부하들을 낙담하게하고, 위임의 효과를 무효화하기 때문이다.)

order / 명령하다, 지시하다 (to request, direct or command)

Local police have ordered that all guns in the region be registered.

(지방 경찰은 그 지역의 모든 권총을 등록하도록 지시하였다.)

orient / 나아가다, 순응하다 (to give direction or guidance to)

They need to know how to find and to troubleshot whatever problems arise, how to orient in order to train their people to function effectively, and how to inspect their equipment at the entry level.

(그들은 발생하는 모든 문제를 찾아내어 해결하고, 올바르게 기능을 하도록 사람들을 훈련하기 위해 방향을 설정하는 방법, 그리고 도입단계에서 장비를 조사하는 방법을 알아야 한다.)

outfit / 채비하다, 공급하다 (to provide someone or something with the clothes)

A van is outfitted with modems and laptop computers.

(어떤 밴은 모뎀과 휴대용 컴퓨터가 장착되어 있다.)

promotion / 승진, 진급, 판촉 (a move to a more important job or rank, a set of advertisement)

They are doing a special promotion of French wines.

(그들은 프랑스 와인을 위해 특별 판촉을 하고 있다.)

re-enlist / 다시 입대하다(시키다) (to enlist again, to enroll for service again)

They both re-enlisted in the Navy a month before the war broke out.
(그들은 전쟁이 발발하기 한 달 전에 해군에 재입대하였다.)

reprimand / 견책하다, 징계하다 (to blame, reprove, or censure)

The officer was severely reprimanded for his unprofessional attitude.
(그 장교는 장교답지 못한 태도로 심하게 비난받았다.)

rotate / 회전하다[시키다] (change regularly, to turn around)

The earth is rotating around the sun.
(지구는 태양 둘레를 돈다.)

serve / 도움이 되다, 이바지하다 (to be used for a particular purpose, especially not the main or original purpose)

His death serves to remind us just how dangerous using drugs can be.
(그의 죽음은 마약이 얼마나 위험한 것인지를 일깨워주고 있다.)

slouch / 단정하지 않게 행동하다 (to stand, sit or move in a lazy way)

A soldier at attention stands erect; he never slouches. Sit up straight!
(차렷을 한 군인은 똑바로 선다. 결코 구부리지 않는다. 똑바로 앉아라.)

surrender / 항복하다, 넘겨주다 (to give up possession of or power over)

The debtor agreed to surrender all claims to the property.
(채무자는 재산에 대한 모든 권리를 넘겨주는 데 동의하였다.)

suspend / 계류하다 [시키다], 중지하다 (to hang, to stop for a time)

The ship was suspended while safety checks were carried on.
(그 배는 안전검사가 진행되는 동안 계류되었다.)

ECL시험 대비 New ALC 필수어휘 완성

troubleshoot / 조사하여 해결하다 [처치하다] (determine and settle problems)

My brother troubleshoots for a large industrial firm.

(내 동생은 대기업에서 문제를 발견하고 처리하는 일을 한다.)

withstand / 저항하다, 반항하다 (to oppose, resist, or endure)

Mobile phones are designed to withstand rough treatment.

(휴대폰은 거칠게 다루어도 견딜 수 있도록 설계되어 있다.)

2. 연습문제

1. The enemy is coming closer. They are ______ .

   ⓐ demanding   ⓑ advancing   ⓒ depressing   ⓓ retreating

2. You should ______ the instructions for us.

   ⓐ clarity   ⓑ clearing   ⓒ clarify   ⓓ clearance

3. Com. Charles ______ his briefing with a safety reminder.

   ⓐ occurred   ⓑ called off   ⓒ concluded   ⓓ considered

4. The troops wore camouflage clothing to hide their appearance.

   ⓐ conceal   ⓑ clear   ⓒ hinder   ⓓ heal

5. James thought the gun was empty, but he guessed wrong. It ______ while he was cleaning it.

   ⓐ extended   ⓑ hesitated

   ⓒ discharged   ⓓ charged

6. I can ______ you, Sergeant, Now, this machine works very well.

   ⓐ dismiss   ⓑ dispel   ⓒ resist   ⓓ disperse

7. He ______ the class early because he was under the weather.

   ⓐ dismissed   ⓑ absent   ⓒ removed   ⓓ dusted

8. He was almost finishing his report when the captain _______ his office.
   ⓐ entered   ⓑ had entered   ⓒ enters   ⓓ has entered

9. The Air Force Academy is the youngest of the U.S. service academies. It was _______ in 1954.
   ⓐ established   ⓑ acquired   ⓒ marked   ⓓ motivated

10. Lt Hall _______ his promotion next year.
   ⓐ will to get   ⓑ getting   ⓒ going to get   ⓓ gets

11. Lt. Paul is on sick leave, and this report must _______ today. Thus, you'll have to do it.
   ⓐ get to   ⓑ get in   ⓒ get up   ⓓ get out

12. The admiral's behaviour is always _______ by his sense of honor.
   ⓐ guided   ⓑ restricted   ⓒ obtained   ⓓ developed

13. A flock of crows often _______ over dead animals in winter.
   ⓐ hover   ⓑ swerve   ⓒ swell   ⓓ lounge

14. Does an overseas assignment _______ the seamen these days?
   ⓐ detect   ⓑ identify   ⓒ interest   ⓓ ignite

15. Even though that country is small, it _______ a large army and navy.
   ⓐ engages   ⓑ defends   ⓒ maintains   ⓓ arranges

16. The captain _______ the airman to report to the clinic at 0700.
   ⓐ watched   ⓑ ordered   ⓒ scolded   ⓓ noticed

17. Before they go overseas, the soldiers will be equipped with special weapons and uniforms.

    ⓐ admired   ⓑ deceived   ⓒ evaluated   ⓓ outfitted

18. He found it too painful to _______ his family for a year while he was stationed in another country.

    ⓐ get along with   ⓑ part with   ⓒ dispatch   ⓓ take part with

19. The seaman made a mistake, so his sergeant _______ him.

    ⓐ recommended   ⓑ reprimanded   ⓒ recited   ⓓ regretted

20. Night watch duty will _______ : every soldier will get a turn everyday.

    ⓐ restore   ⓑ rotate   ⓒ roar   ⓓ roast

21. They _______ their weapons to the enemy.

    ⓐ surrendered   ⓑ revolved   ⓒ rendered   ⓓ resumed

22. The commander found the problem, and then _______ correcting it.

    ⓐ sent for   ⓑ set about   ⓒ dig out   ⓓ ran for

23. The helicopter _______ a rope to save the trapped soldiers in the forest.

    ⓐ spun   ⓑ suspended
    ⓒ seduced   ⓓ shamed

24. Our drill instructors always _______ self-discipline and self-confidence.

    ⓐ shrank   ⓑ subscribed in
    ⓒ stressed   ⓓ shrugged

25. The military branches often joined together to complete the practice exercise. They
   _____ .
   ⓐ dismissed   ⓑ issued   ⓒ united   ⓓ calibrated

26. People driving on the Naval base must _____ to the speed limit.
   ⓐ adhere   ⓑ keep   ⓒ hold   ⓓ fasten

27. Our infantry cannot _____ until the area is cleared.
   ⓐ depress   ⓑ interfere   ⓒ advance   ⓓ deteriorate

28. Davis _____ 5 years to the navy.
   ⓐ defended   ⓑ simulated   ⓒ adopted   ⓓ committed

29. The soldiers were told to _____ his unreasonable order and continue as previously
   planned.
   ⓐ disregard   ⓑ challenge   ⓒ distinguish   ⓓ extinguish

30. The soldiers _____ from the agreed route and got lost.
   ⓐ deviated   ⓑ discriminated   ⓒ revolved   ⓓ disposed

31. The trainer _____ the candles and sat in complete darkness.
   ⓐ surrendered   ⓑ extinguished
   ⓒ surrendered   ⓓ distinguished

32. Frank: Why did Martin get that short haircut?
   Tony: He _____ in the Army
   ⓐ retired   ⓑ promoted   ⓒ previewed   ⓓ enlisted

33. Has a new plan of attack been _____ yet?

    ⓐ denied   ⓑ conflicted   ⓒ cautioned   ⓓ formulated

34. Lieutenant Herman Richmond will be the pilot who _____ this plane.

    ⓐ directs   ⓑ flies   ⓒ collect   ⓓ places

35. Soldiers with dogs were used to _____ the base entrance.

    ⓐ prepare   ⓑ guard   ⓒ crawl   ⓓ instruct

36. No one is allowed to enter the small building. _____ the door!

    ⓐ Guard   ⓑ Praise   ⓒ Mop   ⓓ Crawl

37. The pilots had to _____ the number of test flights for the new aircraft because production was behind schedule.

    ⓐ minimize   ⓑ disperse   ⓒ descend   ⓓ unite

38. James really likes the Navy and plans to sign up for 5 more years. He's going to _____ .

    ⓐ hesitate   ⓑ recruit   ⓒ re-enlist   ⓓ resist

39. The Air Force _____ the Army from the air.

    ⓐ supports   ⓑ gathers   ⓒ detects   ⓓ displays

40. Lt. Edward is going to be sent to _____ a problem at the Air-force base.

    ⓐ trouble   ⓑ trend   ⓒ trade   ⓓ troubleshoot

41. The sergeant caught the private _____ on watch last night.

    ⓐ sleeping   ⓑ slept   ⓒ sleep   ⓓ to sleep

42. I ______ my country. I was in the military seven years.

    ⓐ trained   ⓑ served   ⓒ retired   ⓓ command

43. Mr. Kevin is a very brave man. He has ______ a lot of fighting during the war.

    ⓐ trod   ⓑ avoided   ⓒ withstood   ⓓ surrendered

44. How was the military information arranged?

    ⓐ corroded   ⓑ shattered   ⓒ classified   ⓓ exhibited

45. In the jungle or desert, soldiers must wear special clothes and makeup to disguise themselves.

    ⓐ shift   ⓑ camouflage   ⓒ shield   ⓓ disgust

46. The captain demonstrates all the characteristics of a good leader.

    ⓐ looks   ⓑ takes action   ⓒ admires   ⓓ exhibits

47. Our new warships can withstand terrible storms at sea.

    ⓐ withdraw   ⓑ decay   ⓑ remove   ⓒ endure

48. The order to attack was given out by the commander. He ______ the order.

    ⓐ minimized   ⓑ united   ⓒ issued   ⓓ rescued

49. The men were out of ammunition, but they refused to give up.

    ⓐ defend   ⓑ attack   ⓒ surrender   ⓓ retreat

50. The seamen really look up to their commander.

    ⓐ dislike   ⓑ respect   ⓒ follow   ⓓ accompany

51. Although Sgt Blake was absent without leave from duty, the fact that he had to take his critically ill child to the hospital was an extenuating circumstance. He therefore was not penalized harshly for his offense.

ⓐ This fact made the offense more serious.

ⓑ This fact made the offense seem less serious.

ⓒ This fact had no effect on the seriousness of the offense.

ⓓ This fact couldn't be an excuse

정답 / 해석

1. ⓑ 적이 가까이 다가오고 있다. 그들이 진격하고 있다.

2. ⓒ 우리에게 지시사항을 명확히 해야 한다.

3. ⓒ 찰스 중령은 안전에 대해 경각시킨 뒤에 브리핑을 마무리했다.

4. ⓐ 군인들은 외모를 감추기 위해서 위장복을 입었다.

5. ⓒ 제임스는 총이 장전되어 있지 않다고 생각했으나, 잘못 생각하였다. 그가 총을 소제하는 동안 발사되었다.

6. ⓐ 부사관, 자네는 가도 좋다. 이제 이 기계는 잘 작동한다.

7. ⓐ 그는 몸이 좋지 않아, 수업을 일찍 끝냈다.

8. ⓐ 그 함장[대령, 대위]이 사무실에 들어왔을 때 그는 보고서를 거의 끝내고 있었다.

9. ⓐ 미국 사관학교 가운데 공군사관학교의 역사가 가장 짧다. 공군사관학교는 1954년에 설립되었다.

10. ⓓ 할 대위는 내년에 진급한다.

11. ⓓ 폴 대위는 병가이고, 이 보고서는 오늘 나와야한다. 그러므로 너가 그것을 해야 한다.

12. ⓐ 그 제독의 행동은 항상 명예심에 기초를 둔다.

13. ⓐ 한 떼의 까마귀들이 겨울에는 종종 죽은 동물 위에 배회한다.

14. ⓒ 해외근무가 요즈음 해군에게 관심을 끕니까?

15. ⓒ 그 나라는 작지만 강한 육군과 해군을 유지하고 있다.

16. ⓑ 그 대위는 7시에 의무대에 출두하라고 항공병에게 명령하였다.

17. ⓓ 외국으로 나가기 전에 병사들은 특수 무기와 유니폼을 갖추어야 한다.

18. ⓑ 그는 외국에 주둔해 있는 동안 그의 가족과 헤어지는 것이 매우 고통스러운 것을 알았다.

19. ⓑ 그 수병이 실수를 해서, 담당 부사관이 그를 힐책하였다.

20. ⓑ 밤 근무는 순환한다. 모든 군인은 매일 차례대로 선다.

21. ⓐ 그들은 무기를 적에게 넘겨주었다.

22. ⓑ 그 사령관은 문제를 발견하고 이를 수정하기 시작했다.

23. ⓑ 헬리콥터가 숲 속에 갇힌 군인들을 구하기 위해서 로프를 매달았다.

24. ⓒ 우리의 훈련조교는 항상 자율과 자신감을 강조했다.

25. ⓒ 그 부대들은 종종 군사훈련을 완수하기 위하여 연합한다.

26. ⓐ 해군기지에서 운전하는 사람들은 속도제한을 고수해야한다.

27. ⓒ 그 지역이 소개될 때까지는 우리 보병은 전진할 수 없다.

28. ⓓ 데이비스는 5년간 해군에서 복무했다.

29. ⓐ 군인들을 그의 비합리적인 명령을 무시하고 이전에 계획된 대로 계속하라고 들었다.

30. ⓐ 군인들은 합의된 통로를 이탈하여 실종되었다.

31. ⓑ 그 훈련관은 촛불을 끄고 깜깜한 어둠 속에 앉아 있었다.

32. ⓓ 프랭크: 마틴은 왜 머리를 짧게 깎았지?

　　　　토니: 육군에 입대했답니다.

33. ⓓ 새로운 공격계획이 이미 수립되었느냐?

34. ⓑ 헐만 리차드 대위가 이 항공기를 운항하게 될 것이다.

35. ⓑ 군견을 가진 병사들은 부대 입구를 감시하였다.

36. ⓐ 아무도 그 작은 방에 들여보내서는 안 된다. 그 문을 감시하라!

37. ⓐ 계획에 비해 늦게 생산됨으로 인해 그 비행사는 새 항공기의 평가 비행 횟수를 최소화해야만 했다.

38. ⓒ 제임스는 해군을 좋아하여서, 5년 더 연장할 것이다. 그는 재입대할 것이다.

39. ⓐ 공군은 공중에서 육군을 지원한다.

40. ⓓ 에드워드 대위는 공군기지에서 문제점을 발견수리하기 위하여 파견되었다.

41. ⓐ 그 부사관은 지난 밤 사병이 경계 중에 자고 있는 것을 적발했다.

42. ⓑ 나는 군에 복무하였다. 7년 동안 근무하였다.

43. ⓒ 캐빈씨는 매우 용감한 사람이다. 그는 전쟁 동안 많은 전투를 겪었다.

44. ⓒ 군사정보는 어떻게 정리됩니까?

45. ⓑ 밀림이나 사막에서는 군인들은 위장하기 위해서 특수복과 분장을 해야 한다.

46. ⓓ 그 대령은 훌륭한 지도자의 자질을 보여주고 있다.

47. ⓒ 우리의 새 전함은 바다에서의 심한 폭풍을 견딜 수 있다.

48. ⓒ 공격명령은 사령관이 내렸다. 그가 그 명령을 내렸다.

49. ⓒ 그들은 탄약이 떨어졌으나, 항복하기를 거부하였다.

50. ⓑ 그 수병들은 진실로 그들의 지휘관을 존경한다.

51. ⓑ 블레이크 부사관이 무단 결근했지만, 그가 매우 위중한 자식을 병원으로 데리고 가야 했다는 사실은 참작
　　　이 되는 상황이었다. 그는 그러므로 그의 위반행위에 대해 심하게 처벌되지 않았다.

New American Language Course

absolute / 절대적인, 확실한 (perfect, complete)

Our new president won an absolute majority in the election.
(우리 새 대통령은 선거에서 절대 다수를 얻었다.)

ambiguous / 분명하지 않은, 애매한 (able to be understood in more than one way)

In written form, delegation is less likely to be ambiguous, and it reduces the possibility of distortion or abuses by subordinates.
(서면상으로는 위임이 덜 애매하며, 하급자가 곡해 또는 남용할 가능성이 줄어든다.)

approximately / 약, 대략 (about)

The plane will land in approximately 30 minutes. (그 비행기는 약 30분 후에 착륙할 것이다.)

atomic / 원자의, 원자력에 의한 (powered by nuclear energy)

Atomic energy is often used to drive submarines and cruisers.
(원자에너지는 종종 잠수함과 순양함을 운전하기 위해 사용된다.)

compulsory / 강제된, 의무적인 (must be done because of a rule or law)

A school outfit is no longer compulsory (교복은 더 이상 강제적인 것이 아니다.)

cynical / 냉소적인, 비꼬는 (pessimistic, disbelieving in man's sincerity of motive)

If I have just trained in the skills and knowledge to perform that supervisory function, and I'm denying them that chance, then they're going to get frustrated and cynical, questioning my scruple, and be underworked.

(내가 감독기능을 행할 수 있는 기술과 지식을 훈련시킨 뒤에, 그들에게 기회를 주지 않으면 그들은 좌절하고 냉소적이 되며, 나의 도덕관에 의문을 가지며 열심히 일하지 않는다.)

decisive / 결단력이 있는, 단호한 (determinate, firm)

Capt. Cook is not a very decisive person; he spends too much time weighing the pros and cons.
(쿡 함장은 매우 결단력있는 사람은 아니다; 그는 득실을 계산하는 데 너무 많은 시간 을 보낸다.)

fundamental / 기본의, 필수적인 (basic, essential)

We must understand the fundamental concept of English grammar.
(우리는 영문법의 기본개념을 이해해야 한다.)

fuzzy / 분명치 않은 (not clear, indistinct)

When the relationship between superiors and subordinates is fuzzy, there is a great potential for confusion, conflict, and neglect within the organization.
(상관과 하급자의 관계가 분명치 않으면, 조직내에 혼란, 갈등, 업무소홀의 가능성이 커진다.)

intense / 격렬한, 심한 (very great or extreme)

He's been under intense pressure. (그는 극심한 압력을 받고 있다.)

keen / 날카로운, 예민한 (highly sensitive or perceptive)

Implementing the principles of delegation requires a keen understanding of people and an accurate insight of their limitations.
(위임의 원칙을 수행하기 위해서는 사람들을 깊이 이해하고 그들의 한계를 정확히 통찰해야 한다.)

lean / 기대다, 기울다 (to incline or bend, to cause to lean or rest)

The frame looks to lean a little to the left.
(그 구조물은 약간 왼쪽으로 기울어진 것처럼 보인다.)

makeshift / 임시변통의, 일시적인 (something constructed for temporary use)

In order to train new pilots as quickly as possible, they made a makeshift cockpit out of an old car and jet instruments.

(가능한 빨리 새 조종사를 훈련시키기 위해 그들은 오래된 차와 추진기로 임시 조종실을 만들었다.)

objective / 객관적인, 편견이 없는 (without bias or prejudice)

You must make an objective assessment of your followers.

(당신은 부하들을 객관적으로 평가해야 한다.)

periodic / 주기적인, 정기적인 (occurring at regular intervals or from time to time)

The old man suffers periodic nervous breakdowns.

(그 노인은 주기적인 신경쇠약을 앓고 있다.)

proficient / 능숙한, 숙달된 (competent, skilled)

It's very, very difficult for the boss to be technically proficient in all of the weapons systems.

(상관이 무기체계의 모든 면을 기술적으로 능숙하기는 매우 어렵다.)

stinging / 신랄한, 뼈아픈 (causing pain, either physical or mental)

The sergeant's stinging remarks remained with Hayden throughout the sleepless night.

(그 부사관의 뼈 아픈 말에 헤이든은 밤새 잠을 못이뤘다.)

stringent / 엄중한, 엄격한 (strict or severe)

The company commander has very stringent rules regarding being late for duty. My advice to you would be to be on time!

(그 중대지휘관은 임무를 늦게 수행하는 데 대해 매우 엄격한 규칙을 가지고 있다. 너에게 줄 충고는 시간을 맞추라는 것이다.)

vital / 절대 필요한, 치명적인 (essential, necessary, fatal)

Trust is a vital component in any close relationship.

(신뢰는 모든 밀접한 관계에서 결정적인 요소이다.)

visual / 시각의, 눈에 보이는 (relating to things that you can see)

Television news brings us visual images from around the world.

(TV 뉴스는 전 세계의 모습을 시각적으로 보여준다.)

2. 연습문제

1. The major gave the lieutenant _______ control in the office.
   ⓐ composite   ⓑ absolute   ⓒ fundamental   ⓓ absurd

2. Had the submarine _______ submerged before the enemy attacked it?
   ⓐ already   ⓑ yet   ⓒ still   ⓓ also

3. The sergeant gave us _______ one hour to clean the barracks.
   ⓐ aboard   ⓑ average
   ⓒ approximately   ⓓ abnormal

4. The soldiers were _______ by the sudden explosion of the bomb.
   ⓐ asleep   ⓑ normal   ⓒ religious   ⓓ astonished

5. John just enlisted into the Marine Corps. He's going to start _______ training.
   ⓐ basic   ⓑ advanced   ⓒ complex   ⓓ excited

6. It's _______ for men and women in the armed forces to wear their uniforms properly.
   ⓐ loyal   ⓑ honorable   ⓒ compulsory   ⓓ optional

7. Almost all of the officers at the meeting were in civilian clothes. _______ were wearing uniforms.
   ⓐ Quite a few   ⓑ Few   ⓒ Little   ⓓ A little

8. There is a _____ difference between the two officers: one is a "talker" and the other is a "doer".

ⓐ diagonal　　　ⓑ fundamental　　　ⓒ horizontal　　　ⓓ racial

9. The fighting during the war was very _____ .

ⓐ intense　　　ⓑ stupid　　　ⓒ prime　　　ⓓ auxiliary

10. The drill sergeant forbids the trainees or recruits to _____ their rifles against the tanks.

ⓐ leap　　　ⓑ lie　　　ⓒ lean　　　ⓓ lease

11. Capt Moore doesn't like two junior officers in the base intentionally, so his evaluations of them are never _____ .

ⓐ objective　　　ⓑ subjective　　　ⓒ hardworking　　　ⓓ indecisive

12. The sergeant checks his men's weapons every other week. He holds _____ inspections.

ⓐ random　　　ⓑ perilous　　　ⓒ periodic　　　ⓓ occasional

13. An admiral is _____ to a captain.

ⓐ junior　　　ⓑ senior　　　ⓒ subordinate　　　ⓓ equivalent

14. After several months of practice, Paul could become a(n) _____ marksman.

ⓐ skilled　　　ⓑ dreadful　　　ⓒ terrible　　　ⓓ extinguished

15. Why is the new recruit so _____ ?

ⓐ character　　　ⓑ selfishness　　　ⓒ personality　　　ⓓ unfriendly

16. It's _____ that you carry out your mission in military operations.

ⓐ vital　　　ⓑ proficient　　　ⓒ practical　　　ⓓ inevitable

17. The advance unit has made _______ contact with the enemy.

    ⓐ variable   ⓑ visual   ⓒ blurry   ⓓ ensemble

18. Hey, Lt Jackson, you report to the commander at once!

    ⓐ instantly   ⓑ incessantly   ⓒ incidentally   ⓓ independently

19. The U.S.S. Nautilus was the first American atomic powered submarine.

    ⓐ nuclear   ⓑ molecule   ⓒ toxic   ⓓ particle

20. An officer should always be meticulous in his/her dress. It is of utmost importance that officers maintain their appearance.

    ⓐ very careful with attention to detail   ⓑ wearing lots of ribbons and metals
    ⓒ showing no consideration   ⓓ ready to fight or use force

정답/해석

1. ⓑ 소령은 대위에게 그 사무실에 대한 전적인 통제권을 주었다.

2. ⓐ 적이 공격하기 전에 잠수함이 이미 잠수하였느냐?

3. ⓒ 그 부사관은 우리에게 건물을 청소하도록 약 한 시간을 주었다.

4. ⓓ 그 병사들은 갑작스런 폭탄의 폭발에 놀랐다.

5. ⓐ 존은 해병대에 막 입대 하였다. 그는 기본 군사훈련을 시작할 것이다.

6. ⓒ 남자건 여자건 군에서는 군복을 제대로 입도록 규정하고 있다.

7. ⓑ 그 모임에서 대부분의 장교는 사복을 입고 있었다. 제복을 입은 사람은 거의 없었다.

8. ⓑ 두 장교간에는 근본적인 차이가 있다. 하나는 "말을 앞세우는 사람" 이고 또 한 사람은 "행동가" 이다.

9. ⓐ 그 전쟁 중의 그 전투는 아주 격렬하였다.

10. ⓒ 훈련담당 부사관은 피교육생 또는 신병이 탱크에 총을 기대어 놓는 것을 금지한다.

11. ⓐ 무어 대령[대위]는 그 기지에 있는 두 명의 하급장교를 고의로 싫어하였다. 그래서 그들에 대한 그의 평가는 객관적이지 않다.

12. ⓒ 그 부사관은 부하들의 무기를 매 2주마다 확인한다. 그는 주기적인 검사를 계속 유지한다.

13. ⓑ 제독은 대령보다 높다.

14. ⓐ 여러 달 훈련 한 뒤에 폴은 숙련된 사수가 될 수 있었다.

15. ⓓ 신병은 왜 그렇게 무뚝뚝한가?

16. ⓐ 군사작전에서 사명을 수행하는 것은 매우 중요하다.

17. ⓑ 그 전진 부대는 적을 가시적으로 접촉하였다.

18. ⓐ 야, 잭슨대위, 즉시 지휘관에게 보고해.

19. ⓐ 유에스에스 노틸러스는 미국의 최초 핵추진 잠수함이다.

20. ⓐ 장교는 복장에서 항상 세심해야 한다. 장교가 외모를 유지하는 것은 매우 중요하다.

어휘, 관용구, 문형 종합

기본어휘 / 연습 문제

D

New American
Language Course

at a time / 한번에, 동시에 (at one time, in one group or unit)

He ran up the steps three at a time.

(그는 한 번에 세 계단식 올라갔다.)

be to / 하기로 되어있다, 예정이다 (have to, is going to)

Seoul's transportation system is to be changed drastically starting 1 of January.

(서울의 교통체계는 1월 1일을 시작으로 급격하게 변하게 되어 있다.)

call the shots / 지휘하다, 감독하다 (to be in charge, to direct, control)

No delegation takes place if the commander calls the shots on all important matters in the organization.

(지휘관이 조직의 모든 중요한 문제에 지시를 하면 위임이 되지 않는다.)

call up / 소환하다, 상기시키다 (summon, recall)

The smell of the sea calls up memories of my childhood.

(바다 냄새는 내 어릴 적 추억을 상기한다.)

despite / 멸시, 무례 (contemptuous disregard, lack of respect)

We want neither favor nor despite.

(우리는 편애도 멸시도 원하지 않는다.)

drastically / 격렬하게, 과감하게 (affecting strongly or severely)

The counseling function changes drastically at the top. In sharp contrast to lower levels,

top level leaders no longer are engaged in the day to day counseling function.
(상담기능은 지휘부에서는 크게 바뀐다. 하위계층과 달리, 상위 지도자들은 더 이상 일일 상담기능에 주의를 기울이지 않는다.)

even so / 비록 그렇다 하더라도 (nevertheless, still, however)

She claimed the sauce contained no garlic, but even so the child wouldn't like to taste it.
(그녀는 양념에 마늘이 없다고 단언하였지만, 그래도 아이들은 그것을 시식하려 하지 않았다.)

give in / 굴복하다, 따르다 (to stop competing or arguing and accept)

She had to struggle hard not to give in to a desire to laugh.
(그녀는 웃음을 참기 위해 열심히 노력했다.)

fight off / 격퇴하다, 퇴치하다 (to stop someone who is attacking you)

The woman managed to fight off her attackers.
(그 여자는 그녀에 대한 공격자들을 물리쳤다.)

go through / 통과하다, 경험하다 (endure, suffer, experience)

China has been going through a period of irreversible change these days.
(중국은 요즈음 돌이킬 수 없는 변화의 시기를 겪고 있었다.)

hang on to / 붙잡고 늘어지다, 놓지 않다 (to keep firmly, hold tightly)

The man hung on to the rail in order not to fall to the ground.
(그 사람은 난간에 매달려 땅에 떨어지지 않으려고 하였다.)

in charge of / 관리[감독]하고 있는 (have responsibility or supervision of)

Who's in charge of this group?
(누가 이 그룹을 책임지고 있느냐?)

in comparison to / 비교하여, 비교해 보면 (compared with)

The decoration of the dining room is stark in comparison with that of the conference room.
(식당의 장식은 회의실의 장식과 비교하면 볼품 없다.)

in regard to / 에 관해서 (concerning, in connection with, in reference to)

My teacher spoke to me with regard to my low marks.
(우리 선생님은 내 성적이 낮은 점에 대해 이야기하였다.)

in the course of time / 시간이 경과 한 후에 (after some time has passed)

Don't worry, it will all become clear in the course of time.
(걱정하지 마세요, 시간이 지나면 모든 것이 분명해 질 것입니다.)

in the event of / ~할 경우에는 (if there is)

Take your umbrella in case of rain.
(비올 것을 대비하여 우산을 가져가시오.)

look forward to / 기대하다, 기다리다 (to expect with pleasure or hope)

We are looking forward to summer vacation.
(우리는 여름방학을 기대하고 있다.)

look up to / 존경하다 (to honor or admire)

Young men should look up to older ones, so older men should be good examples.
(젊은이는 나이 든 사람을 존경하고, 또한 나이 든 사람은 좋은 본보기가 되어야 한다.)

relate to / 관계하다, 연관되다 (to be about something or connected with something)

We're only interested in events that relate directly to murder.
(우리는 살해와 직접적으로 관계된 사건에만 관심을 갖고 있다.)

relate on / 떠맡다, 도전하다 (to accept some work or responsibility)

I can't take on any more work at the moment.

(나는 지금 어떤 일도 더 떠맡을 수 없다.)

take on / 떠맡다, 도전하다 (to accept some work or responsibility)

I can't take on any more work at the moment.

(나는 지금 어떤 일도 더 떠맡을 수 없다.)

thereabout(s) / 대략, 그 정도 (near that time)

That officer's been in the army long enough to have established a good record for himself.

He's been in probably six years, thereabouts, or seven, maybe eight.

(그 장교는 군에 충분히 오래 근무하여 좋은 경력을 쌓았다. 그는 6년 정도, 또는 7년 아마 8년 정도 근무했다.)

turn over / 인도하다, 조사하다 (to give, to hand over, to think about carefully)

He turned over the problem for three days before he did anything about it.

(그는 어떤 조치를 취하게 전에 그 문제를 3일 동안 검토해 보았다.)

2. 연습문제

1. The commander talked to the first two seamen, then the next two, and finally the last two. He talked to the seamen two ______ .

   ⓐ at all times　　ⓑ at odd times　　ⓒ all at once　　ⓓ at a time

2. They continue to use the tank ______ the poor condition it's in.

   ⓐ considering　　ⓑ despite　　ⓒ ignorant of　　ⓓ instead of

3. Our tanks were camouflaged: ______ , the enemy spotted them.

   ⓐ even so　　ⓑ even though　　ⓒ even if　　ⓓ even more

4. The other soldiers marched much too quickly for Pvt Kim, so he ______ .

   ⓐ fell on　　ⓑ knocked out　　ⓒ fell behind　　ⓓ knocked down

5. The enemy force withdrew and stopped opposing the army troops. They ______ .

   ⓐ gave in　　ⓑ put off　　ⓒ died down　　ⓓ fought off

6. The troops tried to prevent the enemy invasion. They ______ the enemy.

   ⓐ took on　　　　　　　　ⓑ gave in to

   ⓒ serve chances　　　　　ⓓ fought off

7. Undergraduate pilots must ______ lots of academic and physical training.

   ⓐ go through　　ⓑ go by　　ⓒ go down　　ⓓ go against

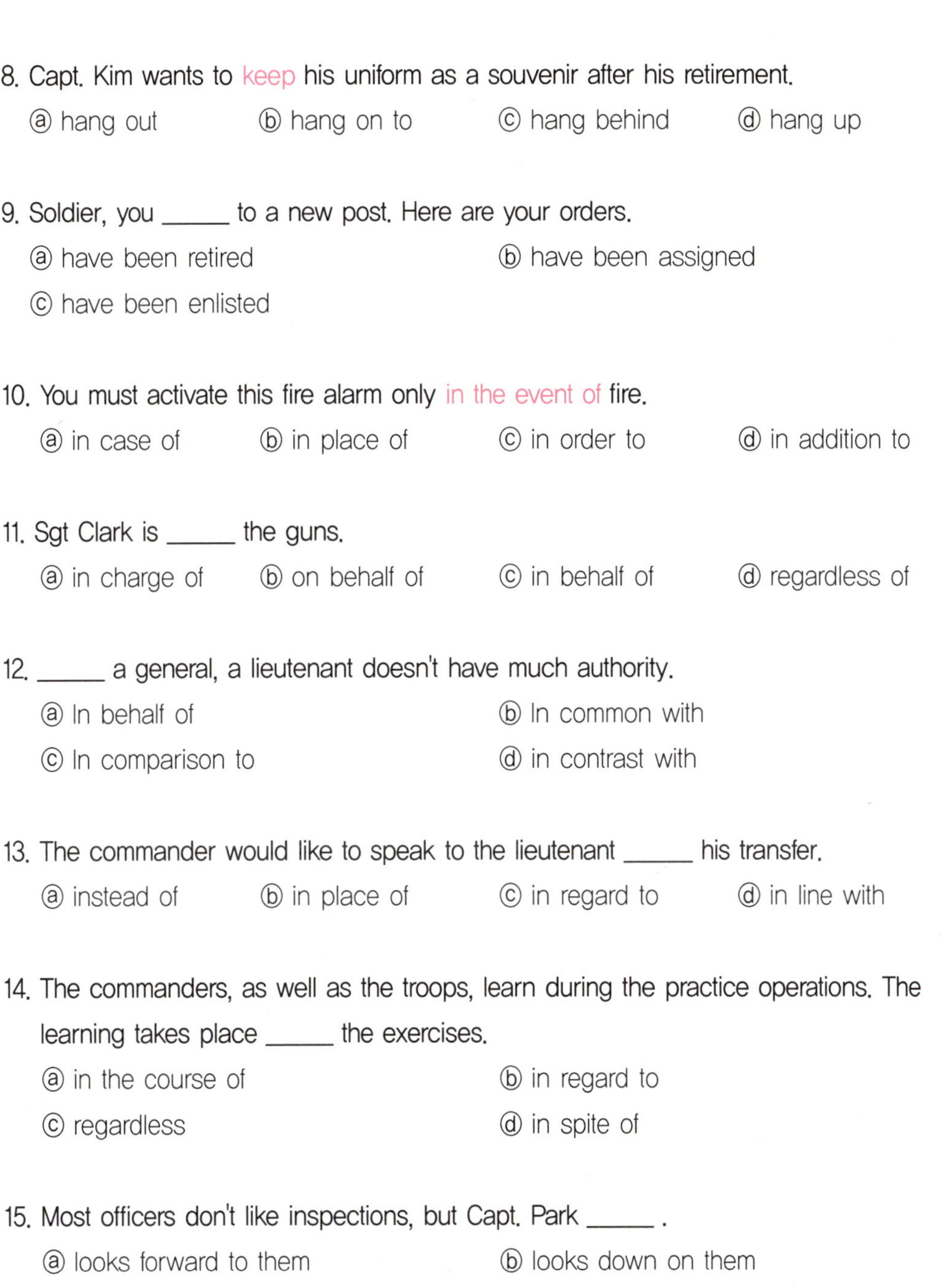

8. Capt. Kim wants to keep his uniform as a souvenir after his retirement.

　ⓐ hang out　　　ⓑ hang on to　　　ⓒ hang behind　　　ⓓ hang up

9. Soldier, you _____ to a new post. Here are your orders.

　ⓐ have been retired　　　　　ⓑ have been assigned

　ⓒ have been enlisted

10. You must activate this fire alarm only in the event of fire.

　ⓐ in case of　　　ⓑ in place of　　　ⓒ in order to　　　ⓓ in addition to

11. Sgt Clark is _____ the guns.

　ⓐ in charge of　　　ⓑ on behalf of　　　ⓒ in behalf of　　　ⓓ regardless of

12. _____ a general, a lieutenant doesn't have much authority.

　ⓐ In behalf of　　　　　ⓑ In common with

　ⓒ In comparison to　　　ⓓ in contrast with

13. The commander would like to speak to the lieutenant _____ his transfer.

　ⓐ instead of　　　ⓑ in place of　　　ⓒ in regard to　　　ⓓ in line with

14. The commanders, as well as the troops, learn during the practice operations. The
learning takes place _____ the exercises.

　ⓐ in the course of　　　　ⓑ in regard to

　ⓒ regardless　　　　　　ⓓ in spite of

15. Most officers don't like inspections, but Capt. Park _____ .

　ⓐ looks forward to them　　　ⓑ looks down on them

　ⓒ looks up to them　　　　　ⓓ look behind them

16. The officers showed a lot of respect for the commander. They _____ .

    ⓐ looked down on him   ⓑ talked back to him

    ⓒ looked up to him   ⓓ looked forward to

17. The first lieutenant is to report to the captain.

    ⓐ might   ⓑ must   ⓒ is willing to   ⓓ can

18. If we don't defeat the enemy, we may probably lose the battle.

    ⓐ come over   ⓑ come out   ⓒ overcome   ⓓ overcast

19. The information concerning the exercise was top secret. All data _____ was protected.

    ⓐ relating to it   ⓒ in the face of it

    ⓑ in the course of it   ⓓ in front of

20. The officers agreed to do the exercise. They decided to _____ the job of organizing the war games.

    ⓐ put off   ⓑ fight off   ⓒ take on   ⓓ issue

21. Why doesn't the colonel want _____ today?

    ⓐ be bothering   ⓑ been bothered   ⓒ to be bothered   ⓓ being bothered

22. The naval commandant _____ his command to the new captain.

    ⓐ checked out   ⓑ turned over

    ⓒ took back   ⓓ turned out

23. I was in San Antonio for six months. I ___ Lankland AFB.

    ⓐ was positioned to   ⓑ was wasted at

    ⓒ was promoted to   ⓓ was stationed at

24. The commander can call an inspection anytime he wants to.

   ⓐ however   ⓑ wherever

   ⓒ whenever   ⓓ whatever

25. LT Stone: Are you going to the reception tonight?

   LT Brick: No, I hate those things.

   LT Stone: It might be good for your career. You could rub elbow with some higher

              ranking officers.

   ⓐ You could dance with them.   ⓑ You could get to know them.

   ⓒ You could assist them.   ⓓ You could have dinner with them.

26. LT Perez: Do you like the new company commander?

   LT Gomez: Most other people like him, but I think he's a pain in the neck.

   ⓐ physically strong   ⓑ negative

   ⓒ cruel   ⓓ bothersome.

27. MAJ Cho: How does LT Oh like the course in Pensacola?

   MAJ Kim: Well, he's really in over his head, but he loves the beaches there.

   ⓐ He doesn't like the course.   ⓑ He can't swim very well.

   ⓒ He's having trouble with the course.   ⓓ He is not concerned about the course.

28. Mr. Swift: If you're not careful, Lieutenant, you're going to fail this course.

   LT Orone: What can I do about it?

   Mr. Swift: Well, for one thing, you can put your nose to the grindstone.

   ⓐ work very hard.   ⓑ stay out of night clubs.

   ⓒ do favors for your instructor   ⓓ have enough time to to it

ECL시험 대비 New ALC 필수어휘 완성

29. CAPT James: Why are you so mad at Parker?

CAPT Short: He went behind my back and presented my plan to th Commandant.

ⓐ imitated me.   ⓑ did it without my permission.

ⓒ did do favors for my instructor   ⓓ told me a lie

30. MSGT Mason: Hey, Captain, did I tell you about the plans for tomorrow's ceremony?

CAPT Brown: I'm all ears.

ⓐ I already heard about them.   ⓑ I've got large ears.

ⓒ I'm listening.   ⓓ Several officers reported already

31. Sgt Rivers: I've never seen PO Torres laugh before. Isn't that kind of strange?

Sgt Fields: You should've seen her at the picnic on Saturday.

She really let her hair down.

ⓐ took off her cap.   ⓑ became very angry

ⓒ was relaxed and casual.   ⓓ was drunken a lot

32. SGT Adams: Sgt. Allen's in my class this week. I had to give him a piece of my mind

yesterday.

SGT Brand: Someone needed to; I almost did that two weeks ago.

ⓐ tell him exactly what I thought.   ⓑ blame him severely

ⓑ give him additional attention.   ⓒ offer my knowledge.

33. Lou: How'd you get the guys to clean up their rooms?

Joe: I finally put my foot down.

ⓐ I exercised my authority.   ⓑ I resorted to physical force.

ⓒ I compromised with them.   ⓓ took a rest for a while.

7. 군사 및 무기

34. Brad: What happened when you flew to the Czech Republic to meet with their generals?

   Chad: They welcomed me with open arms.

   ⓐ They showed their weapons.   ⓑ They were unarmed.

   ⓒ They were warm and friendly.   ⓓ They welcomed me without weapons

35. SGT Hobbs: I talked to the commander yesterday and he approved the change in your

   orders that you asked for.

   PVT Davis: Hey, thanks for sticking your neck out for me.

   ⓐ for taking a risk to help me.   ⓑ taking my place.

   ⓒ letting me use your office.   ⓓ spending so much money

36. Sergeant: Watch it, Private. You'd better stop dragging your feet.

   Pvt Blue: Yes, sir!

   ⓐ doing everything so awkwardly   ⓑ running so strangely.

   ⓒ wearing unpolished shoes.   ⓓ doing everything so slowly.

37. Lt Parker wasn't selected for promotion because when making important decisions he

   just shoots from the hip instead of taking the time to think out a problem.

   ⓐ He pulls his gun from his holster and fires without aiming.

   ⓑ He can't function well because he has a painful hip injury.

   ⓒ He often made serious mistakes and didn't follow the procedure.

   ⓓ He acts or speaks too quickly without thinking of the consequences.

38. Although the captain bends the rules sometimes, the platoon sergeant is much more

   rigid and always goes by the book.

   ⓐ acts strictly according to the rules.   ⓑ disregards the rules.

   ⓒ makes his own rules according to the situation.   ⓓ ignore the rules

ECL시험 대비 New ALC 필수어휘 완성

39. A: Does the General have time to tour the new building?

B: Well, his schedule is real tight right now.

ⓐ The work is piling up.　　　　　ⓑ Every minute is accounted for.

ⓒ The tour is already on his schedule.　　ⓓ He will arrive there on time

40. After the colonel listened to his task, she advised him to polish it up before presenting it.

ⓐ rub it　　　　　　　　　　ⓑ make it shine

ⓒ refine it　　　　　　　　　ⓓ add graphs and material

41. They didn't want to make any mistakes. Therefore, they planned on having a dry run before the actual presentation.

ⓐ a rehearsal　　　　　　　　ⓑ a stamp of approval

ⓒ an early dismissal　　　　　　ⓓ a briefing

42. Serg. Morris blew up when he found out that none of the students showed up for PT.

ⓐ laughed loudly　　　　　　　ⓑ worked out alone

ⓒ smiled sarcastically　　　　　ⓓ got angry

43. The colonel told him to ignore everything else and to give this job priority.

ⓐ place first in order of importance　　ⓑ give attention to after everything is done

ⓒ can be done if there's enough time　　ⓓ spend all money

44. You need more practice before giving your briefing, Captain. Let's go through the whole thing one more time. Take it from the top!

ⓐ start at the beginning　　　　ⓑ wear your dress cap

ⓒ change your introduction　　　ⓓ cancel the beginning

45. If the commander calls on you at the meeting, don't let it throw you. Just relax and answer his questions.

ⓐ Don't be surprised.

ⓑ Don'w say a word

ⓒ Don't stop the meeting.

ⓓ Don't let it disturb you.

정답/해석

1. ⓓ 그 지휘관은 처음 두 명의 수병에게, 다음 두명에게, 그리고 끝으로 마지막 두명에게 말했다. 그는 수병들에게 한 번에 두 명씩 이야기 하였다.

2. ⓑ 그들은 그 탱크가 열악한 상태지만 계속 사용해야 한다.

3. ⓐ 우리 탱크는 위장되어 있었다. 그래도 적은 그것을 발견했다.

4. ⓒ 다른 군인들은 김일병에 비해 너무 빨리 행군하여, 그는 뒤처지게 되었다.

5. ⓐ 적군은 철수했고 육군을 대한 공격을 중지하였다. 그들은 포기하였다.

6. ⓓ 그 부대는 적의 침입을 막고자 노력하였다. 그들은 적을 격퇴시켰다.

7. ⓐ 대학에 재학 중인 조종사들은 많은 학문적 신체적 훈련을 받아야 한다.

8. ⓑ 김 대령[대위]는 자신의 제복을 은퇴 후 기념품으로 보관하고 싶어한다.

9. ⓑ 병사여, 너는 새로운 곳으로 가게 되었다. 여기 명령서가 있다.

10. ⓐ 화재발생 시에만 이 화재경보기를 작동해야 합니다.

11. ⓐ 클라크 부사관은 총기를 담당하고 있다.

12. ⓒ 장군과 비교해서, 대위는 많은 권한이 없다.

13. ⓒ 지휘관은 그 대위의 전출에 대해 이야기하고 싶어한다.

14. ⓐ 그 부대원들과 지휘관은 연습훈련을 통해 교훈을 얻는다. 배움은 연습하면서 얻어진다.

15. ⓐ 대부분의 장교들은 감사를 싫어한다. 그러나 박대위(대령)은 감사를 기다린다.

16. ⓒ 장교들은 지휘관에게 많은 경의를 표했다. 그들은 그를 존경했다.

17. ⓑ 그 중위는 함장에게 보고해야 한다.

ECL시험 대비 New ALC 필수어휘 완성

18. ⓒ 우리가 적을 격퇴하지 않으면, 우리는 아마 전쟁에 패배할 것이다.

19. ⓐ 훈련 관련 정보는 1급 비밀이다. 이와 관련된 모든 자료들은 보호된다.

20. ⓒ 그 장교들은 훈련하기로 합의하였다. 그들은 워게임을 조직하는 일을 맡기로 결정했다.

21. ⓒ 왜 그 대령은 오늘 신경쓰기를 싫어하느냐?

22. ⓑ 해군지휘관이 그의 지휘권을 새 함장에게 넘겼다.

23. ⓓ 나는 샌 안토니오에서 6개월 동안 있었다. 랜크랜드 공군 기지에 배치되었다.

24. ⓒ 지휘관은 하고 싶으면 언제든지 조사를 요구할 수 있다.

25. ⓑ 스톤대위: 오늘 만찬회에 가니?

브릭대위: 아니, 나는 그건 것을 싫어해

스토대위: 너 경력에 도움이 될지 몰라. 몇 몇 상급자들과 사귈 수 있어.

26. ⓓ 페레즈 대위: 너는 새 중대장을 좋아하니?

고메즈 대위: 대부분의 사람들은 그를 좋아하지만, 나는 그가 지겨운 사람이라고 생각해.

27. ⓒ 조소령: 오대위는 펜사콜라에서의 그 과정을 어떻게 생각하니?

김소령: 그래, 그는 실제로 곤란을 겪고 있어. 그러나 그는 그곳의 해안을 좋아한 다.

28. ⓐ 스위프트씨: 대위, 주의하지 않으면, 이 고장에서 탈락할 것입니다.

오론 대위: 어떻게 해야 되지요?

스위프트씨: 먼저, 열심히 노력해야 합니다.

29. ⓑ 제임스 대위: 왜 너는 파커에게 그렇게 성을 내니?

쇼트 대위: 그는 내 몰래 내 계획을 사령관에게 보고했어.

30. ⓒ 메이슨 상사: 대위님, 내일 예식에 대한 계획을 내가 말했습니까?

브라운 대위: 들어 봅시다.

31. ⓒ 리버스 부사관: 나는 토레스 부사관이 전에 웃는 것을 본적이 없다. 그건 좀 이상하지 않니?

필드 부사관: 너는 토요일 소풍에서 그녀를 보았어야 했다. 그녀는 정말 편안하게 행동했다.

32. ⓐ 아담스 부사관: 알렌 부사관이 지난 주 우리 수업에 참석했다. 나는 내 생각을 그에 게 말해야 했다.

브랜드 부사관: 누군가 말할 필요가 있다. 나도 2주전에 그럴 뻔 하였다.

33. ⓐ 루: 어떻게 너는 그 녀석들이 그들의 방을 청소하게 했니?

죠: 나는 마침내 단호하게 행동했어.

34. ⓒ 브래드: 너가 체코에 장성들을 만나러 갔을 때 무슨 일이 있었니?

차드: 그들은 팔을 벌리고 나를 맞이했어.

35. ⓐ 홉스 부사관: 나는 어제 지휘관에게 말해서, 그는 너가 요청한 지시사항의 변경에 대해 승인했다.

데이비스 일병: 나를 위해 위험을 무릅써서 고맙습니다.

36. ⓓ 부사관: 병사, 주의해야 겠어. 늦장부리지 않아야 해.

병사 블루: 예!

37. ⓓ 파크대위는 진급에 선발되지 못했다. 왜냐하면 그는 결정을 내릴 때 문제를 생각할 시간을 가지지 않고 무턱대고 행동하기 때문이다

38. ⓐ 그 부대장은 때로 규칙을 적당히 생각하지만, 그 소대 선임 부사관은 훨씬 더 엄격하며 규정대로 행동한다.

39. ⓑ A: 장군이 새 건물을 돌아다닐 시간이 있습니까?

B: 글쎄, 그의 일과가 지금 아주 꽉 짜여 있습니다.

40. ⓒ 그 대령은 그의 과업을 들은 뒤에, 그에게 발표하기 전에 좀 더 다듬어라고 충고했다.

41. ⓐ 그들은 실수 하기를 원하지 않았다. 그래서, 그들은 실연하기 전에 예행연습을 하기로 계획하였다.

42. ⓓ 학생들이 아무도 PT체조에 나타나지 않자 모리스 부사관은 성이 났다.

43. ⓐ 대령은 그에게 다른 모든 것을 무시하고, 이 일을 우선적으로 하라고 말했다.

44. ⓐ 대위, 브리핑하기 전에 좀 더 연습할 필요가 있다. 전체를 한 번 더 살펴보자. 처음부터 해봐.

45. ⓓ 지휘관이 모임에서 당신을 지명하면, 당황하지 말라. 편안히 그의 질문에 답하라.

New American
Language
Course

New American
Language Course

기타: 사건, 사고 8

A. 명사   B. 동사   C. 형용사   D. 어휘, 관용구, 문형 종합

ECL시험 대비 NEW ALC 必 필수어휘 완성

명사

기본어휘 / 연습 문제

A

New American Language Course

1. 기본어휘　　　명사

blowout / 파열, 펑크 (an occasion when a tire on a moving vehicle suddenly bursts)
We had a blowout on the highway.
(우리 차는 고속도로에서 펑크가 났다.)

confusion / 혼란, 당황 (bewilderment, embarrassment)
There is usually so much confusion after a traffic accident that the drivers have trouble remembering details.
(교통사고 뒤에는 대개 너무 혼란스러워서 운전자들은 세세한 것을 기억하기가 어렵다.)

corrosion / 부식, 침식 (destruction by chemical action)
There is a lot of corrosion on the body of my old car where the paint has come off.
(페인트가 벗겨진 내 낡은 차의 차체에는 많은 부식이 있다.)

frenzy / 격앙, 격분 (a state of great excitement, an attack of madness)
When Henry's car was struck on the side by another car, he went into such a frenzy that he punched the other driver in the nose.
(핸리 차의 측면이 다른 차에 부딪치자, 그는 격분하여 상대 운저자의 코를 때렸다)

impact / 충돌, 영향 (shock, force, the power of a collision)
The anti-smoking campaign has made little impact on young people.
(흡연반대운동은 젊은이에게 거의 영향을 주지 못했다.)

injury / 부상 (physical harm, damage)

I got a slight injury to my knee while jogging.

(나는 죠깅하면서 무릎에 가벼운 부상을 입었다.)

prisoner / 죄수 (someone who is in prison as punishment for a crime)

Federal marshals will escort the prisoners to the scene of the crime.

(연방 보안관은 죄수들을 범죄 현장으로 호송할 것이다.)

static / 잡음, 전파방해 (inteference or noises produced by electrical discharges)

The radio program is often interrupted by static.

(라디오 프로그램이 잡음으로 종종 중단된다.)

surge / 급상승, 큰 파도 (a sudden sharp increase of electric current or voltage in a circuit)

Our nation's household debts surged to 458 trillion won.

(우리나라의 가구부채가 458조원으로 치솟았다.)

tragic / 비극의, 비극적인 (causing or involving great sadness, because someone suffers or dies)

War is a tragic waste of human life.

(전쟁은 인간 생명을 비참하게 소모한다.)

2. 연습문제

1. When they saw the car accident in the highway, other drivers stopped and rendered
   _____ to the people who were injured.
   ⓐ add   ⓑ aid   ⓑ justice   ⓒ abundance

2. George: What was that noise?
   Paul: I don't know, but it sounded like a _____ .
   ⓐ present   ⓑ blowout   ⓒ volume   ⓓ peak

3. The _____ of the terrible blow threw the car forward.
   ⓐ explosive   ⓑ inventory   ⓒ impact   ⓓ improvement

4. Smith suffered a serious _____ in the crash.
   ⓐ injury   ⓑ injure   ⓒ injurious   ⓓ injuring

5. One of the _____ escaped during the night.
   ⓐ theories   ⓑ prisons   ⓒ prisoners   ⓓ principles

6. Fred gave a good _____ for being late. His car wouldn't start.
   ⓐ reason   ⓑ money   ⓒ order   ⓓ mask

7. Five young students were killed in a(n) _____ plane crash.
   ⓐ tragic   ⓑ regular.   ⓒ ambiguous   ⓓ astonished

8. Using salt to melt ice on highways brings about ______ on most cars.
   ⓐ collision　　　ⓑ corrosion　　　ⓒ combustion　　　ⓓ composition

9. Mary: Do you know why this car won't start?
   Ted: I think the ______ is dead.
   ⓐ computer　　　ⓑ battery　　　ⓒ radiator　　　ⓓ air conditioner

10. Diana had wet hands and was using her hair dryer when she got an electric ______ .
    ⓐ cord line　　　ⓑ shock　　　ⓒ switch　　　ⓓ short cut

11. The radio announcement was so full of ______ we couldn't understand the announcer.
    ⓐ hinge　　　ⓑ static　　　ⓒ dynamic　　　ⓓ commentary

12. Have you found the ______ of the leak yet?
    ⓐ source　　　ⓑ fix　　　ⓒ variety　　　ⓓ originality

13. The sudden ______ of electricity caused the computer to crash.
    ⓐ surge　　　ⓑ current　　　ⓒ voltage　　　ⓓ stream

14. The scoundrels who robbed the bank teller last week have been caught. They got away
    with an undetermined amount of money.
    ⓐ wealthy people　　　　　　ⓑ mean, wicked people
    ⓒ kind people　　　　　　　ⓓ clever people

정답 / 해석

1. ⓑ 고속도로에서 교통사고를 목격했을 때, 다른 운전자들은 멈추어서 부상당한 사람들을 도와주었다.

2. ⓑ 조지: 어디서 나는 소리지?

   폴: 잘 몰라요. 하지만 차가 펑크 난 것 같은데요.

3. ⓒ 엄청난 폭발의 영향으로 차가 앞으로 날아갔다.

4. ⓐ 스미스는 충돌로 심한 부상을 입었습니다.

5. ⓒ 죄수들 가운데 1명이 그날 밤에 도주하였다.

6. ⓐ 프레드는 늦은 이유를 말했다. 그의 차가 시동이 걸리지 않았다.

7. ⓐ 다섯 명의 젊은 학생들이 그 비극적인 비행기 사고에서 죽었다.

8. ⓑ 고속도로의 얼음을 녹이기 위해 소금을 사용하면 대부분의 차를 부식시킨다.

9. ⓑ 메리: 왜 이 차가 작동 않는지 아시나요?

   테드: 내 생각에는 건전지 모두 소모된 것 같습니다.

10. ⓑ 다이애나는 젖은 손으로 헤어드라이어를 사용하다 전기 쇼크를 받았다.

11. ⓑ 라디오 방송이 잡음이 많아서 아나운서의 말을 이해할 수 없다.

12. ⓐ 너는 누수의 근원을 이미 찾았느냐?

13. ⓐ 갑작스럽게 전기가 과부하되어 컴퓨터가 고장났다.

14. ⓑ 지난 주 금전출납기를 강도질한 불량배들이 잡혔다. 그들은 액수를 알 수 없는 돈을 가지고 도망갔다.

동사

기본어휘 / 연습 문제

B

New American
Language Course

1. 기본어휘　동사

be involved in / 연관되다, 참여하다 (take part in, be connected with)

You should count all the costs involved in the project.

(너는 그 계획에 소요되는 모든 비용을 계산해야 한다.)

block / 막다, 제한하다 (to obstruct, to restrict or prohibit)

The fallen trees are blocking the road.

(쓰러진 나무가 길을 막고 있다.)

burst / 파열하다, 폭발하다 (to break open or apart)

The balloon would burst if you blow it up a little more.

(조금만 더 불면 그 풍선은 터질 것이다.)

charge / 비난하다, 탓으로 돌리다 (to accuse of wrongdoing, censure)

We charged her with negligence because she forgot the meeting.

(그녀가 모임을 잊었기 때문에 우리는 그녀의 태만을 비난하였다.)

collapse / 부서지다, 붕괴하다 (to fall or cave in, crumble suddenly, to break down)

Despite all their efforts the peace talk collapsed.

(모든 노력에도 불구하고 평화회담은 무산되었다.)

collide / 부딪치다, 충돌하다 (to strike one another against the other)

The bike collided into a cherry tree.

(자전거가 벚나무에 충돌했다.)

crash / 충돌하다 (to collide violently)

The car crashed into a guard rail.

(그 차는 난간에 충돌하였다.)

deflect / 비키다, 피하다 (to direct criticism, attention, or blame away from yourself)

The company was criticized for trying to deflect the blame for the accident.

(그 회사는 그 사고에 대한 비난을 비켜가고자 함으로써 비난받았다.)

depress / 우울하게 하다, 약화시키다 (to press down, to push or pull down, to weaken)

Rising inflation could depress the economy.

(인플레이션이 증가하면 경제를 침체시킨다.)

destroy / 파괴하다 (to damage something so severely)

An earthquakes destroyed the town, killing about 20,000 people.

(지진으로 인해 도시가 파괴되고, 약 2만 명이 죽었다.)

malfunction / 고장하다 (to fail to work correctly)

Just before the crash the pilot reported a malfunction of the plane's navigation system.

(충돌 직전 비행사는 항법장치가 고장 났다고 보고했다.)

protrude / 돌출하다, 튀어나오다 (to stick out or thrust)

A huge mass of rough rock protrudes from the water.

(거대한 거친 바위가 물 바깥으로 돌출해 있다.)

rescue / 구출하다, 구조하다 (to set free as from danger or imprisonment, to save)

The lifeboat rescued the sailors from the sinking boat.

(구명정은 가라앉는 배로부터 선원들을 구조하였다.)

8. 기타: 사건, 사고

shatter / 산산이 부수다, 깨어지다 (to break or burst into pieces, to scatter)

Safety glass doesn't shatter if it is broken.

(안전유리는 깨어져도 흩어지지 않는다.)

spin / 잣다, 질주하다 (to turn round quickly, to drive or travel quickly)

The workers go spinning along the roads on their bikes every morning.

(노동자들이 매일 아침 자전거를 타고 도로를 어지럽게 질주하고 있다.)

2. 연습문제

1. The department store that _______ had never been repaired.
   ⓐ collided   ⓑ collapsed   ⓒ crammed   ⓓ crashed

2. Several cars _______ on the highway in a rainy day.
   ⓐ excelled   ⓑ collided   ⓒ elevated   ⓓ collapsed

3. He's extremely upset because his dog was just _______ by a truck.
   ⓐ bitten   ⓑ killed   ⓒ drowned   ⓓ destroyed

4. During the fire, helicopter pilot _______ more than seventy tourists from the roof of the hotel.
   ⓐ traveled   ⓑ rescued   ⓒ searched   ⓓ enforced

5. The accident was quite terrible, yet everyone _______ the crash by good fortune.
   ⓐ burst   ⓑ lived   ⓒ survived   ⓓ surged

6. The car wouldn't move because it was stuck. The tires were just _______ in the snow.
   ⓐ sustaining   ⓑ hovering   ⓒ spinning   ⓓ flinging

7. The rubber hose _______ because the pressure of tap water was too high.
   ⓐ bustled   ⓑ burst   ⓒ bust   ⓓ boosted

8. 기타: 사건, 사고

8. The typewriter key was stuck, so Anthony couldn't _______ it.
   ⓐ print   ⓑ depress   ⓒ promote   ⓓ deplete

9. My car couldn't be repaired, so I had to _______ .
   ⓐ ger along in it   ⓑ get along with
   ⓒ get rid of it   ⓓ get down to it

10. The helicopter _______ over the forest, looking for the lost soldiers.
    ⓐ hoisted   ⓑ hovered   ⓒ howled   ⓓ hopped

11. His supervisor suggested that they _______ the barricade in front of the demonstrators.
    ⓐ erect   ⓑ endow   ⓒ enlist   ⓓ elect

12. The arrow missed the bear because it was _______ by a branch.
    ⓐ deflected   ⓑ sighted   ⓒ distorted   ⓓ focused

13. Seven people were _______ in that accident.
    ⓐ coordinated   ⓑ invented   ⓒ involved   ⓓ cooperated

14. The police are _______ the car accident.
    ⓐ investigating ⓑ intimidating   ⓒ crushing   ⓓ exploring

15. The car collision blocked the street, so no cars could move.
    ⓐ burst   ⓑ obstructed   ⓒ concealed   ⓓ cracked

16. The iron plates _______ over the back end of the truck, so the policeman stopped it.
    ⓐ protruded   ⓑ revolved   ⓒ distinguished   ⓓ invaded

17. The gas explosion broke the windows.

    ⓐ shattered   ⓑ corroded   ⓒ detonated   ⓓ tore

18. The police _______ the building and demanded that the terrorists come out with their hands up.

    ⓐ composed   ⓑ expended   ⓒ surrounded   ⓓ impressed

19. While Charles was driving in hot weather, his tire _______ from too much heat and air pressure.

    ⓐ obstructed   ⓑ spit   ⓒ burst   ⓓ simulated

20. Oh, no! Some sheep got in the field and _______ the corn.

    ⓐ fixed   ⓑ destroyed   ⓒ harvested   ⓓ cut

21. Unfortunately the truck crashed into the bus.

    ⓐ collided with   ⓑ stopped by   ⓒ carried away   ⓓ corresponded with

정답 / 해석

1. ⓑ 붕궤된 백화점은 결코 수리되지 않았다.

2. ⓑ 비오는 날 여러 대의 차가 고속도로에서 충돌했다.

3. ⓑ 그는 자기 개가 트럭에 치어 죽었기 때문에 매우 기분이 나쁘다.

4. ⓑ 화재가 발생한 동안, 헬리콥터 조종사들은 호텔 지붕에서 70명 이상의 여행객들을 구조하였다.

5. ⓒ 사고는 아주 끔찍했지만, 모두가 운좋게 충돌에서 살아 남았다.

6. ⓒ 차가 처박혀 때문에 움직일 수 없다. 타이어가 눈 속에서 공회전하고 있었다.

7. ⓑ 수돗물의 압력이 너무 높아서 고무호스가 파열되었다.

8. ⓑ 타이프라이트의 키가 움직이지 않아서, 안토니는 그것을 아래로 누를 수가 없다.

9. ⓒ 내 차는 수리할 수가 없다. 그래서 폐차해야 한다.

10. ⓑ 헬리콥터가 숲 위를 배회하면서, 실종된 군인을 찾고 있었다.

11. ⓐ 감독관은 시위자들 앞에 철책선을 세우라고 지시했다.

12. ⓐ 그 화살은 곰에 맞지 않았다. 나무 가지 때문에 화살이 비켜갔기 때문이다.

13. ⓒ 일곱명의 사람들이 그 사건에 연루되어 있다.

14. ⓐ 경찰이 차량사고를 조사하고 있다.

15. ⓑ 차량충돌이 거리를 막아서, 차가 움직일 수 없다.

16. ⓐ 쇠철판이 트럭의 뒤쪽 끝으로 돌출하였다. 그래서 경찰이 그 차를 정지시켰다.

17. ⓐ 가스폭발로 창문이 깨졌다.

18. ⓒ 경찰은 건물을 포위하고, 테러분자들이 손을 들고 나오도록 요구하였다.

19. ⓒ 찰스가 뜨거운 날씨에 운전하는 동안, 그의 타이어가 고열과 공기압으로 폭발하였다.

20. ⓑ 아이쿠, 몇몇 양들이 목초지에 들어가서 옥수수 밭을 망쳐놓았다.

21. ⓐ 불행히도 그 트럭은 버스와 충돌하였다.

형용사

기본어휘 / 연습 문제

C

New American Language Course

erect / 똑바로 선, 똑바로 세우다 (to build or put up, in an upright position)

Stand still with your arms by your side and your head erect.

(양팔을 옆구리에 붙이고 머리를 똑바로 세운 체로 움직이지 마라.)

excessive / 지나친, 과도한 (too much, immoderate)

Excessive drinking can hurt your health.

(지나친 음주는 건강을 해칠 수 있다.)

fatal / 치명적인 (very serious, resulting in death, decisive)

The soldier was fatally wounded in the chest.

(그 군인은 가슴에 치명적인 상처를 입었다.)

minor / 보다 작은, 부전공의 (lesser in size or extent, a secondary area of academic study)

She minors in English.

(그녀는 영어를 부전공으로 하고 있다.)

unusual / 유별난, 이상한 (not normal, common, or ordinary)

You're in a very unusual situation.

(당신은 아주 특수한 상황에 놓여있다.)

2. 연습문제

1. Mark: Did they use _______ force to take your purse?

   Edward: Yes! They broke my arm!

   ⓐ strict　　　　ⓑ excessive　　　　ⓒ special　　　　ⓓ ridiculous

2. Tom shouldn't have tried to cross the railroad tracks ahead of the train. That was a(n) _______ mistake.

   ⓐ complete　　　　ⓑ fatal　　　　ⓒ entire　　　　ⓓ little

3. The legs of the desk are not even. The desk top is not _______ .

   ⓐ accurate　　　　ⓑ level　　　　ⓒ skilled　　　　ⓓ straight

4. The driver was so lucky; fortunately he received only _______ injuries.

   ⓐ minor　　　　ⓑ within　　　　ⓒ conscious　　　　ⓓ particular

5. That stamp is not very common. In fact, it's very _______ .

   ⓐ unusual　　　　ⓑ regular　　　　ⓒ dead　　　　ⓓ similar

6. The blade of this fan isn't _______ . Could you fix it?

   ⓐ hovering　　　　ⓑ suspending　　　　ⓒ rotating　　　　ⓓ lifting

7. The thermostat isn't working correctly. It's _______ .

   ⓐ functioning　　　　ⓑ separating　　　　ⓒ malfunctioning　　　　ⓓ circulating

1. ⓑ 마크: 그들은 지갑을 뺏으려고 폭력을 사용했습니까?

   에드워드: 예! 그들은 나의 팔을 부러뜨렸습니다.

2. ⓑ 톰은 기차 앞에서 철로를 가로지르지 않았어야 했다. 그것은 치명적인 실수였다.

3. ⓑ 책상다리가 고르지 않다. 책상 위가 평평하지 않다.

4. ⓐ 그 운전자는 아주 운이 좋았다. 다행히 그는 작은 부상을 업었다.

5. ⓐ 그 우표는 그다지 흔하지 않다. 사실 매우 특별한 것이다.

6. ⓒ 이 팬의 날개가 회전하지 않는다. 고칠 수 있니?

7. ⓒ 온도조절계가 잘 작동하지 않고 있다. 그것이 고장 났다.

어휘, 관용구, 문형 종합

기본어휘 / 연습 문제

D

New American Language Course

1. 기본어휘

blow (out) / 펑크나다 (burst)

Kathy was turning the corner when one of the front tires blew out.
(케시의 앞 바퀴 중 하나가 펑크 났을 때 그녀는 코너를 돌고 있었다.)

blow up / 폭발하다, 폭파시키다 (to break or destroy by explosion)

The terrorists blew up the plane by means of a concealed bomb.
(테러리스트는 감춘 폭탄으로 비행기를 폭파하였다.)

break in on / 뛰어들다, 방해하다 (to interrupt, to enter suddenly)

A stranger broke in on the conference without knocking.
(낯선 사람이 노크도 없이 회의장에 뛰어들었다.)

burn down / 타버리다, 태워버리다 (to destroy a building or something large with fire)

The entire house burned down in 30 minutes.
(그 집은 모두 30분 안에 타 버렸다.)

see about / 처리하다, 조치하다 (to deal with or organize something)

I should go and see about this job.
(내가 가서 이 일을 처리해야 한다.)

2. 연습문제

1. While I was watching TV yesterday, the announcer _______ my favorite soap opera to show the President's speech.

   ⓐ broke in on   ⓑ broke up   ⓒ broke away   ⓓ broke out

2. The Jones' house _______ last night.

   ⓐ burned down   ⓑ looked for   ⓒ set about   ⓓ sent for

3. She'll have to _______ getting that broken chair fixed.

   ⓐ see about   ⓑ come by   ⓒ go by   ⓑ come to

4. She had a flat tire in the highway, and a kind man stopped to give her a hand.

   ⓐ to steal her car   ⓑ to help her
   ⓒ to pass out   ⓓ to drive away

5. The taxi driver _______ leaving the scene of an accident.

   ⓐ was assumed   ⓑ was charged with
   ⓒ chipped in   ⓓ was constructed to

6. The construction workers _______ the bridge.

   ⓐ blew over   ⓑ blew off   ⓒ blew up   ⓓ blew out

7. One of his front tires _______ , and he had to stop carefully.

   ⓐ blew out   ⓑ dropped by   ⓒ turned down

8. Lynne: I see you got your car fixed. How much did they charge you?

   Alice: An arm and a leg.

   ⓐ It was very expensive.

   ⓑ It was much cheaper than I expected.

   ⓒ I paid half the cost. I'll pay the balance later.

   ⓓ It was free

9. His car always breaks down on Loop 410 during rush hour.

   ⓐ ceases operation   ⓑ uses too much gas

   ⓒ exceeds the speed limit   ⓓ runs slowly

10. The detective vowed that he would get to the bottom of the crime by examining all the

    facts and circumstances surrounding the incident.

    ⓐ investigate thoroughly.   ⓑ overlook

    ⓒ deep-sea diving.   ⓓ report from the first

정답/해석

1. ⓐ 어제 TV를 보고 있는 동안 아나운서가 내가 좋아하는 연속극을 중도에 막고 대통령의 연설을 보여 주었다.

2. ⓐ 존 가족의 집은 지난 밤 불에 타 버렸다.

3. ⓐ 그녀는 부러진 의자 수리를 처리해야 할 것입니다.

4. ⓑ 그녀는 고속도로에서 타이어가 펑크나자, 친절한 사람이 그녀를 도우기 위해 멈췄다.

5. ⓑ 택시운전사는 사고 현장을 방치한 죄가 있었다.

6. ⓒ 건설작업자들은 다리를 폭파하였다.

7. ⓐ 그의 차 앞바퀴 중 하나가 펑크 났다. 그는 조심해서 멈추어섰다.

8. ⓐ 린: 차 수리했구나. 비용이 얼마였니?

앨리스: 비용이 많이 들었어.

9. ⓐ 그의 차는 출퇴근 시간에 410번 우회도로에서 항상 고장이 난다.

10. ⓐ 그 형사는 그 사건을 둘러 싼 모든 사실과 상황을 조사하여 그 범죄의 진상을 규명하겠다고 공언했다.

ECL시험 대비 NEW ALC 필수어휘 완성

| 초판 1쇄 인쇄 / 2009년 11월 27일 | 초판 1쇄 발행 / 2009년 11월 30일 |

| 저 자 / 이준용 · 황기동 | 펴낸이 / 이정수 | 펴낸곳 / 연경문화사 | 등록 / 1-995호 |

| 주소 / 서울시 마포구 서교동 465-7 | 대표전화 / 02-332-3923 | 팩시밀리 / 02-332-3928 | 이메일 / ykmedia@korea.com |

| 값 19,000원 | ISBN 978-89-8298-110-4   13740 |

본서의 무단 복제 행위를 금하며, 잘못된 책은 바꾸어 드립니다.